The Souls of Black Folk

and Related Readings

McDougal Littell
A HOUGHTON MIFFLIN COMPANY
Evanston, Illinois • Boston • Dallas

Acknowledgments

Broadside Press: "Booker T. and W. E. B." by Dudley Randall, from *Poem Counterpoem* by Margaret Danner and Dudley Randall. Copyright © 1966 by Dudley Randall. Reprinted by permission of Broadside Press.

Scribner: "Address to the Fourth International Convention of the Negro Peoples of the World" by Marcus Garvey, from *Philosophy and Opinions of Marcus Garvey*, edited by Amy Jacques-Garvey. Copyright 1923, 1925 by Amy Jacques-Garvey. Reprinted with the permission of Scribner, a Division of Simon & Schuster, Inc.

Doubleday: Excerpt from *Coming of Age In Mississippi* by Anne Moody. Copyright © 1968 by Anne Moody. Used by permission of Doubleday, a division of Bantam Doubleday Dell Publishing Group, Inc.

Pocket Books: Excerpt from *Warriors Don't Cry* by Melba Pattillo Beals. Copyright © 1994, 1995 by Melba Beals. Reprinted with the permission of Pocket Books, a Division of Simon & Schuster, Inc.

George Braziller, Inc.: "After Dreaming of President Johnson," from *The African In Me* by Howard Gordon. Copyright © 1992 by Howard Gordon. Reprinted by courtesy of George Braziller, Inc.

Continued on page 384

Cover photo: UPI/Corbis-Bettmann.
Author photo: Corbis/Bettmann.

Printed in the United States of America.

ISBN 0-395-90107-3

23456789 - QNT - 03 02 01 00 99 98

Contents

The Souls of Black Folk

W.E.B. Du Bois

HEREIN IS WRITTEN

The Forethought

Herein lie buried many things which if read with patience may show the strange meaning of being black here at the dawning of the Twentieth Century. This meaning is not without interest to you, Gentle Reader; for the problem of the Twentieth Century is the problem of the color line. I pray you, then, receive my little book in all charity, studying my words with me, forgiving mistake and foible for sake of the faith and passion that is in me, and seeking the grain of truth hidden there.

I have sought here to sketch, in vague, uncertain outline, the spiritual world in which ten thousand thousand Americans live and strive. First, in two chapters I have tried to show what Emancipation meant to them, and what was its aftermath. In a third chapter I have pointed out the slow rise of personal leadership, and criticised candidly the leader who bears the chief burden of his race to-day. Then, in two other chapters I have sketched in swift outline the two worlds within and without the Veil, and thus have come to the central problem of training men for life. Venturing now into deeper detail, I have in two chapters studied the struggles of the massed millions of the black peasantry, and in another have sought to make clear the present relations of the sons of master and man. Leaving, then, the white world, I have stepped within the Veil, raising it that you may view faintly its deeper recesses,—the meaning of its religion, the passion of its human sorrow, and the struggle of its greater souls. All this I have ended with a tale twice told but seldom written, and a chapter of song.

Some of these thoughts of mine have seen the light before in other guise. For kindly consenting to their republication here, in altered and extended form, I must thank the publishers of the *Atlantic Monthly, The World's Work,* the *Dial, The New World,* and the *Annals of the American Academy of Political and Social Science.* Before each chapter, as now printed, stands a bar of the Sorrow Songs,—some echo of haunting melody from the only American music which welled up from black souls in the dark past. And, finally, need I add that I who speak here am bone of the bone and flesh of the flesh of them that live within the Veil?

—W. E. B. Du B.
*Atlanta, Ga.,
Feb. 1, 1903.*

Chapter I

Of Our Spiritual Strivings

O water, voice of my heart, crying in the sand,
    All night long crying with a mournful cry,
As I lie and listen, and cannot understand
        The voice of my heart in my side or the voice of
        the sea,
    O water, crying for rest, is it I, is it I?
    All night long the water is crying to me.

Unresting water, there shall never be rest
    Till the last moon droop and the last tide fail,
And the fire of the end begin to burn in the west;
        And the heart shall be weary and wonder and cry like
        the sea,
    All life long crying without avail,
        As the water all night long is crying to me.

ARTHUR SYMONS.

Between me and the other world there is ever an unasked question: unasked by some through feelings of delicacy; by others through the difficulty of rightly framing it. All, nevertheless, flutter round it. They approach me in a half-hesitant sort of way, eye me curiously or compassionately, and then, instead of saying directly, How does it feel to be a problem? they say, I know an excellent colored man in my town; or, I fought at Mechanicsville; or, Do not these Southern outrages make your blood boil? At these I smile, or am interested, or reduce the boiling to a simmer, as the occasion may require. To the real question, How does it feel to be a problem? I answer seldom a word.

And yet, being a problem is a strange experience,—peculiar even for one who has never been anything else, save perhaps in babyhood and in Europe. It is in the early days of rollicking boyhood that the revelation first bursts upon one, all in a day, as it were. I remember well when the shadow swept across me. I was a little thing, away up in the hills of New England, where the dark Housatonic winds between Hoosac and Taghkanic to the sea. In a wee wooden schoolhouse, something put it into the boys' and girls' heads to buy gorgeous visiting-cards—ten cents a package—and exchange. The exchange was merry, till one girl, a tall newcomer, refused my card,—refused it peremptorily, with a glance. Then it dawned upon me with a certain suddenness that I was different from the others; or like, mayhap, in heart and life and longing, but shut out from their world by a vast veil. I had thereafter no desire to tear down that veil, to creep through; I held all beyond it in common contempt, and lived above it in a region of blue sky and great wandering shadows. That sky was bluest when I could beat my mates at examination-time, or beat them at a foot-race, or even beat their stringy heads. Alas, with the years all this fine contempt began to fade; for the words I longed for, and all their dazzling oppor-tunities, were theirs, not mine. But they should not keep these prizes, I said; some, all, I would wrest from them. Just how I would do it I could never decide: by reading law, by healing the sick, by telling the wonderful tales that swam in my head,—some way.

With other black boys the strife was not so fiercely sunny: their youth shrunk into tasteless sycophancy, or into silent hatred of the pale world about them and mocking distrust of everything white; or wasted itself in a bitter cry, Why did God make me an outcast and a stranger in mine own house? The shades of the prison-house closed round about us all: walls strait and stubborn to the whitest, but relentlessly narrow, tall, and unscalable to sons of night who must plod darkly on in resignation, or beat unavailing palms against the stone, or steadily, half hopelessly, watch the streak of blue above.

After the Egyptian and Indian, the Greek and Roman, the Teuton and Mongolian, the Negro is a sort of seventh son, born with a veil, and gifted with second-sight in this American world,—a world which yields him no true self-consciousness, but only lets him see himself through the revelation of the other world. It is a peculiar sensation, this double-consciousness, this sense of always looking at one's self through the eyes of others, of measuring one's soul by the tape of a world that looks on in amused contempt and pity. One ever feels his twoness,—an American, a Negro; two souls, two thoughts, two unreconciled strivings; two warring ideals in one dark body, whose dogged strength alone keeps it from being torn asunder.

The history of the American Negro is the history of this strife,—this longing to attain self-conscious manhood, to merge his double self into a better and truer self. In this merging he wishes neither of the older selves to be lost. He would not Africanize America, for America has too much to teach the world and Africa. He would not bleach his Negro soul in a flood of white Americanism, for he knows that Negro blood has a message for the world. He simply wishes to make it possible for a man to be both a Negro and an American, without being cursed and spit upon by his fellows, without having the doors of Opportunity closed roughly in his face.

This, then, is the end of his striving: to be a co-worker in the kingdom of culture, to escape both death and isolation, to husband and use his best powers and his latent genius. These powers of body and mind have in the past been strangely wasted, dispersed, or forgotten. The shadow of a mighty Negro past flits through the tale of Ethiopia the Shadowy and of Egypt the Sphinx. Through history, the powers of single black men flash here and there like falling stars, and die sometimes before the world has rightly gauged their brightness. Here in America, in the few days since Emancipation, the black man's turning hither and thither in hesitant and doubtful striving has often made his very strength to lose effectiveness, to seem like absence of power, like weakness. And yet it is not weakness,—it is the contradiction of double aims. The double-aimed struggle of the black artisan—on the one hand to escape white contempt for a nation of mere hewers of wood and drawers of water, and on the other hand to plough and nail and dig for a poverty-stricken horde—could only result in making him a poor craftsman, for he had but half a heart in either cause. By the poverty and ignorance of his people, the Negro minister or doctor was tempted toward quackery and demagogy; and by the criticism of the other world, toward ideals that made him ashamed of his lowly tasks. The would-be black *savant* was confronted by the paradox that the knowledge his people needed was a twice-told tale to his white neighbors, while the knowledge which would teach the white world was Greek to his own flesh and blood. The innate love of harmony and beauty that set the ruder souls of his people a-dancing and a-singing raised but confusion and doubt in the soul of the black artist; for the beauty revealed to him was the soul-beauty of a race which his larger audience despised, and he could not articulate the message of another people. This waste of double aims, this seeking to satisfy two unreconciled ideals, has wrought sad havoc with the courage and faith and deeds of ten thousand thousand people,—has sent them often wooing false gods and invoking false means of salvation, and at times has even seemed about to make them ashamed of themselves.

Away back in the days of bondage they thought to see in one divine event the end of all doubt and disappointment; few men ever worshipped Freedom with half such unquestioning faith as did the American Negro for two centuries. To him, so far as he thought and dreamed, slavery was indeed the sum of all villainies, the cause of all sorrow, the root of all prejudice; Emancipation was the key to a promised land of sweeter beauty than ever stretched before the eyes of wearied Israelites. In song and exhortation swelled one refrain—Liberty; in his tears and curses the God he implored had Freedom in his right hand. At last it came,—suddenly, fearfully, like a dream. With one wild carnival of blood and passion came the message in his own plaintive cadences:—

> "Shout, O children!
> Shout, you're free!
> For God has bought your liberty!"

Years have passed away since then,—ten, twenty, forty; forty years of national life, forty years of renewal and development, and yet the swarthy spectre sits in its accustomed seat at the Nation's feast. In vain do we cry to this our vastest social problem:—

"Take any shape but that, and my firm nerves
Shall never tremble!"

The Nation has not yet found peace from its sins; the freedman has not yet found in freedom his promised land. Whatever of good may have come in these years of change, the shadow of a deep disappointment rests upon the Negro people,—a disappointment all the more bitter because the unattained ideal was unbounded save by the simple ignorance of a lowly people.

The first decade was merely a prolongation of the vain search for freedom, the boon that seemed ever barely to elude their grasp,—like a tantalizing will-o'-the-wisp, maddening and misleading the headless host. The holocaust of war, the terrors of the Ku-Klux Klan, the lies of the carpet-baggers,* the disorganization of industry, and the contradictory advice of friends and foes, left the bewildered serf with no new watchword beyond the old cry for freedom. As the time flew, however, he began to grasp a new idea. The ideal of liberty demanded for its attainment powerful means, and these the Fifteenth Amendment* gave him. The ballot, which before he had looked upon as a visible sign of freedom, he now regarded as the chief means of gaining and perfecting the liberty with which war had partially endowed him. And why not? Had not votes made war and emancipated millions? Had not votes enfranchised the freedom? Was anything impossible to a power that had done all this? A million black men started with renewed zeal to vote

---

* This mark indicates that the word appears in the Glossary.

themselves into the kingdom. So the decade flew away, the revolution of 1876* came, and left the half-free serf weary, wondering, but still inspired. Slowly but steadily, in the following years, a new vision began gradually to replace the dream of political power,—a powerful movement, the rise of another ideal to guide the unguided, another pillar of fire by night after a clouded day. It was the ideal of "book-learning"; the curiosity, born of compulsory ignorance, to know and test the power of the cabalistic letters of the white man, the longing to know. Here at last seemed to have been discovered the mountain path to Canaan;* longer than the highway of Emancipation and law, steep and rugged, but straight, leading to heights high enough to overlook life.

Up the new path the advance guard toiled, slowly, heavily, doggedly; only those who have watched and guided the faltering feet, the misty minds, the dull understandings, of the dark pupils of these schools know how faithfully, how piteously, this people strove to learn. It was weary work. The cold statistician wrote down the inches of progress here and there, noted also where here and there a foot had slipped or some one had fallen. To the tired climbers, the horizon was ever dark, the mists were often cold, the Canaan was always dim and far away. If, however, the vistas disclosed as yet no goal, no resting-place, little but flattery and criticism, the journey at least gave leisure for reflection and self-examination; it changed the child of Emancipation to the youth with dawning self-consciousness, self-realization, self-respect. In those sombre forests of his striving his own soul rose before him, and he saw himself,—darkly as through a veil; and yet he saw in himself some faint revelation of his power, of his mission. He began to have a dim feeling that, to attain his place in the world, he must be himself, and not another. For the first time he sought to analyze the burden he bore upon his back, that dead-weight of social degradation partially masked behind a half-named Negro problem. He felt his poverty; without a cent, without a home, without land, tools, or savings, he had entered into competition with rich, landed, skilled neighbors. To be a poor man is hard, but to be a poor race in a land of dollars is the very bottom of hardships. He felt the weight of his ignorance,—not simply of letters, but of life, of business, of the humanities; the accumulated sloth and shirking and awkwardness of decades and centuries shackled his hands and feet. Nor was his burden all poverty and ignorance. The red stain of bastardy, which two centuries of systematic legal defilement of Negro women had stamped upon his race, meant not only the loss of ancient African chastity, but also the hereditary weight of a mass of corruption from white adulterers, threatening almost the obliteration of the Negro home.

A people thus handicapped ought not to be asked to race with the world, but rather allowed to give all its time and thought to its own social problems. But alas! while sociologists gleefully count his bastards and his prostitutes, the very soul of the toiling, sweating black man is darkened by the shadow of a vast despair. Men call the shadow prejudice, and learnedly explain it as the natural defence of culture against barbarism, learning against ignorance, purity against crime, the "higher" against the "lower" races. To which the Negro cries Amen! and swears that to so much of this strange prejudice as is founded on just homage to civilization, culture, righteousness, and progress, he humbly bows and meekly does obeisance.

But before that nameless prejudice that leaps beyond all this he stands helpless, dismayed, and well-nigh speechless; before that personal disrespect and mockery, the ridicule and systematic humiliation, the distortion of fact and wanton license of fancy, the cynical ignoring of the better and the boisterous welcoming of the worse, the all-pervading desire to inculcate disdain for everything black, from Toussaint to the devil,—before this there rises a sickening despair that would disarm and discourage any nation save that black host to whom "discouragement" is an unwritten word.

But the facing of so vast a prejudice could not but bring the inevitable self-questioning, self-disparagement, and lowering of ideals which ever accompany repression and breed in an atmosphere of contempt and hate. Whisperings and portents came borne upon the four winds: Lo! we are diseased and dying, cried the dark hosts; we cannot write, our voting is vain; what need of education, since we must always cook and serve? And the Nation echoed and enforced this self-criticism, saying: Be content to be servants, and nothing more; what need of higher culture for half-men? Away with the black man's ballot, by force or fraud,—and behold the suicide of a race! Nevertheless, out of the evil came something of good,—the more careful adjustment of education to real life, the clearer perception of the Negroes' social responsibilities, and the sobering realization of the meaning of progress.

So dawned the time of *Sturm und Drang:** storm and stress to-day rocks our little boat on the mad waters of the world-sea; there is within and without the sound of conflict, the burning of body and rending of soul; inspiration strives with doubt, and faith with vain questionings. The bright ideals of the past,—

physical freedom, political power, the training of brains and the training of hands,—all these in turn have waxed and waned, until even the last grows dim and overcast. Are they all wrong,—all false? No, not that, but each alone was over-simple and incomplete,—the dreams of a credulous race-childhood, or the fond imaginings of the other world which does not know and does not want to know our power. To be really true, all these ideals must be melted and welded into one. The training of the schools we need to-day more than ever,—the training of deft hands, quick eyes and ears, and above all the broader, deeper, higher culture of gifted minds and pure hearts. The power of the ballot we need in sheer self-defence,—else what shall save us from a second slavery? Freedom, too, the long-sought, we still seek,—the freedom of life and limb, the freedom to work and think, the freedom to love and aspire. Work, culture, liberty,—all these we need, not singly but together, not successively but together, each growing and aiding each, and all striving toward that vaster ideal that swims before the Negro people, the ideal of human brotherhood, gained through the unifying ideal of Race; the ideal of fostering and developing the traits and talents of the Negro, not in opposition to or contempt for other races, but rather in large conformity to the greater ideals of the American Republic, in order that some day on American soil two world-races may give each to each those characteristics both so sadly lack. We the darker ones come even now not altogether empty-handed: there are to-day no truer exponents of the pure human spirit of the Declaration of Independence than the American Negroes; there is no true American music but the wild sweet melodies of the Negro slave; the American fairy tales and folklore are Indian and

African; and, all in all, we black men seem the sole oasis of simple faith and reverence in a dusty desert of dollars and smartness. Will America be poorer if she replace her brutal dyspeptic blundering with light-hearted but determined Negro humility? or her coarse and cruel wit with loving jovial good-humor? or her vulgar music with the soul of the Sorrow Songs?

Merely a concrete test of the underlying principles of the great republic is the Negro Problem, and the spiritual striving of the freedmen's sons is the travail of souls whose burden is almost beyond the measure of their strength, but who bear it in the name of an historic race, in the name of this the land of their fathers' fathers, and in the name of human opportunity.

And now what I have briefly sketched in large outline let me on coming pages tell again in many ways, with loving emphasis and deeper detail, that men may listen to the striving in the souls of black folk.

Chapter II

Of the Dawn of Freedom

Careless seems the great Avenger;
　　History's lessons but record
One death-grapple in the darkness
　　'Twixt old systems and the Word;
Truth forever on the scaffold,
　　Wrong forever on the throne;
Yet that scaffold sways the future,
　　And behind the dim unknown
Standeth God within the shadow
　　Keeping watch above His own.

　　　　　　　　　　　　LOWELL.

The problem of the twentieth century is the problem of the color-line,—the relation of the darker to the lighter races of men in Asia and Africa, in America and the islands of the sea. It was a phase of this problem that caused the Civil War; and however much they who marched South and North in 1861 may have fixed on the technical points of union and local autonomy as a shibboleth, all nevertheless knew, as we know, that the question of Negro slavery was the real cause of the conflict. Curious it was, too, how this deeper question ever forced itself to the surface despite effort and disclaimer. No sooner had Northern armies touched Southern soil than this old question, newly guised, sprang from the earth,—What shall be done with Negroes? Peremptory military commands this way and that, could not answer the query; the Emancipation Proclamation* seemed but to broaden and intensify the difficulties; and the War Amendments made the Negro problems of to-day.

It is the aim of this essay to study the period of history from 1861 to 1872 so far as it relates to the American Negro. In effect, this tale of the dawn of Freedom is an account of that government of men called the Freedmen's Bureau,—one of the most singular and interesting of the attempts made by a great nation to grapple with vast problems of race and social condition.

The war has naught to do with slaves, cried Congress, the President, and the Nation; and yet no sooner had the armies, East and West, penetrated Virginia and Tennessee than fugitive slaves appeared within their lines. They came at night, when the flickering camp-fires shone like vast unsteady stars along the black horizon: old men and thin, with gray and tufted hair; women with frightened eyes, dragging whimpering hungry children; men and girls, stalwart and gaunt,—a horde of starving vagabonds, homeless, helpless, and pitiable, in their dark distress. Two methods of treating these newcomers seemed equally logical to opposite sorts of minds. Ben Butler,* in Virginia, quickly declared slave property contraband of war, and put the fugitives to work; while Fremont,* in Missouri, declared the slaves free under martial law. Butler's action was approved, but Fremont's was hastily countermanded, and his successor, Halleck, saw things differently. "Hereafter," he commanded, "no slaves should be allowed to come into your lines at all; if any come without your knowledge, when owners call for them deliver them." Such a policy was difficult to enforce; some of the black refugees declared themselves freemen, others showed that their masters had deserted them, and still others were captured with forts and plantations. Evidently, too, slaves were a source of strength to the Confederacy, and were being used as laborers and producers. "They constitute a military resource," wrote Secretary Cameron, late in 1861; "and being such, that they should not be turned over to the enemy is too plain to discuss." So gradually the tone of the army chiefs changed; Congress forbade the rendition of fugitives, and Butler's "contrabands" were welcomed as military laborers. This complicated rather than solved the problem, for now the scattering fugitives became a steady stream, which flowed faster as the armies marched.

Then the long-headed man with care-chiselled face who sat in the White House saw the inevitable, and emancipated the slaves of rebels on New Year's, 1863. A month later Congress called earnestly for the Negro soldiers whom the act of July, 1862, had half grudgingly allowed to enlist. Thus the barriers were levelled and the deed was done. The stream of fugitives swelled to a flood, and anxious army officers kept inquiring: "What must be done with slaves, arriving almost daily? Are we to find food and shelter for women and children?"

It was a Pierce of Boston who pointed out the way, and thus became in a sense the founder of the Freedmen's Bureau. He was a firm friend of Secretary Chase;* and when, in 1861, the care of slaves and abandoned lands developed upon the Treasury officials, Pierce was specially detailed from the ranks to study the conditions. First, he cared for the refugees at Fortress Monroe; and then, after Sherman* had captured Hilton Head, Pierce was sent there to found his Port Royal experiment of making free working-men out of slaves. Before his experiment was barely started, however, the problem of the fugitives had assumed such proportions that it was taken from the hands of the over-burdened Treasury Department and given to the army officials. Already centres of massed freedmen were forming at Fortress Monroe, Washington, New Orleans, Vicksburg and Corinth, Columbus, Ky., and Cairo, Ill., as well as at Port Royal. Army chaplains found here new and fruitful fields; "superintendents of contrabands" multiplied, and some attempt at systematic work was made by enlisting the able-bodied men and giving work to the others.

Then came the Freedmen's Aid societies, born of the touching appeals from Pierce and from these other centres of distress. There was the American Missionary Association, sprung from the *Amistad,*⃰ and now full-grown for work; the various church organizations, the National Freedmen's Relief Association, the American Freedmen's Union, the Western Freedmen's Aid Commission,—in all fifty or more active organizations, which sent clothes, money, school-books, and teachers southward. All they did was needed, for the destitution of the freedmen was often reported as "too appalling for belief," and the situation was daily growing worse rather than better.

And daily, too, it seemed more plain that this was no ordinary matter of temporary relief, but a national crisis; for here loomed a labor problem of vast dimensions. Masses of Negroes stood idle, or, if they worked spasmodically, were never sure of pay; and if perchance they received pay, squandered the new thing thoughtlessly. In these and other ways were camp-life and the new liberty demoralizing the freedmen. The broader economic organization thus clearly demanded sprang up here and there as accident and local conditions determined. Here it was that Pierce's Port Royal plan of leased plantations and guided workmen pointed out the rough way. In Washington the military governor, at the urgent appeal of the superintendent, opened confiscated estates to the cultivation of the fugitives, and there in the shadow of the dome gathered black farm villages. General Dix gave over estates to the freedmen of Fortress Monroe, and so on, South and West. The government and benevolent societies furnished the means of cultivation, and the Negro turned again slowly to work. The systems of control, thus started, rapidly grew, here and there, into strange little governments, like that of General Banks in Louisiana, with its ninety thousand black subjects, its fifty thousand guided laborers, and its annual budget of one hundred thousand dollars and more. It made out four thousand pay-rolls a year, registered all freedmen, inquired into grievances and redressed them, laid and collected taxes, and established a system of public schools. So, too, Colonel Eaton, the superintendent of Tennessee and Arkansas, ruled over one hundred thousand freedmen, leased and cultivated seven thousand acres of cotton land, and fed ten thousand paupers a year. In South Carolina was General Saxton, with his deep interest in black folk. He succeeded Pierce and the Treasury officials, and sold forfeited estates, leased abandoned plantations, encouraged schools, and received from Sherman, after that terribly picturesque march to the sea, thousands of the wretched camp followers.

Three characteristic things one might have seen in

Sherman's raid through Georgia, which threw the new situation in shadowy relief: the Conqueror, the Conquered, and the Negro. Some see all significance in the grim front of the destroyer, and some in the bitter sufferers of the Lost Cause. But to me neither soldier nor fugitive speaks with so deep a meaning as that dark human cloud that clung like remorse on the rear of those swift columns, swelling at times to half their size, almost engulfing and choking them. In vain were they ordered back, in vain were bridges hewn from beneath their feet; on they trudged and writhed and surged, until they rolled into Savannah, a starved and naked horde of tens of thousands. There too came the characteristic military remedy: "The islands from Charleston south, the abandoned rice-fields along the rivers for thirty miles back from the sea, and the country bordering the St. John's River, Florida, are reserved and set apart for the settlement of Negroes now made free by act of war." So read the celebrated "Field-order Number Fifteen."

All these experiments, orders, and systems were bound to attract and perplex the government and the nation. Directly after the Emancipation Proclamation, Representative Eliot had introduced a bill creating a Bureau of Emancipation; but it was never reported. The following June a committee of inquiry, appointed by the Secretary of War, reported in favor of a temporary bureau for the "improvement, protection, and employment of refugee freedmen," on much the same lines as were afterwards followed. Petitions came in to President Lincoln from distinguished citizens and organizations, strongly urging a comprehensive and unified plan of dealing with the freedmen, under a bureau which should be "charged with the study of plans and execution of measures for easily guiding, and in every way judiciously and humanely aiding, the passage of our emancipated and yet to be emancipated blacks from the old condition of forced labor to their new state of voluntary industry."

Some half-hearted steps were taken to accomplish this, in part, by putting the whole matter again in charge of the special Treasury agents. Laws of 1863 and 1864 directed them to take charge of and lease abandoned lands for periods not exceeding twelve months, and to "provide in such leases, or otherwise, for the employment and general welfare" of the freedmen. Most of the army officers greeted this as a welcome relief from perplexing "Negro affairs," and Secretary Fessenden, July 29, 1864, issued an excellent system of regulations, which were afterward closely followed by General Howard. Under Treasury agents, large quantities of land were leased in the Mississippi Valley, and many Negroes were employed; but in August, 1864, the new regulations were suspended for reasons of "public policy," and the army was again in control.

Meanwhile Congress had turned its attention to the subject; and in March the House passed a bill by a majority of two establishing a Bureau for Freedmen in the War Department. Charles Sumner,* who had charge of the bill in the Senate, argued that freedmen and abandoned lands ought to be under the same department, and reported a substitute for the House bill attaching the Bureau to the Treasury Department. This bill passed, but too late for action by the House. The debates wandered over the whole policy of the administration and the general question of slavery, without touching very closely the specific merits of the measure in hand. Then the national election took place; and the administration, with a vote of renewed confidence from the country, addressed itself to the matter more seriously. A conference between the two branches of Congress agreed upon a carefully drawn measure which contained the chief provisions of Sumner's bill, but made the proposed organization a department independent of both the War and the Treasury officials. The bill was conservative, giving the new department "general superintendence of all freedmen." Its purpose was to "establish regulations" for them, protect them, lease them lands, adjust their wages, and appear in civil and military courts as their "next friend." There were many limitations attached to the powers thus granted, and the organization was made permanent. Nevertheless, the Senate defeated the bill, and a new conference committee was appointed. This committee reported a new bill, February 28, which was whirled through just as the session closed, and became the act of 1865 establishing in the War Department a "Bureau of Refugees, Freedmen, and Abandoned Lands."

This last compromise was a hasty bit of legislation, vague and uncertain in outline. A Bureau was created, "to continue during the present War of Rebellion, and for one year thereafter," to which was given "the supervision and management of all abandoned lands and the control of all subjects relating to refugees and freedmen," under "such rules and regulations as may be presented by the head of the Bureau and approved by the President." A Commissioner, appointed by the President and Senate, was to control the Bureau, with an office force not exceeding ten clerks. The President might also appoint assistant commissioners in the seceded States, and to all these offices military officials might be detailed at regular pay. The Secretary of War could issue rations, clothing, and fuel to the destitute, and all abandoned property was placed in the hands of the Bureau for eventual lease and sale to ex-slaves in forty-acre parcels.

Thus did the United States government definitely assume charge of the emancipated Negro as the ward of the nation. It was a tremendous undertaking. Here at a stroke of the pen was erected a government of millions of men,—and not ordinary men either, but black men emasculated by a peculiarly complete system of slavery, centuries old; and now, suddenly, violently, they come into a new birthright, at a time of war and passion, in the midst of the stricken and embittered population of their former masters. Any man might well have hesitated to assume charge of such a work, with vast responsibilities, indefinite powers, and limited resources. Probably no one but a soldier would have answered such a call promptly; and, indeed, no one but a soldier could be called, for Congress had appropriated no money for salaries and expenses.

Less than a month after the weary Emancipator passed to his rest, his successor assigned Major-Gen. Oliver O. Howard to duty as Commissioner of the new Bureau. He was a Maine man, then only thirty-five years of age. He had marched with Sherman to the sea, had fought well at Gettysburg, and but the year before had been assigned to the command of the Department of Tennessee. An honest man, with too much faith in human nature, little aptitude for business and intricate detail, he had had large opportunity of becoming acquainted at first hand with much of the work before him. And of that work it has been truly said that "no approximately correct history of civilization can ever be written which does not throw out in bold relief, as one of the great landmarks of political and social progress, the organization and administration of the Freedmen's Bureau."

On May 12, 1865, Howard was appointed; and he

assumed the duties of his office promptly on the 15th, and began examining the field of work. A curious mess he looked upon: little despotisms, communistic experiments, slavery, peonage, business speculations, organized charity, unorganized almsgiving,—all reeling on under the guise of helping the freedmen, and all enshrined in the smoke and blood of the war and the cursing and silence of angry men. On May 19 the new government—for a government it really was—issued its constitution; commissioners were to be appointed in each of the seceded states, who were to take charge of "all subjects relating to refugees and freedmen," and all relief and rations were to be given by their consent alone. The Bureau invited continued coöperation with benevolent societies, and declared: "It will be the object of all commissioners to introduce practicable systems of compensated labor," and to establish schools. Forthwith nine assistant commissioners were appointed. They were to hasten to their fields of work; seek gradually to close relief establishments, and make the destitute self-supporting; act as courts of law where there were no courts, or where Negroes were not recognized in them as free; establish the institution of marriage among ex-slaves, and keep records; see that freedmen were free to choose their employers, and help in making fair contracts for them; and finally, the circular said: "Simple good faith, for which we hope on all hands for those concerned in the passing away of slavery, will especially relieve the assistant commissioners in the discharge of their duties toward the freedmen, as well as promote the general welfare."

No sooner was the work thus started, and the general system and local organization in some measure begun, than two grave difficulties appeared which changed largely the theory and outcome of

Bureau work. First, there were the abandoned lands of the South. It had long been the more or less definitely expressed theory of the North that all the chief problems of Emancipation might be settled by establishing the slaves on the forfeited lands of their masters,—a sort of poetic justice, said some. But this poetry done into solemn prose meant either wholesale confiscation of private property in the South, or vast appropriations. Now Congress had not appropriated a cent, and no sooner did the proclamations of general amnesty appear than the eight hundred thousand acres of abandoned lands in the hands of the Freedmen's Bureau melted quickly away. The second difficulty lay in perfecting the local organization of the Bureau throughout the wide field of work. Making a new machine and sending out officials of duly ascertained fitness for a great work of social reform is no child's task; but this task was even harder, for a new central organization had to be fitted on a heterogeneous and confused but already existing system of relief and control of ex-slaves; and the agents available for this work must be sought for in an army still busy with war operations,—men in the very nature of the case ill fitted for delicate social work,— or among the questionable camp followers of an invading host. Thus, after a year's work, vigorously as it was pushed, the problem looked even more difficult to grasp and solve than at the beginning. Nevertheless, three things that year's work did, well worth the doing: it relieved a vast amount of physical suffering; it transported seven thousand fugitives from congested centres back to the farm; and, best of all, it inaugurated the crusade of the New England schoolma'am.

The annals of this Ninth Crusade* are yet to be written,—the tale of a mission that seemed to our age far more quixotic than the quest of St. Louis seemed to his. Behind the mists of ruin and rapine waved the calico dresses of women who dared, and after the hoarse mouthings of the field guns rang the rhythm of the alphabet. Rich and poor they were, serious and curious. Bereaved now of a father, now of a brother, now of more than these, they came seeking a life work in planting New England schoolhouses among the white and black of the South. They did their work well. In that first year they taught one hundred thousand souls, and more.

Evidently, Congress must soon legislate again on the hastily organized Bureau, which had so quickly grown into wide significance and vast possibilities. An institution such as that was well-nigh as difficult to end as to begin. Early in 1866 Congress took up the matter, when Senator Trumbull, of Illinois, introduced a bill to extend the Bureau and enlarge its powers. This measure received, at the hands of Congress, far more thorough discussion and attention than its predecessor. The war cloud had thinned enough to allow a clearer conception of the work of Emancipation. The champions of the bill argued that the strengthening of the Freedmen's Bureau was still a military necessity; that it was needed for the proper carrying out of the Thirteenth Amendment, and was a work of sheer justice to the ex-slave, at a trifling cost to the government. The opponents of the measure declared that the war was over, and the necessity for war measures past; that the Bureau, by reason of its extraordinary powers, was clearly unconstitutional in time of peace, and was destined to irritate the South and pauperize the freedmen, at a final cost of possibly hundreds of millions. These two arguments were unanswered, and indeed unanswerable: the one that the extraordinary powers of the Bureau threatened the civil rights of all citizens; and the other that the government must have power to do what manifestly must be done, and that present abandonment of the freedmen meant their practical re-enslavement. The bill which finally passed enlarged and made permanent the Freedmen's Bureau. It was promptly vetoed by President Johnson as "unconstitutional," "unnecessary," and "extrajudicial," and failed of passage over the veto. Meantime, however, the breach between Congress and the President began to broaden, and a modified form of the lost bill was finally passed over the President's second veto, July 16.

The act of 1866 gave the Freedmen's Bureau its final form,—the form by which it will be known to posterity and judged of men. It extended the existence of the Bureau to July, 1868; it authorized additional assistant commissioners, the retention of army officers mustered out of regular service, the sale of certain forfeited lands to freedmen on nominal terms, the sale of Confederate public property for Negro schools, and a wider field of judicial interpretation and cognizance. The government of the unreconstructed South was thus put very largely in the hands of the Freedmen's Bureau, especially as in many cases the departmental military commander was now made also assistant commissioner. It was thus that the Freedmen's Bureau became a full-fledged government of men. It made laws, executed them and interpreted them; it laid and collected taxes, defined and punished crime, maintained and used military force, and dictated such measures as it thought necessary and proper for the accomplishment of its varied ends. Naturally, all these powers were not exercised continuously nor to their fullest extent; and yet, as General Howard has said, "scarcely any subject that has to be legislated upon in civil society failed, at one time or another, to demand the action of this singular Bureau."

To understand and criticise intelligently so vast a work, one must not forget an instant the drift of things in the later sixties. Lee* had surrendered, Lincoln was dead, and Johnson and Congress were at loggerheads; the Thirteenth Amendment* was adopted, the Fourteenth pending, and the Fifteenth declared in force in 1870. Guerrilla raiding, the ever-present flickering after-flame of war, was spending its forces against the Negroes, and all the Southern land was awakening as from some wild dream to poverty and social revolution. In a time of perfect calm, amid willing neighbors and streaming wealth, the social uplifting of four million slaves to an assured and self-sustaining place in the body politic and economic would have been a herculean task; but when to the inherent difficulties of so delicate and nice a social operation were added the spite and hate of conflict, the hell of war; when suspicion and cruelty were rife, and gaunt Hunger wept beside Bereavement,—in such a case, the work of any instrument of social regeneration was in large part foredoomed to failure. The very name of the Bureau stood for a thing in the South which for two centuries and better men had refused even to argue,—that life amid free Negroes was simply unthinkable, the maddest of experiments.

The agents that the Bureau could command varied all the way from unselfish philanthropists to narrow-minded busybodies and thieves; and even though it be true that the average was far better than the worst, it was the occasional fly that helped spoil the ointment.

Then amid all crouched the freed slave, bewildered between friend and foe. He had emerged from slavery,—not the worst slavery in the world, not a slavery that made all life unbearable, rather a slavery that had here and there something of kindliness, fidelity, and happiness,—but withal slavery, which, so far as human aspiration and desert were concerned, classed the black man and the ox together. And the Negro knew full well that, whatever their deeper convictions may have been, Southern men had fought with desperate energy to perpetuate this slavery under which the black masses, with half-articulate thought, had writhed and shivered. They welcomed freedom with a cry. They shrank from the master who still strove for their chains; they fled to the friends that had freed them, even though those friends stood ready to use them as a club for driving the recalcitrant South back into loyalty. So the cleft between the white and black South grew. Idle to say it never should have been; it was as inevitable as its results were pitiable. Curiously incongruous elements were left arrayed against each other,—the North, the government, the carpet-bagger, and the slave, here; and there, all the South that was white, whether gentleman or vagabond, honest man or rascal, lawless murderer or martyr to duty.

Thus it is doubly difficult to write of this period calmly, so intense was the feeling, so mighty the human passions that swayed and blinded men. Amid it all, two figures ever stand to typify that day to coming ages,—the one, a gray-haired gentleman, whose fathers had quit themselves like men, whose sons lay in nameless graves; who bowed to the evil of slavery because its abolition threatened untold ill to all; who stood at last, in the evening of life, a blighted, ruined form, with hate in his eyes;—and the other, a form hovering dark and mother-like, her awful face black with the mists of centuries, had aforetime quailed at that white master's command, had bent in love over the cradles of his sons and daughters, and closed in death the sunken eyes of his wife,—aye, too, at his behest had laid herself low to his lust, and borne a tawny man-child to the world, only to see her dark boy's limbs scattered to the winds by midnight marauders riding after "damned Niggers." These were the saddest sights of that woful day; and no man clasped the hands of these two passing figures of the present-past; but, hating, they went to their long home, and, hating, their children's children live today.

Here, then, was the field of work for the Freedmen's Bureau; and since, with some hesitation, it was continued by the act of 1868 until 1869, let us look upon four years of its work as a whole. There were, in 1868, nine hundred Bureau officials scattered from Washington to Texas, ruling, directly and indirectly, many millions of men. The deeds of these rulers fall mainly under seven heads: the relief of physical suffering, the overseeing of the beginnings of free labor, the buying and selling of land, the establishment of schools, the paying of bounties, the administration of justice, and the financiering of all these activities.

Up to June, 1869, over half a million patients had been treated by Bureau physicians and surgeons, and sixty hospitals and asylums had been in operation. In fifty months twenty-one million free rations were distributed at a cost of over four million dollars. Next came the difficult question of labor. First, thirty thousand black men were transported from the refuges and relief stations back to the farms, back to the critical trial of a new way of working. Plain instructions went out from Washington: the laborers must be free to choose their employers, no fixed rate of wages was prescribed, and there was to be no peonage or forced labor. So far, so good; but where local agents differed *toto cœlo** in capacity and character, where the *personnel* was continually changing, the outcome was necessarily varied. The largest element of success lay in the fact that the majority of the freedmen were willing, even eager, to work. So labor contracts were written,—fifty thousand in a single State,—laborers advised, wages guaranteed, and employers supplied. In truth, the organization became a vast labor bureau,—not perfect, indeed, notably defective here and there, but on the whole successful beyond the dreams of thoughtful men. The two great obstacles which confronted the officials were the tyrant and the idler,—the slaveholder who was determined to perpetuate slavery under another name; and the freedman who regarded freedom as perpetual rest,— the Devil and the Deep Sea.

In the work of establishing the Negroes as peasant proprietors, the Bureau was from the first handicapped and at last absolutely checked. Something was done, and larger things were planned; abandoned lands were leased so long as they remained in the hands of the Bureau, and a total revenue of nearly half a million dollars derived from black tenants. Some other lands to which the nation had gained title were sold on easy terms, and public lands were opened for settlement to the very few freedmen who had tools and capital. But the vision of "forty acres and a mule"—the righteous and reasonable ambition to become a landholder, which the nation had all but categorically promised the freedmen—was destined in most cases to bitter disappointment. And those men of marvellous hindsight who are today seeking to preach the Negro back to the present peonage of the soil know well, or ought to know, that the opportunity of binding the Negro peasant willingly to the soil was lost on that day when the

Commissioner of the Freedmen's Bureau had to go to South Carolina and tell the weeping freedmen, after their years of toil, that their land was not theirs, that there was a mistake—somewhere. If by 1874 the Georgia Negro alone owned three hundred and fifty thousand acres of land, it was by grace of his thrift rather than by bounty of the government.

The greatest success of the Freedmen's Bureau lay in the planting of the free school among Negroes, and the idea of free elementary education among all classes in the South. It not only called the school-mistresses through the benevolent agencies and built them schoolhouses, but it helped discover and support such apostles of human culture as Edmund Ware, Samuel Armstrong, and Erastus Cravath.* The opposition to Negro education in the South was at first bitter, and showed itself in ashes, insult, and blood; for the South believed an educated Negro to be a dangerous Negro. And the South was not wholly wrong; for education among all kinds of men always has had, and always will have, an element of danger and revolution, of dissatisfaction and discontent. Nevertheless, men strive to know. Perhaps some inkling of this paradox, even in the unquiet days of the Bureau, helped the bayonets allay an opposition to human training which still to-day lies smouldering in the South, but not flaming. Fisk, Atlanta, Howard, and Hampton were founded in these days, and six million dollars were expended for educational work, seven hundred and fifty thousand dollars of which the freedmen themselves gave of their poverty.

Such contributions, together with the buying of land and various other enterprises, showed that the ex-slave was handling some free capital already. The chief initial source of this was labor in the army, and his pay and bounty as a soldier. Payments to Negro soldiers were at first complicated by the ignorance of the recipients, and the fact that the quotas of colored regiments from Northern States were largely filled by recruits from the South, unknown to their fellow soldiers. Consequently, payments were accompanied by such frauds that Congress, by joint resolution in 1867, put the whole matter in the hands of the Freedmen's Bureau. In two years six million dollars was thus distributed to five thousand claimants, and in the end the sum exceeded eight million dollars. Even in this system fraud was frequent; but still the work put needed capital in the hands of practical paupers, and some, at least, was well spent.

The most perplexing and least successful part of the Bureau's work lay in the exercise of its judicial functions. The regular Bureau court consisted of one representative of the employer, one of the Negro, and one of the Bureau. If the Bureau could have maintained a perfectly judicial attitude, this arrangement would have been ideal, and must in time have gained confidence; but the nature of its other activities and the character of its personnel prejudiced the Bureau in favor of the black litigants, and led without doubt to much injustice and annoyance. On the other hand, to leave the Negro in the hands of Southern courts was impossible. In a distracted land where slavery had hardly fallen, to keep the strong from wanton abuse of the weak, and the weak from gloating insolently over the half-shorn strength of the strong, was a thankless, hopeless task. The former masters of the land were peremptorily ordered about, seized, and imprisoned, and punished over and again, with scant courtesy from army officers. The former slaves were intimidated, beaten, raped, and butchered by angry and revengeful men. Bureau courts tended to become centres simply for punishing whites, while the regular civil courts tended to become solely institutions for perpetuating the slavery of blacks. Almost every law and method ingenuity could devise was employed by the legislatures to reduce the Negroes to serfdom,—to make them the slaves of the State, if not of individual owners; while the Bureau officials too often were found striving to put the "bottom rail on top," and gave the freedmen a power and independence which they could not yet use. It is all well enough for us of another generation to wax wise with advice to those who bore the burden in the heat of the day. It is full easy now to see that the man who lost home, fortune, and family at a stroke, and saw his land ruled by "mules and niggers," was really benefited by the passing of slavery. It is not difficult now to say to the young freedman, cheated and cuffed about who has seen his father's head beaten to a jelly and his own mother namelessly assaulted, that the meek shall inherit the earth. Above all, nothing is more convenient than to heap on the Freedmen's Bureau all the evils of that evil day, and damn it utterly for every mistake and blunder that was made.

All this is easy, but it is neither sensible nor just. Someone had blundered, but that was long before Oliver Howard was born; there was criminal aggression and heedless neglect, but without some system of control there would have been far more than there was. Had that control been from within, the Negro would have been re-enslaved, to all intents and purposes. Coming as the control did from without, perfect men and methods would have bettered all things; and even with imperfect agents and questionable methods, the work accomplished was not undeserving of commendation.

Such was the dawn of Freedom; such was the work of the Freedmen's Bureau, which, summed up in brief, may be epitomized thus: for some fifteen million dollars, beside the sums spent before 1865, and the dole of benevolent societies, this Bureau set going a system of free labor, established a beginning of peasant proprietorship, secured the recognition of black freedmen before courts of law, and founded the free common school in the South. On the other hand, it failed to begin the establishment of good-will between ex-masters and freedmen, to guard its work wholly from paternalistic methods which discouraged self-reliance, and to carry out to any considerable extent its implied promises to furnish the freedmen with land. Its successes were the result of hard work, supplemented by the aid of philanthropists and the eager striving of black men. Its failures were the result of bad local agents, the inherent difficulties of the work, and national neglect.

Such an institution, from its wide powers, great responsibilities, large control of moneys, and generally conspicuous position, was naturally open to repeated and bitter attack. It sustained a searching Congressional investigation at the instance of Fernando Wood in 1870. Its archives and few remaining functions were with blunt discourtesy transferred from Howard's control, in his absence, to the supervision of Secretary of War Belknap in 1872, on the Secretary's recommendation. Finally, in consequence of grave intimations of wrong-doing made by the Secretary and his subordinates, General Howard was court-martialed in 1874. In both of these trials the Commissioner of the Freedmen's Bureau was officially exonerated from any wilful misdoing, and his work commended. Nevertheless, many unpleasant things were brought to light,—the methods of transacting the business of the Bureau were faulty; several cases of defalcation were proved, and other frauds strongly suspected; there were some business transactions which savored of dangerous speculation, if not dishonesty; and around it all lay the smirch of the Freedmen's Bank.

Morally and practically, the Freedmen's Bank was part of the Freedmen's Bureau, although it had no legal connection with it. With the prestige of the government back of it, and a directing board of unusual respectability and national reputation, this banking institution had made a remarkable start in the development of that thrift among black folk which slavery had kept them from knowing. Then in one sad day came the crash,—all the hard-earned dollars of the freedmen disappeared; but that was the least of the loss,—all the faith in saving went too, and much of the faith in men; and that was a loss that a Nation which to-day sneers at Negro shiftlessness has never yet made good. Not even ten additional years of slavery could have done so much to throttle the thrift of the freedmen as the mismanagement and bankruptcy of the series of savings banks chartered by the Nation for their especial aid. Where all the blame should rest, it is hard to say; whether the Bureau and the Bank died chiefly by reason of the blows of its selfish friends or the dark machinations of its foes, perhaps even time will never reveal, for here lies unwritten history.

Of the foes without the Bureau, the bitterest were those who attacked not so much its conduct or policy under the law as the necessity for any such institution at all. Such attacks came primarily from the Border States and the South; and they were summed up by Senator Davis, of Kentucky, when he moved to entitle the act of 1866 a bill "to promote strife and conflict between the white and black races . . . by a grant of unconstitutional power." The argument gathered tremendous strength South and North; but its very strength was its weakness. For, argued the plain common-sense of the nation, if it is unconstitutional, unpractical, and futile for the nation to stand guardian over its helpless wards, then there is left but one alternative,—to make those wards their own guardians by arming them with the ballot. Moreover, the path of the practical politician pointed the same way; for, argued this opportunist, if we cannot peacefully reconstruct the South with white votes, we certainly can with black votes. So justice and force joined hands.

The alternative thus offered the nation was not between full and restricted Negro suffrage; else every sensible man, black and white, would easily have chosen the latter. It was rather a choice between suffrage and slavery, after endless blood and gold had flowed to sweep human bondage away. Not a single Southern legislature stood ready to admit a Negro, under any conditions, to the polls; not a single Southern legislature believed free Negro labor was possible without a system of restrictions that took all its freedom away; there was scarcely a white man in the South who did not honestly regard Emancipation as a crime, and its practical nullification as a duty. In such a situation, the granting of the ballot to the black man was a necessity, the very least a guilty nation could grant a wronged race, and the only method of compelling the South to accept the results of the war. Thus Negro suffrage ended a civil war by beginning a race feud. And some felt gratitude toward the race thus sacrificed in its swaddling clothes on the altar of national integrity; and some felt and feel only indifference and contempt.

Had political exigencies been less pressing, the opposition to government guardianship of Negroes less bitter, and the attachment to the slave system less strong, the social seer can well imagine a far better policy,—a permanent Freedmen's Bureau, with a national system of Negro schools; a carefully supervised employment and labor office; a system of impartial protection before the regular courts; and such institutions for social betterment as savings-banks, land and building associations, and social settlements. All this vast expenditure of money and brains might have formed a great school of prospective citizenship, and solved in a way we have not yet solved the most perplexing and persistent of the Negro problems.

That such an institution was unthinkable in 1870 was due in part to certain acts of the Freedmen's Bureau itself. It came to regard its work as merely temporary, and Negro suffrage as a final answer to all present perplexities. The political ambition of many of its agents and *protégés* led it far afield into questionable activities, until the South, nursing its own deep prejudices, came easily to ignore all the good deeds of the Bureau and hate its very name with perfect hatred. So the Freedmen's Bureau died, and its child was the Fifteenth Amendment.

The passing of a great human institution before its work is done, like the untimely passing of a single soul, but leaves a legacy of striving for other men. The legacy of the Freedmen's Bureau is the heavy heritage of this generation. To-day, when new and vaster problems are destined to strain every fibre of the national mind and soul, would it not be well to count this legacy honestly and carefully? For this much all men know: despite compromise, war, and struggle, the Negro is not free. In the backwoods of the Gulf States, for miles and miles, he may not leave the plantation of his birth; in well-nigh the whole rural

South the black farmers are peons, bound by law and custom to an economic slavery, from which the only escape is death or the penitentiary. In the most cultured sections and cities of the South the Negroes are a segregated servile caste, with restricted rights and privileges. Before the courts, both in law and custom, they stand on a different and peculiar basis. Taxation without representation is the rule of their political life. And the result of all this is, and in nature must have been, lawlessness and crime. That is the large legacy of the Freedmen's Bureau, the work it did not do because it could not.

I have seen a land right merry with the sun, where children sing, and rolling hills lie like passioned women wanton with harvest. And there in the King's Highways sat and sits a figure veiled and bowed, by which the traveller's footsteps hasten as they go. On the tainted air broods fear. Three centuries' thought has been the raising and unveiling of that bowed human heart, and now behold a century new for the duty and the deed. The problem of the Twentieth Century is the problem of the color-line.

Chapter III

Of Mr. Booker T. Washington and Others

From birth till death enslaved; in word, in deed, unmanned!

· · · · · · · ·

Hereditary bondsmen! Know ye not
Who would be free themselves must strike the blow?

BYRON.

Easily the most striking thing in the history of the American Negro since 1876 is the ascendancy of Mr. Booker T. Washington. It began at the time when war memories and ideals were rapidly passing; a day of astonishing commercial development was dawning; a sense of doubt and hesitation overtook the freedmen's sons,—then it was that his leading began. Mr. Washington came, with a single definite programme, at the psychological moment when the nation was a little ashamed of having bestowed so much sentiment on Negroes, and was concentrating its energies on Dollars. His programme of industrial education, conciliation of the South, and submission and silence as to civil and political rights, was not wholly original; the Free Negroes from 1830 up to war-time

The Souls of Black Folk   43

had striven to build industrial schools, and the American Missionary Association had from the first taught various trades; and Price* and others had sought a way of honorable alliance with the best of the Southerners. But Mr. Washington first indissolubly linked these things; he put enthusiasm, unlimited energy, and perfect faith into his programme, and changed it from a by-path into a veritable Way of Life. And the tale of the methods by which he did this is a fascinating study of human life.

It startled the nation to hear a Negro advocating such a programme after many decades of bitter complaint; it startled and won the applause of the South, it interested and won the admiration of the North; and after a confused murmur of protest, it silenced if it did not convert the Negroes themselves.

To gain the sympathy and coöperation of the various elements comprising the white South was Mr. Washington's first task; and this, at the time Tuskegee was founded, seemed, for a black man, well-nigh impossible. And yet ten years later it was done in the word spoken at Atlanta: "In all things purely social we can be as separate as the five fingers, and yet one as the hand in all things essential to mutual progress." This "Atlanta Compromise" is by all odds the most notable thing in Mr. Washington's career. The South interpreted it in different ways: the radicals received it as a complete surrender of the demand for civil and political equality; the conservatives, as a generously conceived working basis for mutual understanding. So both approved it, and to-day its author is certainly the most distinguished Southerner since Jefferson Davis,* and the one with the largest personal following.

Next to this achievement comes Mr. Washington's work in gaining place and consideration in the North. Others less shrewd and tactful had formerly essayed to sit on these two stools and had fallen between them; but as Mr. Washington knew the heart of the South from birth and training, so by singular insight he intuitively grasped the spirit of the age which was dominating the North. And so thoroughly did he learn the speech and thought of triumphant commercialism, and the ideals of material prosperity, that the picture of a lone black boy poring over a French grammar amid the weeds and dirt of a neglected home soon seemed to him the acme of absurdities. One wonders what Socrates* and St. Francis of Assisi* would say to this.

And yet this very singleness of vision and thorough oneness with his age is a mark of the successful man. It is as though Nature must needs make men narrow in order to give them force. So Mr. Washington's cult has gained unquestioning followers, his work has wonderfully prospered, his friends are legion, and his enemies are confounded. To-day he stands as the one recognized spokesman of his ten million fellows, and one of the most notable figures in a nation of seventy millions. One hesitates, therefore, to criticise a life which, beginning with so little, has done so much. And yet the time is come when one may speak in all sincerity and utter courtesy of the mistakes and shortcomings of Mr. Washington's career, as well as of his triumphs, without being thought captious or envious, and without forgetting that it is easier to do ill than well in the world.

The criticism that has hitherto met Mr. Washington has not always been of this broad character. In the South especially has he had to walk warily to avoid the harshest judgments,—and naturally so, for he is dealing with the one subject of deepest sensitiveness to that section. Twice—once when at the Chicago celebration of the Spanish-American War* he alluded to the color-prejudice that is "eating away the vitals of the South," and once when he dined with President Roosevelt*—has the resulting Southern criticism been violent enough to threaten seriously his popularity. In the North the feeling has several times forced itself into words, that Mr. Washington's counsels of submission overlooked certain elements of true manhood, and that his educational programme was unnecessarily narrow. Usually, however, such criticism has not found open expression, although, too, the spiritual sons of the Abolitionists* have not been prepared to acknowledge that the schools founded before Tuskegee, by men of broad ideals and self-sacrificing spirit, were wholly failures or worthy of ridicule. While, then, criticism has not failed to follow Mr. Washington, yet the prevailing public opinion of the land has been but too willing to deliver the solution of a wearisome problem into his hands, and say, "If that is all you and your race ask, take it."

Among his own people, however, Mr. Washington has encountered the strongest and most lasting opposition, amounting at times to bitterness, and even today continuing strong and insistent even though largely silenced in outward expression by the public opinion of the nation. Some of this opposition is, of course, mere envy; the disappointment of displaced demagogues and the spite of narrow minds. But aside from this, there is among educated and thoughtful colored men in all parts of the land a feeling of deep regret, sorrow, and apprehension at the wide currency and ascendancy which some of Mr. Washington's theories have gained. These same men admire his sincerity of purpose, and are willing to forgive much to honest endeavor which is doing something worth the doing. They coöperate with Mr. Washington as far as they conscientiously can; and, indeed, it is no ordinary tribute to this man's tact and power that, steering as he must between so many diverse interests and opinions, he so largely retains the respect of all.

But the hushing of the criticism of honest opponents is a dangerous thing. It leads some of the best of the critics to unfortunate silence and paralysis of effort, and others to burst into speech so passionately and intemperately as to lose listeners. Honest and earnest criticism from those whose interests are most nearly touched,—criticism of writers by readers, of government by those governed, of leaders by those led,—this is the soul of democracy and the safeguard of modern society. If the best of the American Negroes receive by outer pressure a leader whom they had not recognized before, manifestly there is here a certain palpable gain. Yet there is also irreparable loss,—a loss of that peculiarly valuable education which a group receives when by search and criticism it finds and commissions its own leaders. The way in which this is done is at once the most elementary and the nicest problem of social growth. History is but the record of such group-leadership; and yet how infinitely changeful is its type and character! And of all types and kinds, what can be more instructive than the leadership of a group within a group?—that curious double movement where real progress may be negative and actual advance be relative retrogression. All this is the social student's inspiration and despair.

Now in the past the American Negro has had instructive experience in the choosing of group leaders, founding thus a peculiar dynasty which in the light of present conditions is worth while studying. When sticks and stones and beasts form the sole environment of a people, their attitude is largely one of determined opposition to and conquest of natural forces. But when to earth and brute is added an environment of men and ideas, then the attitude of the imprisoned group may take three main forms,—a feeling of revolt and revenge; an attempt to adjust all thought and action to the will of the greater group; or, finally, a determined effort at self-realization and self-development despite environing opinion. The influence of all of these attitudes at various times can be traced in the history of the American Negro, and in the evolution of his successive leaders.

Before 1750, while the fire of African freedom still burned in the veins of the slaves, there was in all leadership or attempted leadership but the one motive of revolt and revenge,—typified in the terrible Maroons,* the Danish blacks,* and Cato of Stono,* and veiling all the Americas in fear of insurrection. The liberalizing tendencies of the latter half of the eighteenth century brought, along with kindlier relations between black and white, thoughts of ultimate adjustment and assimilation. Such aspiration was especially voiced in the earnest songs of Phyllis,* in the martyrdom of Attucks,* the fighting of Salem and Poor,* the intellectual accomplishments of Banneker* and Derham,* and the political demands of the Cuffes.*

Stern financial and social stress after the war cooled much of the previous humanitarian ardor. The disappointment and impatience of the Negroes at the persistence of slavery and serfdom voiced itself in two movements. The slaves in the South, aroused undoubtedly by vague rumors of the Haytian revolt,* made three fierce attempts at insurrection,—in 1800 under Gabriel* in Virginia, in 1822 under Vesey* in Carolina, and in 1831 again in Virginia under the terrible Nat Turner.* In the Free States, on the other hand, a new and curious attempt at self-development was made. In Philadelphia and New York color-prescription led to a withdrawal of Negro communicants from white churches and the formation of a peculiar socio-religious institution among the Negroes known as the African Church,—an organization still living and controlling in its various branches over a million of men.

Walker's wild appeal* against the trend of the times showed how the world was changing after the coming of the cotton-gin. By 1830 slavery seemed hopelessly fastened on the South, and the slaves thoroughly cowed into submission. The free Negroes of the North, inspired by the mulatto immigrants from the West Indies, began to change the basis of their demands; they recognized the slavery of slaves, but insisted that they themselves were freemen, and sought assimilation and amalgamation with the nation on the same terms with other men. Thus, Forten* and Purvis* of Philadelphia, Shad* of Wilmington, Du Bois* of New Haven, Barbadoes* of Boston, and others, strove singly and together as men, they said, not as slaves; as "people of color," not as "Negroes." The trend of the times, however, refused them recognition save in individual and exceptional cases, considered them as one with all the despised blacks, and they soon found themselves striving to keep even the rights they formerly had of voting and working and moving as freemen. Schemes of migration and colonization arose among them; but these they refused to entertain, and they eventually turned to the Abolition movement as a final refuge.

Here, led by Remond,* Nell,* Wells-Brown,* and Douglass, a new period of self-assertion and self-development dawned. To be sure, ultimate freedom and assimilation was the ideal before the leaders, but the assertion of the manhood rights of the Negro by

himself was the main reliance, and John Brown's raid*
was the extreme of its logic. After the war and
emancipation, the great form of Frederick Douglass,
the greatest of American Negro leaders, still led the
host. Self-assertion, especially in political lines, was
the main programme, and behind Douglass came
Elliot,* Bruce,* and Langston,* and the Reconstruction politicians, and, less conspicuous but of
greater social significance, Alexander Crummell* and
Bishop Daniel Payne.*

Then came the Revolution of 1876,* the suppression of the Negro votes, the changing and shifting
of ideals, and the seeking of new lights in the great
night. Douglass, in his old age, still bravely stood for
the ideals of his early manhood,—ultimate assimilation *through* self-assertion, and on no other terms.
For a time Price arose as a new leader, destined, it
seemed, not to give up, but to re-state the old ideals in
a form less repugnant to the white South. But he
passed away in his prime. Then came the new leader.
Nearly all the former ones had become leaders by the
silent suffrage of their fellows, had sought to lead
their own people alone, and were usually, save
Douglass, little known outside their race. But Booker
T. Washington arose as essentially the leader not of
one race but of two,—a compromiser between the
South, the North, and the Negro. Naturally the
Negroes resented, at first bitterly, signs of compromise
which surrendered their civil and political rights, even
though this was to be exchanged for larger chances of
economic development. The rich and dominating
North, however, was not only weary of the race
problem, but was investing largely in Southern
enterprises, and welcomed any method of peaceful
coöperation. Thus, by national opinion, the Negroes
began to recognize Mr. Washington's leadership; and

the voice of criticism was hushed.

Mr. Washington represents in Negro thought the old attitude of adjustment and submission; but adjustment at such a peculiar time as to make his programme unique. This is an age of unusual economic development, and Mr. Washington's programme naturally takes an economic cast, becoming a gospel of Work and Money to such an extent as apparently almost completely to overshadow the higher aims of life. Moreover, this is an age when the more advanced races are coming in closer contact with the less developed races, and the race-feeling is therefore intensified; and Mr. Washington's programme practically accepts the alleged inferiority of the Negro races. Again, in our own land, the reaction from the sentiment of war time has given impetus to race-prejudice against Negroes, and Mr. Washington withdraws many of the high demands of Negroes as men and American citizens. In other periods of intensified prejudice all the Negro's tendency to self-assertion has been called forth; at this period a policy of submission is advocated. In the history of nearly all other races and peoples and doctrine preached at such crises has been that manly self-respect is worth more than lands and houses, and that a people who voluntarily surrender such respect, or cease striving for it, are not worth civilizing.

In answer to this, it has been claimed that the Negro can survive only through submission. Mr. Washington distinctly asks that black people give up, at least for the present, three things,—

First, political power,

Second, insistence on civil rights,

Third, higher education of Negro youth,—
and concentrate all their energies on industrial education, and accumulation of wealth, and the

conciliation of the South. This policy has been courageously and insistently advocated for over fifteen years, and has been triumphant for perhaps ten years. As a result of this tender of the palm-branch, what has been the return? In these years there have occurred:

1. The disfranchisement of the Negro.

2. The legal creation of a distinct status of civil inferiority for the Negro.

3. The steady withdrawal of aid from institutions for the higher training of the Negro.

These movements are not, to be sure, direct results of Mr. Washington's teachings; but his propaganda has, without a shadow of doubt, helped their speedier accomplishment. The question then comes: Is it possible, and probable, that nine millions of men can make effective progress in economic lines if they are deprived of political rights, made a servile caste, and allowed only the most meagre chance for developing their exceptional men? If history and reason give any distinct answer to these questions, it is an emphatic *No*. And Mr. Washington thus faces the triple paradox of his career:

1. He is striving nobly to make Negro artisans business men and property-owners; but it is utterly impossible, under modern competitive methods, for workingmen and property-owners to defend their rights and exist without the right of suffrage.

2. He insists on thrift and self-respect, but at the same time counsels a silent submission to civic inferiority such as is bound to sap the manhood of any race in the long run.

3. He advocates common-school and industrial training, and depreciates institutions of higher learning; but neither the Negro common-schools, nor

Tuskegee itself, could remain open a day were it not for teachers trained in Negro colleges, or trained by their graduates.

This triple paradox in Mr. Washington's position is the object of criticism by two classes of colored Americans. One class is spiritually descended from Toussaint the Savior, through Gabriel, Vesey, and Turner, and they represent the attitude of revolt and revenge; they hate the white South blindly and distrust the white race generally, and so far as they agree on definite action, think that the Negro's only hope lies in emigration beyond the borders of the United States. And yet, by the irony of fate, nothing has more effectually made this programme seem hopeless than the recent course* of the United States toward weaker and darker peoples in the West Indies, Hawaii, and the Philippines,—for where in the world may we go and be safe from lying and brute force?

The other class of Negroes who cannot agree with Mr. Washington has hitherto said little aloud. They deprecate the sight of scattered counsels, of internal disagreement; and especially they dislike making their just criticism of a useful and earnest man an excuse for a general discharge of venom from small-minded opponents. Nevertheless, the questions involved are so fundamental and serious that it is difficult to see how men like the Grimkes,* Kelly Miller,* J. W. E. Bowen,* and other representatives of this group, can much longer be silent. Such men feel in conscience bound to ask of this nation three things:

1. The right to vote.
2. Civic equality.
3. The education of youth according to ability.

They acknowledge Mr. Washington's invaluable service in counselling patience and courtesy in such demands; they do not ask that ignorant black men vote when ignorant whites are debarred, or that any reasonable restrictions in the suffrage should not be applied; they know that the low social level of the mass of the race is responsible for much discrimination against it, but they also know, and the nation knows, that relentless color-prejudice is more often a cause than a result of the Negro's degradation; they seek the abatement of this relic of barbarism, and not its systematic encouragement and pampering by all agencies of social power from the Associated Press to the Church of Christ. They advocate, with Mr. Washington, a broad system of Negro common schools supplemented by thorough industrial training; but they are surprised that a man of Mr. Washington's insight cannot see that no such educational system ever has rested or can rest on any other basis than that of the well-equipped college and university, and they insist that there is a demand for a few such institutions throughout the South to train the best of the Negro youth as teachers, professional men, and leaders.

This group of men honor Mr. Washington for his attitude of conciliation toward the white South; they accept the "Atlanta Compromise" in its broadest interpretation; they recognize, with him, many signs of promise, many men of high purpose and fair judgment, in this section; they know that no easy task has been laid upon a region already tottering under heavy burdens. But, nevertheless, they insist that the way to truth and right lies in straightforward honesty, not in indiscriminate flattery; in praising those of the South who do well and criticising uncompromisingly those who do ill; in taking advantage of the opportunities at hand and urging their fellows to do the same, but at the same time in remembering that only a firm adherence to their higher ideals and aspirations will ever keep those ideals within the realm of possibility. They do not expect that the free right to vote, to enjoy civic rights, and to be educated, will come in a moment; they do not expect to see the bias and prejudices of years disappear at the blast of a trumpet; but they are absolutely certain that the way for a people to gain their reasonable rights is not by voluntarily throwing them away and insisting that they do not want them; that the way for a people to gain respect is not by continually belittling and ridiculing themselves; that, on the contrary, Negroes must insist continually, in season and out of season, that voting is necessary to modern manhood, that color discrimination is barbarism, and that black boys need education as well as white boys.

In failing thus to state plainly and unequivocally the legitimate demands of their people, even at the cost of opposing an honored leader, the thinking classes of American Negroes would shirk a heavy responsibility,—a responsibility to themselves, a responsibility to the struggling masses, a responsibility to the darker races of men whose future depends so largely on this American experiment, but especially a responsibility to this nation,—this common Fatherland. It is wrong to encourage a man or a people in evil-doing; it is wrong to aid and abet a national crime simply because it is unpopular not to do so. The growing spirit of kindliness and reconciliation between the North and South after the frightful difference of a generation ago ought to be a source of deep congratulation to all, and especially to those whose mistreatment caused the war; but if that reconciliation is to be marked by the industrial slavery and civic death of those same black men, with permanent legislation into a position of inferiority, then those black men, if they are really men, are called upon by every consideration of patriotism and loyalty to oppose such a course by all civilized methods, even though such opposition involves disagreement with Mr. Booker T. Washington. We have no right to sit silently by while the inevitable seeds are sown for a harvest of disaster to our children, black and white.

First, it is the duty of black men to judge the South discriminatingly. The present generation of Southerners are not responsible for the past, and they should not be blindly hated or blamed for it. Furthermore, to no class is the indiscriminate endorsement of the recent course of the South toward Negroes more nauseating than to the best thought of the South. The South is not "solid"; it is a land in the ferment of social change, wherein forces of all kinds are fighting for supremacy; and to praise the ill the South is today perpetrating is just as wrong as to condemn the good. Discriminating and broad-minded criticism is what the South needs,—needs it for the sake of her own white sons and daughters, and for the insurance of robust, healthy mental and moral development.

To-day even the attitude of the Southern whites toward the blacks is not, as so many assume, in all cases the same; the ignorant Southerner hates the Negro, the workingmen fear his competition, the money-makers wish to use him as a laborer, some of the educated see a menace in his upward development, while others—usually the sons of the masters—wish to help him to rise. National opinion has enabled this last class to maintain the Negro common schools, and to protect the Negro partially in property, life, and limb. Through the pressure of the money-makers, the Negro is in danger of being reduced to semi-slavery, especially in the country districts; the workingmen, and those of the educated who fear the Negro, have united to disfranchise him, and some have urged his deportation; while the passions of the ignorant are easily aroused to lynch and abuse any black man. To praise this intricate whirl of thought and prejudice is nonsense; to inveigh indiscriminately against "the South" is unjust; but to use the same breath in praising Governor Aycock,* exposing Senator Morgan,* arguing with Mr. Thomas Nelson Page,* and denouncing Senator Ben Tillman,* is not only sane, but the imperative duty of thinking black men.

It would be unjust to Mr. Washington not to acknowledge that in several instances he has opposed movements in the South which were unjust to the Negro; he sent memorials to the Louisiana and Alabama constitutional conventions, he has spoken against lynching, and in other ways has openly or silently set his influence against sinister schemes and unfortunate happenings. Notwithstanding this, it is equally true to assert that on the whole the distinct impression left by Mr. Washington's propaganda is, first, that the South is justified in its present attitude toward the Negro because of the Negro's degradation; secondly, that the prime cause of the Negro's failure to rise more quickly is his wrong education in the past; and, thirdly, that his future rise depends primarily on his own efforts. Each of these propositions is a dangerous half-truth. The supplementary truths must never be lost sight of: first, slavery and race-prejudice are potent if not sufficient causes of the Negro's position; second, industrial and common-school training were necessarily slow in planting because they had to await the black teachers trained by higher institutions,—it being extremely doubtful if any essentially different development was possible, and certainly a Tuskegee was unthinkable before 1880; and, third, while it is a great truth to say that the

Negro must strive and strive mightily to help himself, it is equally true that unless his striving be not simply seconded, but rather aroused and encouraged, by the initiative of the richer and wiser environing group, he cannot hope for great success.

In his failure to realize and impress this last point, Mr. Washington is especially to be criticised. His doctrine has tended to make the whites, North and South, shift the burden of the Negro problem to the Negro's shoulders and stand aside as critical and rather pessimistic spectators; when in fact the burden belongs to the nation, and the hands of none of us are clean if we bend not our energies to righting these great wrongs.

The South ought to be led, by candid and honest criticism, to assert her better self and do her full duty to the race she has cruelly wronged and is still wronging. The North—her co-partner in guilt—cannot salve her conscience by plastering it with gold. We cannot settle this problem by diplomacy and suaveness, by "policy" alone. If worse come to worst, can the moral fibre of this country survive the slow throttling and murder of nine millions of men?

The black men of America have a duty to perform, a duty stern and delicate,—a forward movement to oppose a part of the work of their greatest leader. So far as Mr. Washington preaches Thrift, Patience, and Industrial Training for the masses, we must hold up his hands and strive with him, rejoicing in his honors and glorying in the strength of this Joshua called of God and of man to lead the headless host. But so far as Mr. Washington apologizes for injustice, North or South, does not rightly value the privilege and duty of voting, belittles the emasculating effects of caste distinctions, and opposes the higher training and ambition of our brighter minds,—so far as he, the

South, or the Nation, does this,—we must unceasingly and firmly oppose them. By every civilized and peaceful method we must strive for the rights which the world accords to men, clinging unwaveringly to those great words which the sons of the Fathers would fain forget: "We hold these truths to be self-evident: That all men are created equal; that they are endowed by their Creator with certain unalienable rights; that among these are life, liberty, and the pursuit of happiness."

Chapter IV

Of the Meaning of Progress

Willst Du Deine Macht verkünden,
Wähle sie die frei von Sünden,
Steh'n in Deinem ew'gen Haus!
Deine Geister sende aus!
Die Unsterblichen, die Reinen,
Die nicht fühlen, die nicht weinen!
Nicht die zarte Jungfrau wähle,
Nicht der Hirtin weiche Seele!

SCHILLER.

Once upon a time I taught school in the hills of Tennessee, where the broad dark vale of the Mississippi begins to roll and crumple to greet the Alleghanies. I was a Fisk student then, and all Fisk men thought that Tennessee—beyond the Veil—was theirs alone, and in vacation time they sallied forth in lusty bands to meet the county school-commissioners. Young and happy, I too went, and I shall not soon forget that summer, seventeen years ago.

First, there was a Teachers' Institute at the countyseat; and there distinguished guests of the superintendent taught the teachers fractions and spelling and other mysteries,—white teachers in the morning, Negroes at night. A picnic now and then, and a supper, and the rough world was softened by laughter and song. I remember how—But I wander.

There came a day when all the teachers left the Institute and began the hunt for schools. I learn from hearsay (for my mother was mortally afraid of firearms) that the hunting of ducks and bears and men is wonderfully interesting, but I am sure that the man who has never hunted a country school has something to learn of the pleasures of the chase. I see now the white, hot roads lazily rise and fall and wind before me under the burning July sun; I feel the deep weariness of heart and limb as ten, eight, six miles stretch relentlessly ahead; I feel my heart sink heavily as I hear again and again, "Got a teacher? Yes." So I walked on and on—horses were too expensive—until I had wandered beyond railways, beyond stage lines, to a land of "varmints" and rattlesnakes, where the coming of a stranger was an event, and men lived and died in the shadow of one blue hill.

Sprinkled over hill and dale lay cabins and farmhouses, shut out from the world by the forests and the rolling hills toward the east. There I found at last a little school. Josie told me of it; she was a thin, homely girl of twenty, with a dark-brown face and thick, hard hair. I had crossed the stream at Watertown, and rested under the great willows; then I had gone to the little cabin in the lot where Josie was resting on her way to town. The gaunt farmer made me welcome, and Josie, hearing my errand, told me anxiously that they wanted a school over the hill; that but once since the war had a teacher been there; that she herself longed to learn,—and thus she ran on, talking fast and loud, with much earnestness and energy.

Next morning I crossed the tall round hill, lingered to look at the blue and yellow mountains stretching toward the Carolinas, then plunged into the wood, and came out at Josie's home. It was a dull frame cottage with four rooms, perched just below the brow of the hill, amid peach-trees. The father was a quiet, simple soul, calmly ignorant, with no touch of vulgarity. The mother was different,—strong, bustling, and energetic, with a quick, restless tongue, and an ambition to live "like folks." There was a crowd of children. Two boys had gone away. There remained two growing girls; a shy midget of eight; John, tall, awkward, and eighteen; Jim, younger, quicker, and better looking; and two babies of indefinite age. Then there was Josie herself. She seemed to be the centre of the family: always busy at service, or at home, or berry-picking; a little nervous and inclined to scold, like her mother, yet faithful, too, like her father. She had about her a certain fineness, the shadow of an unconscious moral heroism that would willingly give all of life to make life broader, deeper, and fuller for her and hers. I saw much of this family afterwards, and grew to love them for their honest efforts to be decent and comfortable, and for their knowledge of their own ignorance. There was with them no affectation. The mother would scold the father for being so "easy"; Josie would roundly berate the boys for carelessness; and all knew that it was a hard thing to dig a living out of a rocky side-hill.

I secured the school. I remember the day I rode horseback out to the commissioner's house with a pleasant young white fellow who wanted the white school. The road ran down the bed of a stream; the sun laughed and the water jingled, and we rode on. "Come in," said the commissioner,—"come in. Have a seat. Yes, that certificate will do. Stay to dinner.

What do you want a month?" "Oh," thought I, "this is lucky"; but even then fell the awful shadow of the Veil, for they ate first, then I—alone.

The schoolhouse was a log hut, where Colonel Wheeler used to shelter his corn. It sat in a lot behind a rail fence and thorn bushes, near the sweetest of springs. There was an entrance where a door once was, and within, a massive rickety fireplace; great chinks between the logs served as windows. Furniture was scarce. A pale blackboard crouched in the corner. My desk was made of three boards, reinforced at critical points, and my chair, borrowed from the landlady, had to be returned every night. Seats for the children—these puzzled me much. I was haunted by a New England vision of neat little desks and chairs, but, alas! the reality was rough plank benches without backs, and at times without legs. They had the one virtue of making naps dangerous,—possibly fatal, for the floor was not to be trusted.

It was a hot morning late in July when the school opened. I trembled when I heard the patter of little feet down the dusty road, and saw the growing row of dark solemn faces and bright eager eyes facing me. First came Josie and her brothers and sisters. The longing to know, to be a student in the great school at Nashville, hovered like a star above this child-woman amid her work and worry, and she studied doggedly. There were the Dowells from their farm over toward Alexandria,—Fanny, with her smooth black face and wondering eyes; Martha, brown and dull; the pretty girl-wife of a brother, and the younger brood.

There were the Burkes,—two brown and yellow lads, and a tiny haughty-eyed girl. Fat Reuben's little chubby girl came, with golden face and old-gold hair, faithful and solemn. 'Thenie was on hand early,—a jolly, ugly, good-hearted girl, who slyly dipped snuff and looked after her little bow-legged brother. When her mother could spare her, 'Tildy came,—a midnight beauty, with starry eyes and tapering limbs; and her brother, correspondingly homely. And then the big boys,—the hulking Lawrences; the lazy Neills, unfathered sons of mother and daughter; Hickman, with a stoop in his shoulders; and the rest.

There they sat, nearly thirty of them, on the rough benches, their faces shading from a pale cream to a deep brown, the little feet bare and swinging, the eyes full of expectation, with here and there a twinkle of mischief, and the hands grasping Webster's blue-black spelling-book. I loved my school, and the fine faith the children had in the wisdom of their teacher was truly marvellous. We read and spelled together, wrote a little, picked flowers, sang, and listened to stories of the world beyond the hill. At times the school would dwindle away, and I would start out. I would visit Mun Eddings, who lived in two very dirty rooms, and ask why little Lugene, whose flaming face seemed ever ablaze with the dark-red hair uncombed, was absent all last week, or why I missed so often the inimitable rags of Mack and Ed. Then the father, who worked Colonel Wheeler's farm on shares, would tell me how the crops needed the boys; and the thin, slovenly mother, whose face was pretty when washed, assured me that Lugene must mind the baby. "But we'll start them again next week." When the Lawrences stopped, I knew that the doubts of the old folks about book-learning had conquered again, and so, toiling up the hill, and getting as far into the cabin as possible, I put Cicero "pro Archia Poeta"* into the simplest English with local applications, and usually convinced them— for a week or so.

On Friday nights I often went home with some of the children,—sometimes to Doc Burke's farm. He was a great, loud, thin Black, ever working, and trying to buy the seventy-five acres of hill and dale where he lived; but people said that he would surely fail, and the "white folks would get it all." His wife was a magnificent Amazon, with saffron face and shining hair, uncorseted and barefooted, and the children were strong and beautiful. They lived in a one-and-a-half-room cabin in the hollow of the farm, near the spring. The front room was full of great fat white beds, scrupulously neat; and there were bad chromos on the walls, and a tired centre-table. In the tiny back kitchen I was often invited to "take out and help" myself to fried chicken and wheat biscuit, "meat" and corn pone, string-beans and berries. At first I used to be a little alarmed at the approach of bedtime in the one lone bedroom, but embarrassment was very deftly avoided. First, all the children nodded and slept, and were stowed away in one great pile of goose feathers; next, the mother and the father discreetly slipped away to the kitchen while I went to bed; then, blowing out the dim light, they retired in the dark. In the morning all were up and away before I thought of awaking. Across the road, where fat Reuben lived, they all went outdoors while the teacher retired, because they did not boast the luxury of a kitchen.

I liked to stay with the Dowells, for they had four rooms and plenty of good country fare. Uncle Bird had a small, rough farm, all woods and hills, miles from the big road; but he was full of tales,—he preached now and then,—and with his children, berries, horses, and wheat he was happy and prosperous. Often, to keep the peace, I must go where life was less lovely; for instance, 'Tildy's mother was incorrigibly dirty, Reuben's larder was limited seriously, and herds of untamed insects wandered over the Eddingses' beds. Best of all I loved to go to Josie's, and sit on the porch, eating peaches, while the mother bustled and talked: how Josie had bought the sewing-machine; how Josie worked at service in winter, but that four dollars a month was "mighty little" wages; how Josie longed to go away to school, but that it "looked like" they never could get far enough ahead to let her; how the crops failed and the well was yet unfinished; and, finally, how "mean" some of the white folks were.

For two summers I lived in this little world; it was dull and humdrum. The girls looked at the hill in wistful longing, and the boys fretted and haunted Alexandria. Alexandria was "town,"—a straggling, lazy village of houses, churches, and shops, and an aristocracy of Toms, Dicks, and Captains. Cuddled on the hill to the north was the village of the colored folks, who lived in three- or four-room unpainted cottages, some neat and homelike, and some dirty. The dwellings were scattered rather aimlessly, but they centred about the twin temples of the hamlet, the Methodist, and the Hard-Shell Baptist churches. These, in turn, leaned gingerly on a sad-colored schoolhouse. Hither my little world wended its crooked way on Sunday to meet other worlds, and gossip, and wonder, and make the weekly sacrifice with frenzied priest at the altar of the "old-time religion." Then the soft melody and mighty cadences of Negro song fluttered and thundered.

I have called my tiny community a world, and so its isolation made it; and yet there was among us but a half-awakened common consciousness, sprung from common joy and grief, at burial, birth, or wedding; from a common hardship in poverty, poor land, and low wages; and, above all, from the sight of the Veil that hung between us and Opportunity. All this caused us to think some thoughts together; but these, when ripe for speech, were spoken in various languages. Those whose eyes twenty-five and more years before had seen "the glory of the coming of the Lord," saw in every present hindrance or help a dark fatalism bound to bring all things right in His own good time. The mass of those to whom slavery was a dim recollection of childhood found the world a puzzling thing: it asked little of them, and they answered with little, and yet it ridiculed their offering. Such a paradox they could not understand, and therefore sank into listless indifference, or shiftlessness, or reckless bravado. There were, however, some—such as Josie, Jim, and Ben—to whom War, Hell, and Slavery were but childhood tales, whose young appetites had been whetted to an edge by school and story and half-awakened thought. Ill could they be content, born without and beyond the World. And their weak wings beat against their barriers,—barriers of caste, of youth, of life; at last, in dangerous moments, against everything that opposed even a whim.

The ten years that follow youth, the years when first the realization comes that life is leading somewhere,—these were the years that passed after I left my little school. When they were past, I came by chance once more to the walls of Fisk University, to the halls of the chapel of melody. As I lingered there in the joy and pain of meeting old school-friends, there swept over me a sudden longing to pass again beyond the blue hill, and to see the homes and the school of other days, and to learn how life had gone with my school-children; and I went.

Josie was dead, and the gray-haired mother said simply, "We've had a heap of trouble since you've been away." I had feared for Jim. With a cultured parentage and a social caste to uphold him, he might have made a venturesome merchant or a West Point cadet. But here he was, angry with life and reckless; and when Farmer Durham charged him with stealing wheat, the old man had to ride fast to escape the stones which the furious fool hurled after him. They told Jim to run away; but he would not run, and the constable came that afternoon. It grieved Josie, and great awkward John walked nine miles every day to see his little brother through the bars of Lebanon jail. At last the two came back together in the dark night. The mother cooked supper, and Josie emptied her purse, and the boys stole away. Josie grew thin and silent, yet worked the more. The hill became steep for the quiet old father, and with the boys away there was little to do in the valley. Josie helped them to sell the old farm, and they moved nearer town. Brother Dennis, the carpenter, built a new house with six rooms; Josie toiled a year in Nashville, and brought back ninety dollars to furnish the house and change it to a home.

When the spring came, and the birds twittered, and the stream ran proud and full, little sister Lizzie, bold and thoughtless, flushed with the passion of youth, bestowed herself on the tempter, and brought home a nameless child. Josie shivered and worked on, with the vision of schooldays all fled, with a face wan and tired,—worked until, on a summer's day, some one married another; then Josie crept to her mother like a hurt child, and slept—and sleeps.

I paused to scent the breeze as I entered the valley. The Lawrences have gone,—father and son forever,— and the other son lazily digs in the earth to live. A new young widow rents out their cabin to fat Reuben. Reuben is a Baptist preacher now, but I fear as lazy as ever, though his cabin has three rooms; and little Ella has grown into a bouncing woman, and is ploughing corn on the hot hillside. There are babies a-plenty, and one half-witted girl. Across the valley is a house I did not know before, and there I found, rocking one baby and expecting another, one of my schoolgirls, a daughter of Uncle Bird Dowell. She looked somewhat worried with her new duties, but soon bristled into pride over her neat cabin and the tale of her thrifty husband, and the horse and cow, and the farm they were planning to buy.

My log schoolhouse was gone. In its place stood Progress; and Progress, I understand, is necessarily ugly. The crazy foundation stones still marked the former site of my poor little cabin, and not far away, on six weary boulders, perched a jaunty board house, perhaps twenty by thirty feet, with three windows and a door that locked. Some of the window-glass was broken, and part of an old iron stove lay mournfully under the house. I peeped through the window half reverently, and found things that were more familiar. The blackboard had grown by about two feet, and the seats were still without backs. The county owns the lot now, I hear, and every year there is a session of school. As I sat by the spring and looked on the Old and the New I felt glad, very glad, and yet—

After two long drinks I started on. There was the great double log-house on the corner. I remembered the broken, blighted family that used to live there. The strong, hard face of the mother, with its wilderness of hair, rose before me. She had driven her husband away, and while I taught school a strange man lived there, big and jovial, and people talked. I felt sure that Ben and 'Tildy would come to naught from such a home. But this is an odd world; for Ben is a busy farmer in Smith County, "doing well, too," they say, and he had cared for little 'Tildy until last spring, when a lover married her. A hard life the lad had led, toiling for meat, and laughed at because he was homely and crooked. There was Sam Carlon, an impudent old skinflint, who had definite notions about "niggers," and hired Ben a summer and would not pay him. Then the hungry boy gathered his sacks together, and in broad daylight went into Carlon's corn; and when the hard-fisted farmer set upon him, the angry boy flew at him like a beast. Doc Burke saved a murder and a lynching that day.

The story reminded me again of the Burkes, and an impatience seized me to know who won in the battle, Doc or the seventy-five acres. For it is a hard thing to make a farm out of nothing, even in fifteen years. So I hurried on, thinking of the Burkes. They used to have a certain magnificent barbarism about them that I liked. They were never vulgar, never immoral, but rather rough and primitive, with an unconventionality that spent itself in loud guffaws, slaps on the back, and naps in the corner. I hurried by the cottage of the misborn Neill boys. It was empty, and they were grown into fat, lazy farm-hands. I saw the home of the Hickmans, but Albert, with his stooping shoulders, had passed from the world. Then I came to the Burkes' gate and peered through; the inclosure looked rough and untrimmed, and yet there were the same fences around the old farm save to the left, where lay twenty-five other acres. And lo! the cabin in the hollow had climbed the hill and swollen to a half-finished six-room cottage.

The Burkes held a hundred acres, but they were still in debt. Indeed, the gaunt father who toiled night and day would scarcely be happy out of debt, being so used to it. Some day he must stop, for his massive frame is showing decline. The mother wore shoes, but the lion-like physique of other days was broken. The children had grown up. Rob, the image of his father, was loud and rough with laughter. Birdie, my school baby of six, had grown to a picture of maiden beauty, tall and tawny. "Edgar is gone," said the mother, with head half bowed,—"gone to work in Nashville; he and his father couldn't agree."

Little Doc, the boy born since the time of my school, took me horseback down the creek next morning toward Farmer Dowell's. The road and the stream were battling for mastery, and the stream had the better of it. We splashed and waded, and the merry boy, perched behind me, chattered and laughed. He showed me where Simon Thompson had bought a bit of ground and a home; but his daughter Lana, a plump, brown, slow girl, was not there. She had married a man and a farm twenty miles away. We wound on down the stream till we came to a gate that I did not recognize, but the boy insisted that it was "Uncle Bird's." The farm was fat with the growing crop. In that little valley was a strange stillness as I rode up; for death and marriage had stolen youth and left age and childhood there. We sat and talked that night after the chores were done. Uncle Bird was grayer, and his eyes did not see so well, but he was still jovial. We talked of the acres bought,—one hundred and twenty-five,—of the new guest-chamber added, of Martha's marrying. Then we talked of death: Fanny and Fred were gone; a shadow hung over the other daughter, and when it lifted she was to go to Nashville to school. At last we spoke of the neighbors, and as night fell, Uncle Bird told me how, on a night like that, 'Thenie came wandering back to her home over yonder, to escape the blows of her husband. And next morning she died in the home that her little bow-legged brother, working and saving, had bought for their widowed mother.

My journey was done, and behind me lay hill and dale, and Life and Death. How shall man measure Progress there where the dark-faced Josie lies? How many heartfuls of sorrow shall balance a bushel of wheat? How hard a thing is life to the lowly, and yet how human and real! And all this life and love and strife and failure,—is it the twilight of nightfall or the flush of some faint-dawning day?

Thus sadly musing, I rode to Nashville in the Jim Crow car.*

Chapter V

Of the Wings of Atalanta

O black boy of Atlanta!
 But half was spoken;
The slave's chains and the master's
 Alike are broken;
The one curse of the races
 Held both in tether;
They are rising—all are rising—
 The black and white together.

WHITTIER.

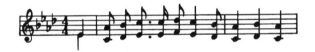

South of the North, yet north of the South, lies the City of a Hundred Hills, peering out from the shadows of the past into the promise of the future. I have seen her in the morning, when the first flush of day had half-roused her; she lay gray and still on the crimson soil of Georgia; then the blue smoke began to curl from her chimneys, the tinkle of bell and scream of whistle broke the silence, the rattle and roar of busy life slowly gathered and swelled, until the seething whirl of the city seemed a strange thing in a sleepy land.

Once, they say, even Atlanta slept dull and drowsy at the foot-hills of the Alleghanies, until the iron baptism of war awakened her with its sullen waters, aroused and maddened her, and left her listening to the sea. And the sea cried to the hills and the hills answered the sea, till the city rose like a widow and cast away her weeds, and toiled for her daily bread; toiled steadily, toiled cunningly,—perhaps with some bitterness, with a touch of *réclame*,*—and yet with real earnestness, and real sweat.

It is a hard thing to live haunted by the ghost of an untrue dream; to see the wide vision of empire fade into real ashes and dirt; to feel the pang of the conquered, and yet know that with all the Bad that fell on one black day, something was vanquished that deserved to live, something killed that in justice had not dared to die; to know that with the Right that triumphed, triumphed something of Wrong, something sordid and mean, something less than the broadest and best. All this is bitter hard; and many a man and city and people have found in it excuse for sulking, and brooding, and listless waiting.

Such are not men of the sturdier make; they of Atlanta turned resolutely toward the future; and that future held aloft vistas of purple and gold:—Atlanta, Queen of the cotton kingdom; Atlanta, Gateway to the Land of the Sun; Atlanta, the new Lachesis,* spinner of web and woof for the world. So the city crowned her hundred hills with factories, and stored her shops with cunning handiwork, and stretched long iron ways to greet the busy Mercury* in his coming. And the Nation talked of her striving.

Perhaps Atlanta was not christened for the winged maiden of dull Bœotia;* you know the tale,—how swarthy Atalanta, tall and wild, would marry only him who out-raced her; and how the wily Hippomenes laid three apples of gold in the way. She fled like a shadow, paused, startled over the first apple, but even as he stretched his hand, fled again; hovered over the second, then, slipping from his hot grasp, flew over river, vale, and hill; but as she lingered over the third, his arms fell round her, and looking on each other, the blazing passion of their love profaned the sanctuary of Love, and they were cursed. If Atlanta be not named for Atalanta, she ought to have been.

Atalanta is not the first or the last maiden whom greed of gold has led to defile the temple of Love; and not maids alone, but men in the race of life, sink from the high and generous ideals of youth to the gambler's code of the Bourse;* and in all our Nation's striving is not the Gospel of Work befouled by the Gospel of Pay? So common is this that one-half think it normal; so unquestioned, that we almost fear to question if the end of racing is not gold, if the aim of man is not rightly to be rich. And if this is the fault of America, how dire a danger lies before a new land and a new city, lest Atlanta, stooping for mere gold, shall find that gold accursed!

It was no maiden's idle whim that started this hard racing; a fearful wilderness lay about the feet of that city after the War,—feudalism, poverty, the rise of the Third Estate,* serfdom, the re-birth of Law and Order, and above and between all, the Veil of Race. How heavy a journey for weary feet! what wings must Atalanta have to flit over all this hollow and hill, through sour wood and sullen water, and by the red waste of sun-baked clay! How fleet must Atalanta be if she will not be tempted by gold to profane the Sanctuary!

The Sanctuary of our fathers has, to be sure, few Gods,—some sneer, "all too few." There is the thrifty Mercury of New England, Pluto* of the North, and Ceres* of the West; and there, too, is the half-forgotten Apollo* of the South, under whose ægis the maiden ran,—and as she ran she forgot him, even as there in Bœotia Venus was forgot. She forgot the old ideal of the Southern gentleman,—that new-world heir of the grace and courtliness of patrician, knight, and noble; forgot his honor with his foibles, his kindliness with his carelessness, and stooped to apples of gold,—to men busier and sharper, thriftier and more unscrupulous. Golden apples are beautiful—I remember the lawless days of boyhood, when orchards in crimson and gold tempted me over fence and field—and, too, the merchant who has dethroned the planter is no despicable *parvenu*.* Work and wealth are the mighty levers to lift this old new land; thrift and toil and saving are the highways to new hopes and new possibilities; and yet the warning is needed lest the wily Hippomenes tempt Atalanta to thinking that golden apples are the goal of racing, and not mere incidents by the way.

Atlanta must not lead the South to dream of material prosperity as the touchstone of all success; already the fatal might of this idea is beginning to spread; it is replacing the finer type of Southerner with vulgar money-getters; it is burying the sweeter beauties of Southern life beneath pretence and ostentation. For every social ill the panacea of Wealth has been urged,—wealth to overthrow the remains of the slave feudalism; wealth to raise the "cracker" Third Estate; wealth to employ the black serfs, and the prospect of wealth to keep them working; wealth as the end and aim of politics, and as the legal tender for law and order; and, finally, instead of Truth, Beauty, and Goodness, wealth as the ideal of the Public School.

Not only is this true in the world which Atlanta typifies, but it is threatening to be true of a world beneath and beyond that world,—the Black World beyond the Veil. To-day it makes little difference to Atlanta, to the South, what the Negro thinks or dreams or wills. In the soul-life of the land he is to-day, and naturally will long remain, unthought of, half forgotten; and yet when he does come to think and will and do for himself,—and let no man dream that day will never come,—then the part he plays will not be one of sudden learning, but words and thoughts he has been taught to lisp in his race-childhood. To-day the ferment of his striving toward self-realization is to the strife of the white world like a wheel within a wheel: beyond the Veil are smaller but like problems of ideals, of leaders and the led, of serfdom, of poverty, of order and subordination, and, through all, the Veil of Race. Few know of these problems, few who know notice them; and yet there they are, awaiting student, artist, and seer,—a field for somebody sometime to discover. Hither has the temptation of Hippomenes penetrated; already in this smaller world, which now indirectly and anon directly must influence the larger for good or ill, the habit is forming of interpreting the world in dollars. The old leaders of Negro opinion, in the little groups where there is a Negro social consciousness, are being replaced by new; neither the black preacher nor the black teacher leads as he did two decades ago. Into their places are pushing the farmers and gardeners, the well-paid porters and artisans, the business-men,—all those with property and money. And with all this change, so curiously parallel to that of the Other-world, goes too the same inevitable change in ideals. The South laments to-day the slow, steady disappearance of a certain type of Negro,—the faithful, courteous slave of other days, with his incorruptible honesty and dignified humility. He is passing away just as surely as the old type of Southern gentleman is passing, and from not dissimilar causes,—the sudden transformation of a fair far-off ideal of Freedom into the hard reality of bread-winning and the consequent deification of Bread.

In the Black World, the Preacher and Teacher embodied once the ideals of this people—the strife for another and a juster world, the vague dream of righteousness, the mystery of knowing; but to-day the danger is that these ideals, with their simple beauty and weird inspiration, will suddenly sink to a question of cash and a lust for gold. Here stands this black young Atalanta, girding herself for the race that must be run; and if her eyes be still toward the hills and sky as in the days of old, then we may look for noble running; but what if some ruthless or wily or even thoughtless Hippomenes lay golden apples before her? What if the Negro people be wooed from a strife for righteousness, from a love of knowing, to regard dollars as the be-all and end-all of life? What if to the Mammonism* of America be added the rising Mammonism of the re-born South, and the Mammonism of this South be reinforced by the budding Mammonism of its half-wakened black millions? Whither, then, is the new-world quest of Goodness and Beauty and Truth gone glimmering? Must this, and that fair flower of Freedom which, despite the jeers of latter-day striplings, sprung from our fathers' blood, must that too degenerate into a dusty quest of gold,—into lawless lust with Hippomenes?

The hundred hills of Atlanta are not all crowned with factories. On one, toward the west, the setting sun throws three buildings in bold relief against the sky. The beauty of the group lies in its simple unity:— a broad lawn of green rising from the red street and mingled roses and peaches; north and south, two plain and stately halls; and in the midst, half hidden in ivy, a larger building, boldly graceful, sparingly decorated, and with one low spire. It is a restful group,—one never looks for more; it is all here, all intelligible. There I live, and there I hear from day to day the low hum of restful life. In winter's twilight, when the red sun glows, I can see the dark figures pass between the halls to the music of the night-bell. In the morning, when the sun is golden, the clang of the day-bell brings the hurry and laughter of three hundred young hearts from hall and street, and from the busy city below,—children all dark and heavy-haired,—to join their clear young voices in the music of the morning sacrifice. In a half-dozen class-rooms they gather then,—here to follow the love-song of Dido,* here to listen to the tale of Troy divine; there to wander among the stars, there to wander among men and nations,—and elsewhere other well-worn ways of knowing this queer world. Nothing new, no time-saving devices,—simply old time-glorified methods of delving for Truth, and searching out the hidden beauties of life, and learning the good of living. The riddle of existence is the college curriculum that was laid before the Pharaohs,* that was taught in the groves by Plato,* that formed the *trivium** and *quadrivium*, and is to-day laid before the freedmen's sons by Atlanta University. And this course of study will not change; its methods will grow more deft and effectual, its content richer by toil of scholar and sight of seer; but the true college will ever have one goal,— not to earn meat, but to know the end and aim of that life which meat nourishes.

The vision of life that rises before these dark eyes has in it nothing mean or selfish. Not at Oxford* or at Leipsic, not at Yale or Columbia, is there an air of higher resolve or more unfettered striving; the determination to realize for men, both black and white, the broadest possibilities of life, to seek the better and the best, to spread with their own hands the Gospel of Sacrifice,—all this is the burden of their talk and dream. Here, amid a wide desert of caste and proscription, amid the heart-hurting slights and jars and vagaries of a deep race-dislike, lies this green oasis, where hot anger cools, and the bitterness of disappointment is sweetened by the springs and breezes of Parnassus;* and here men may lie and listen, and learn of a future fuller than the past, and hear the voice of Time:

"Entbehren sollst du, sollst entbehren."*

They made their mistakes, those who planted Fisk and Howard and Atlanta before the smoke of battle had lifted; they made their mistakes, but those mistakes were not the things at which we lately laughed somewhat uproariously. They were right when they sought to found a new educational system upon the University: where, forsooth, shall we ground knowledge save on the broadest and deepest knowledge? The roots of the tree, rather than the leaves, are the sources of its life; and from the dawn of history, from Academus* to Cambridge, the culture of the University has been the broad foundation-stone on which is built the kindergarten's A B C.

But these builders did make a mistake in minimizing the gravity of the problem before them; in thinking it a matter of years and decades; in therefore building quickly and laying their foundation carelessly, and lowering the standard of knowing, until they had scattered haphazard through the South some dozen poorly equipped high schools and miscalled them universities. They forgot, too, just as their successors are forgetting, the rule of inequality:—that of the million black youth, some were fitted to know and some to dig; that some had the talent and capacity of university men, and some the talent and capacity of blacksmiths; and that true training meant neither that all should be college men nor all artisans, but that the one should be made a missionary of culture to an untaught people, and the other a free workman among serfs. And to seek to make the blacksmith a scholar is almost as silly as the more modern scheme of making the scholar a blacksmith; almost, but not quite.

The function of the university is not simply to teach bread-winning, or to furnish teachers for the public schools or to be a centre of polite society; it is, above all, to be the organ of that fine adjustment between real life and the growing knowledge of life, an adjustment which forms the secret of civilization. Such an institution the South of to-day sorely needs. She has religion, earnest, bigoted:—religion that on both sides the Veil often omits the sixth,* seventh, and eighth commandments, but substitutes a dozen supplementary ones. She has, as Atlanta shows, growing thrift and love of toil; but she lacks that broad knowledge of what the world knows and knew of human living and doing, which she may apply to the thousand problems of real life to-day confronting her. The need of the South is knowledge and culture,—not in dainty limited quantity, as before the war, but in broad busy abundance in the world of work; and until she has this, not all the Apples of Hesperides, be they golden and bejewelled, can save her from the curse of the Bœotian lovers.

The Wings of Atalanta are the coming universities

of the South. They alone can bear the maiden past the temptation of golden fruit. They will not guide her flying feet away from the cotton and gold; for—ah, thoughtful Hippomenes!—do not the apples lie in the very Way of Life? But they will guide her over and beyond them, and leave her kneeling in the Sanctuary of Truth and Freedom and broad Humanity, virgin and undefiled. Sadly did the Old South err in human education, despising the education of the masses, and niggardly in the support of colleges. Her ancient university foundations dwindled and withered under the foul breath of slavery; and even since the war they have fought a failing fight for life in the tainted air of social unrest and commercial selfishness, stunted by the death of criticism, and starving for lack of broadly cultured men. And if this is the white South's need and danger, how much heavier the danger and need of the freedmen's sons! how pressing here the need of broad ideals and true culture, the conservation of soul from sordid aims and petty passions! Let us build the Southern university—William and Mary, Trinity, Georgia, Texas, Tulane, Vanderbilt, and the others—fit to live; let us build, too, the Negro universities:—Fisk, whose foundation was ever broad; Howard, at the heart of the Nation; Atlanta at Atlanta, whose ideal of scholarship has been held above the temptation of numbers. Why not here, and perhaps elsewhere, plant deeply and for all time centres of learning and living, colleges that yearly would send into the life of the South a few white men and a few black men of broad culture, catholic tolerance, and trained ability, joining their hands to other hands, and giving to this squabble of the Races a decent and dignified peace?

Patience, Humility, Manners, and Taste, common schools and kindergartens, industrial and technical schools, literature and tolerance,—all these spring from knowledge and culture, the children of the university. So must men and nations build, not otherwise, not upside down.

Teach workers to work,—a wise saying; wise when applied to German boys and American girls; wiser when said of Negro boys, for they have less knowledge of working and none to teach them. Teach thinkers to think,—a needed knowledge in a day of loose and careless logic; and they whose lot is gravest must have the carefulest training to think aright. If these things are so, how foolish to ask what is the best education for one or seven or sixty million souls! shall we teach them trades, or train them in liberal arts? Neither and both: teach the workers to work and the thinkers to think; make carpenters of carpenters, and philosophers of philosophers, and fops of fools. Nor can we pause here. We are training not isolated men but a living group of men,—nay, a group within a group. And the final product of our training must be neither a psychologist nor a brickmason, but a man. And to make men, we must have ideals, broad, pure, and inspiring ends of living,—not sordid money-getting, not apples of gold. The worker must work for the glory of his handiwork, not simply for pay; the thinker must think for truth, not for fame. And all this is gained only by human strife and longing; by ceaseless training and education; by founding Right on righteousness and Truth on the unhampered search for Truth; by founding the common school on the university, and the industrial school on the common school; and weaving thus a system, not a distortion, and bringing a birth, not an abortion.

When night falls on the City of a Hundred Hills, a wind gathers itself from the seas and comes murmuring westward. And at its bidding, the smoke of the drowsy factories sweeps down upon the mighty city and covers it like a pall, while yonder at the University the stars twinkle above Stone Hall. And they say that yon gray mist is the tunic of Atalanta pausing over her golden apples. Fly, my maiden, fly, for yonder comes Hippomenes!

VI

Of the Training of Black Men

Why, if the Soul can fling the Dust aside,
And naked on the Air of Heaven ride,
    Were't not a Shame—were't not a Shame for him
In this clay carcase crippled to abide?

OMAR KHAYYÁM (FITZGERALD).

From the shimmering swirl of waters where many, many thoughts ago the slave-ship first saw the square tower of Jamestown,* have flowed down to our day three streams of thinking: one swollen from the larger world here and over-seas, saying, the multiplying of human wants in culture-lands calls for the world-wide coöperation of men in satisfying them. Hence arises a new human unity, pulling the ends of earth nearer, and all men, black, yellow, and white. The larger humanity strives to feel in this contact of living Nations and sleeping hordes a thrill of new life in the world, crying, "If the contact of Life and Sleep be Death, shame on such Life." To be sure, behind this thought lurks the afterthought of force and dominion,—the making of brown men to delve when the temptation of beads and red calico cloys.

The second thought streaming from the death-ship and the curving river is the thought of the older South,—the sincere and passionate belief that somewhere between men and cattle, God created a *tertium quid,** and called it a Negro,—a clownish, simple creature, at times even lovable within its limitations, but straitly foreordained to walk within the Veil. To be sure, behind the thought lurks the afterthought,—some of them with favoring chance might become men, but in sheer self-defence we dare not let them, and we build about them walls so high, and hang between them and the light a veil so thick, that they shall not even think of breaking through.

And last of all there trickles down that third and darker thought,—the thought of the things themselves, the confused, half-conscious mutter of men who are black and whitened, crying "Liberty, Freedom, Opportunity—vouchsafe to us, O boastful World, the chance of living men!" To be sure, behind the thought lurks the afterthought,—suppose, after all, the World is right and we are less than men? Suppose this mad impulse within is all wrong, some mock mirage from the untrue?

So here we stand among thoughts of human unity, even through conquest and slavery; the inferiority of black men, even if forced by fraud; a shriek in the night for the freedom of men who themselves are not yet sure of their right to demand it. This is the tangle of thought and afterthought wherein we are called to solve the problem of training men for life.

Behind all its curiousness, so attractive alike to sage and *dilettante,** lie its dim dangers, throwing across us shadows at once grotesque and awful. Plain it is to us that what the world seeks through desert and wild we have within our threshold,—a stalwart laboring force, suited to the semi-tropics; if, deaf to the voice of the Zeitgeist,* we refuse to use and develop these men, we risk poverty and loss. If, on the other hand, seized by the brutal afterthought, we debauch the race thus caught in our talons, selfishly sucking their blood and brains in the future as in the past, what shall save us from national decadence? Only that saner selfishness, which Education teaches, can find the rights of all in the whirl of work.

Again, we may decry the color-prejudice of the South, yet it remains a heavy fact. Such curious kinks of the human mind exist and must be reckoned with soberly. They cannot be laughed away, nor always successfully stormed at, nor easily abolished by act of legislature. And yet they must not be encouraged by being let alone. They must be recognized as facts, but unpleasant facts; things that stand in the way of civilization and religion and common decency. They can be met in but one way,—by the breadth and broadening of human reason, by catholicity of taste and culture. And so, too, the native ambition and aspiration of men, even though they be black, backward, and ungraceful, must not lightly be dealt with. To stimulate wildly weak and untrained minds is to play with mighty fires; to flout their striving idly is to welcome a harvest of brutish crime and shameless lethargy in our very laps. The guiding of thought and the deft coordination of deed is at once the path of honor and humanity.

And so, in this great question of reconciling three vast and partially contradictory streams of thought, the one panacea of Education leaps to the lips of all:—such human training as will best use the labor of all men without enslaving or brutalizing; such training as will give us poise to encourage the prejudices that bulwark society, and to stamp out those that in sheer barbarity deafen us to the wail of prisoned souls within the Veil, and the mounting fury of shackled men.

But when we have vaguely said that Education will set this tangle straight, what have we uttered but a truism? Training for life teaches living; but what training for the profitable living together of black men and white? A hundred and fifty years ago our task would have seemed easier. Then Dr. Johnson* blandly assured us that education was needful solely for the embellishments of life, and was useless for ordinary vermin. To-day we have climbed to heights where we would open at least the outer courts of knowledge to all, display its treasures to many, and select the few to whom its mystery of Truth is revealed, not wholly by birth or the accidents of the stock market, but at least in part according to deftness and aim, talent and character. This programme, however, we are sorely puzzled in carrying out through that part of the land where the blight of slavery fell hardest, and where we are dealing with two backward peoples. To make here in human education that ever necessary combination of the permanent and the contingent—of the ideal and the practical in workable equilibrium—has been there, as it ever must be in every age and place, a matter of infinite experiment and frequent mistakes.

In rough approximation we may point out four varying decades of work in Southern education since the Civil War. From the close of the war until 1876, was the period of uncertain groping and temporary relief. There were army schools, mission schools, and schools of the Freedman's Bureau in chaotic disarrangement seeking system and coöperation. Then followed ten years of constructive definite effort toward the building of complete school systems in the South. Normal schools and colleges were founded for the freedmen, and teachers trained there to man the public schools. There was the inevitable tendency of war to underestimate the prejudices of the master and the ignorance of the slave, and all seemed clear sailing out of the wreckage of the storm. Meantime, starting in this decade yet especially developing from 1885 to 1895, began the industrial revolution of the South. The land saw glimpses of a new destiny and the stirring of new ideals. The educational system striving to complete itself saw new obstacles and a field of work ever broader and deeper. The Negro colleges, hurriedly founded, were inadequately equipped, illogically distributed, and of varying efficiency and grade; the normal and high schools were doing little more than common-school work, and the common schools were training but a third of the children who ought to be in them, and training these too often poorly. At the same time the white South, by reason of its sudden conversion from the slavery ideal, by so much the more became set and strengthened in its racial prejudice, and crystallized it into harsh law and harsher custom; while the marvellous pushing forward of the poor white daily threatened to take even bread and butter from the mouths of the heavily handicapped sons of the freedmen. In the midst, then, of the larger problem of Negro education sprang up the more practical question of work, the inevitable economic quandary that faces a people in the transition from slavery to freedom, and especially those who make that change amid hate and prejudice, lawlessness and ruthless competition.

The industrial school springing to notice in this decade, but coming to full recognition in the decade beginning with 1895, was the proffered answer to this combined educational and economic crisis, and an answer of singular wisdom and timeliness. From the very first in nearly all the schools some attention had been given to training in handiwork, but now was this training first raised to a dignity that brought it in direct touch with the South's magnificent industrial development, and given an emphasis which reminded black folk that before the Temple of Knowledge swing the Gates of Toil.

Yet after all they are but gates, and when turning our eyes from the temporary and the contingent in the Negro problem to the broader question of the permanent uplifting and civilization of black men in America, we have a right to inquire, as this enthusiasm for material advancement mounts to its height, if after all the industrial school is the final and sufficient answer in the training of the Negro race; and to ask gently, but in all sincerity, the ever-recurring query of the ages, Is not life more than meat, and the body more than raiment? And men ask this to-day all the more eagerly because of sinister signs in recent educational movements. The tendency is here, born of slavery and quickened to renewed life by the crazy imperialism of the day, to regard human beings as among the material resources of a land to be trained with an eye single to future dividends. Race-prejudices, which keep brown and black men in their "places," we are coming to regard as useful allies with such a theory, no matter how much they may dull the ambition and sicken the hearts of struggling human beings. And above all, we daily hear that an education that encourages aspiration, that sets the loftiest of ideals and seeks as an end culture and character rather than bread-winning, is the privilege of white men and the danger and delusion of black.

Especially has criticism been directed against the former educational efforts to aid the Negro. In the four periods I have mentioned, we find first, boundless, planless enthusiasm and sacrifice; then the preparation of teachers for a vast public-school system; then the launching and expansion of that school system amid increasing difficulties; and finally the training of workmen for the new and growing industries. This development has been sharply ridiculed as a logical anomaly and flat reversal of nature. Soothly we have been told that first industrial and manual training should have taught the Negro to work, then simple schools should have taught him to read and write, and finally, after years, high and normal schools could have completed the system, as intelligence and wealth demanded.

That a system logically so complete was historically impossible, it needs but a little thought to prove. Progress in human affairs is more often a pull than a push, a surging forward of the exceptional man, and the lifting of his duller brethren slowly and painfully to his vantage-ground. Thus it was no accident that gave birth to universities centuries before the common schools, that made fair Harvard the first flower of our wilderness. So in the South: the mass of the freedmen at the end of the war lacked the intelligence so necessary to modern workingmen. They must first have the common school to teach them to read, write, and cipher; and they must have higher schools to teach teachers for the common schools. The white teachers who flocked South went to establish such a common-school system. Few held the idea of founding colleges; most of them at first would have laughed at the idea. But they faced, as all men since them have faced, that central paradox of the South,— the social separation of the races. At that time it was the sudden volcanic rupture of nearly all relations between black and white, in work and government and family life. Since then a new adjustment of relations in economic and political affairs has grown up,—an adjustment subtle and difficult to grasp, yet singularly ingenious, which leaves still that frightful chasm at the color-line across which men pass at their peril. Thus, then and now, there stand in the South two separate worlds; and separate not simply in the higher realms of social intercourse, but also in church and school, on railway and street-car, in hotels and theatres, in streets and city sections, in books and newspapers, in asylums and jails, in hospitals and graveyards. There is still enough of contact for large economic and group coöperation, but the separation is so thorough and deep that it absolutely precludes for the present between the races anything like that sympathetic and effective group-training and leader-ship of the one by the other, such as the American Negro and all backward peoples must have for effectual progress.

This the missionaries of '68 soon saw; and if effective industrial and trade schools were imprac-ticable before the establishment of a common-school system, just as certainly no adequate common schools could be founded until there were teachers to teach them. Southern whites would not teach them; Northern whites in sufficient numbers could not be had. If the Negro was to learn, he must teach himself, and the most effective help that could be given him was the establishment of schools to train Negro teachers. This conclusion was slowly but surely reached by every student of the situation until simultaneously, in widely separated regions, without consultation or systematic plan, there arose a series of institutions designed to furnish teachers for the untaught. Above the sneers of critics at the obvious defects of this procedure must ever stand its one crushing rejoinder: in a single generation they put thirty thousand black teachers in the South; they wiped out the illiteracy of the majority of the black people of the land, and they made Tuskegee possible.

Such higher training-schools tended naturally to deepen broader development: at first they were common and grammar schools, then some became high schools. And finally, by 1900, some thirty-four had one year or more of studies of college grade. This development was reached with different degrees of speed in different institutions: Hampton is still a high school, while Fisk University started her college in 1871, and Spelman Seminary about 1896. In all cases the aim was identical,—to maintain the standards of the lower training by giving teachers and leaders the best practicable training; and above all, to furnish the black world with adequate standards of human culture and lofty ideals of life. It was not enough that the teachers of teachers should be trained in technical normal methods; they must also, so far as possible, be broad-minded, cultured men and women, to scatter civilization among a people whose ignorance was not simply of letters, but of life itself.

It can thus be seen that the work of education in the South began with higher institutions of training, which threw off as their foliage common schools, and later industrial schools, and at the same time strove to shoot their roots ever deeper toward college and university training. That this was an inevitable and necessary development, sooner or later, goes without saying; but there has been, and still is, a question in many minds if the natural growth was not forced, and if the higher training was not either overdone or done with cheap and unsound methods. Among white Southerners this feeling is widespread and positive. A prominent Southern journal voiced this in a recent editorial.

"The experiment that has been made to give the colored students classical training has not been satisfactory. Even though many were able to pursue the course, most of them did so in a parrot-like way, learning what was taught, but not seeming to appropriate the truth and import of their instruction, and graduating without sensible aim or valuable occupation for their future. The whole scheme has proved a waste of time, efforts, and the money of the state."

While most fair-minded men would recognize this as extreme and overdrawn, still without doubt many are asking, Are there a sufficient number of Negroes ready for college training to warrant the undertaking? Are not too many students prematurely forced into this work? Does it not have the effect of dissatisfying the young Negro with his environment? And do these graduates succeed in real life? Such natural questions cannot be evaded, nor on the other hand must a Nation naturally skeptical as to Negro ability assume an unfavorable answer without careful inquiry and patient openness to conviction. We must not forget that most Americans answer all queries regarding the Negro *a priori,** and that the least that human courtesy can do is to listen to evidence.

The advocates of the higher education of the Negro would be the last to deny the incompleteness and glaring defects of the present system: too many institutions have attempted to do college work, the work in some cases has not been thoroughly done, and quantity rather than quality has sometimes been sought. But all this can be said of higher education throughout the land; it is the almost inevitable incident of educational growth, and leaves the deeper question of the legitimate demand for the higher training of Negroes untouched. And this latter question can be settled in but one way,—by a first-hand study of the facts. If we leave out of view all institutions which have not actually graduated students from a course higher than that of a New England high school, even though they be called colleges; if then we take the thirty-four remaining institutions, we may clear up many misapprehensions by asking searchingly, What kind of institutions are they? what do they teach? and what sort of men do they graduate?

And first we may say that this type of college, including Atlanta, Fisk, and Howard, Wilberforce and Claflin, Shaw, and the rest, is peculiar, almost unique. Through the shining trees that whisper before me as I write, I catch glimpses of a boulder of New England granite, covering a grave, which graduates of Atlanta University have placed there,—

"GRATEFUL MEMORY OF THEIR FOR-
MER TEACHER AND FRIEND AND OF
THE UNSELFISH LIFE HE LIVED, AND
THE NOBLE WORK HE WROUGHT;
THAT THEY, THEIR CHILDREN, AND
THEIR CHILDREN'S CHILDREN MIGHT
BE BLESSED."

This was the gift of New England to the freed Negro: not alms, but a friend; not cash, but character. It was not and is not money these seething millions want, but love and sympathy, the pulse of hearts beating with red blood;—a gift which to-day only their own kindred and race can bring to the masses, but which once saintly souls brought to their favored children in the crusade of the sixties, that finest thing in American history, and one of the few things untainted by sordid greed and cheap vainglory. The teachers in these institutions came not to keep the Negroes in their place, but to raise them out of the defilement of the places where slavery had wallowed them. The colleges they founded were social settlements; homes where the best of the sons of the freedmen came in close and sympathetic touch with the best traditions of New England. They lived and ate together, studied and worked, hoped and harkened in the dawning light. In actual formal content their curriculum was doubtless old-fashioned, but in educational power it was supreme, for it was the contact of living souls.

From such schools about two thousand Negroes have gone forth with the bachelor's degree. The number in itself is enough to put at rest the argument that too large a proportion of Negroes are receiving higher training. If the ratio to population of all Negro students throughout the land, in both college and secondary training, be counted, Commissioner Harris assures us "it must be increased to five times its present average" to equal the average of the land.

Fifty years ago the ability of Negro students in any appreciable numbers to master a modern college course would have been difficult to prove. To-day it is proved by the fact that four hundred Negroes, many of whom have been reported as brilliant students, have received the bachelor's degree from Harvard, Yale, Oberlin, and seventy other leading colleges. Here we have, then, nearly twenty-five hundred Negro graduates, of whom the crucial query must be made, How far did their training fit them for life? It is of course extremely difficult to collect satisfactory data on such a point,—difficult to reach the men, to get trustworthy testimony, and to gauge that testimony by any generally acceptable criterion of success. In 1900, the Conference at Atlanta University undertook to study these graduates, and published the results. First they sought to know what these graduates were doing, and succeeded in getting answers from nearly two-thirds of the living. The direct testimony was in almost all cases corroborated by the reports of the colleges where they graduated, so that in the main the reports were worthy of credence. Fifty-three per cent of these graduates were teachers,—presidents of institutions, heads of normal schools, principals of city school-systems, and the like. Seventeen per cent were clergymen; another seventeen per cent were in the professions, chiefly as physicians. Over six per cent were merchants, farmers, and artisans, and four per cent were in the government civil-service. Granting even that a considerable proportion of the third unheard from are unsuccessful, this is a record of usefulness. Personally I know many hundreds of these graduates, and have corresponded with more than a thousand; through others I have followed carefully the life-work of scores; I have taught some of them and some of the pupils whom they have taught, lived in homes which they have builded, and looked at life through their eyes. Comparing them as a class with my fellow students in New England and in Europe, I cannot hesitate in saying that nowhere have I met men and women with a broader spirit of helpfulness, with deeper devotion to their life-work, or with more consecrated determination to succeed in the face of bitter difficulties than among Negro college-bred men. They have, to be sure, their proportion of ne'er-do-weels, their pedants and lettered fools, but they have a surprisingly small proportion of them; they have not that culture of manner which we instinctively associate with university men, forgetting that in reality it is the heritage from cultured homes, and that no people a generation removed from slavery can escape a certain unpleasant rawness and *gaucherie,** despite the best of training.

With all their larger vision and deeper sensibility, these men have usually been conservative, careful leaders. They have seldom been agitators, have withstood the temptation to head the mob, and have worked steadily and faithfully in a thousand communities in the South. As teachers, they have given the South a commendable system of city schools and large numbers of private normal-schools and academies. Colored college-bred men have worked side by side with white college graduates at Hampton; almost from the beginning the backbone of Tuskegee's teaching force has been formed of graduates from Fisk and Atlanta. And to-day the institute is filled with college graduates, from the energetic wife of the principal down to the teacher of agriculture, including nearly half of the executive council and a majority of the heads of departments. In the professions, college men are slowly but surely leavening the Negro church, are healing and preventing the devastations of disease, and beginning to furnish legal protection for the liberty and property of the toiling masses. All this is needful work. Who would do it if Negroes did not? How could Negroes do it if they were not trained carefully for it? If white people need colleges to furnish teachers, ministers, lawyers, and doctors, do black people need nothing of the sort?

If it is true that there are an appreciable number of Negro youth in the land capable by character and talent to receive that higher training, the end of which is culture, and if the two and a half thousand who have had something of this training in the past have in the main proved themselves useful to their race and generation, the question then comes, What place in the future development of the South ought the Negro college and college-bred man to occupy? That the present social separation and acute race-sensitiveness must eventually yield to the influences of culture, as the South grows civilized, is clear. But such transformation calls for singular wisdom and patience. If, while the healing of this vast sore is progressing, the races are to live for many years side by side, united in economic effort, obeying a common government, sensitive to mutual thought and feeling, yet subtly and silently separate in many matters of deeper human intimacy,—if this unusual and dangerous development is to progress amid peace and order, mutual respect and growing intelligence, it will call for social surgery at once the delicatest and nicest in modern history. It will demand broad-minded, upright men, both white and black, and in its final accomplishment American civilization will triumph. So far as white men are concerned, this fact is to-day being recognized in the South, and a happy renaissance of university education seems imminent. But the very voices that cry hail to this good work are, strange to relate, largely silent or antagonistic to the higher education of the Negro.

Strange to relate! for this is certain, no secure civilization can be built in the South with the Negro as an ignorant, turbulent proletariat. Suppose we seek to remedy this by making them laborers and nothing more: they are not fools, they have tasted of the Tree of Life, and they will not cease to think, will not cease attempting to read the riddle of the world. By taking away their best equipped teachers and leaders, by slamming the door of opportunity in the faces of their bolder and brighter minds, will you make them satisfied with their lot? or will you not rather transfer their leading from the hands of men taught to think to the hands of untrained demagogues? We ought not to forget that despite the pressure of poverty, and despite the active discouragement and even ridicule of friends, the demand for higher training steadily increases among Negro youth: there were, in the years from 1875 to 1880, 22 Negro graduates from Northern colleges; from 1885 to 1890 there were 43, and from 1895 to 1900, nearly 100 graduates. From Southern Negro colleges there were, in the same three periods, 143, 413, and over 500 graduates. Here, then, is the plain thirst for training; by refusing to give this Talented Tenth the key to knowledge, can any sane man imagine that they will lightly lay aside their yearning and contentedly become hewers of wood and drawers of water?

No. The dangerously clear logic of the Negro's position will more and more loudly assert itself in that day when increasing wealth and more intricate social organization preclude the South from being, as it so largely is, simply an armed camp for intimidating black folk. Such waste of energy cannot be spared if the South is to catch up with civilization. And as the black third of the land grows in thrift and skill, unless skilfully guided in its larger philosophy, it must more and more brood over the red past and the creeping, crooked present, until it grasps a gospel of revolt and revenge and throws its new-found energies athwart the current of advance. Even to-day the masses of the Negroes see all too clearly the anomalies of their position and the moral crookedness of yours. You may marshal strong indictments against them, but their counter-cries, lacking though they be in formal logic, have burning truths within them which you may not wholly ignore, O Southern Gentlemen! If you deplore their presence here, they ask, Who brought us? When you cry, Deliver us from the vision of intermarriage, they answer that legal marriage is infinitely better than systematic concubinage and prostitution. And if in just fury you accuse their vagabonds of violating women, they also in fury quite as just may reply: The rape which your gentlemen have done against helpless black women in defiance of your own laws is written on the foreheads of two millions of mulattoes, and written in ineffaceable blood. And finally, when you fasten crime upon this race as its peculiar trait, they answer that slavery was the arch-crime, and lynching and lawlessness its twin abortions; that color and race are not crimes, and yet it is they which in this land receive most unceasing condemnation, North, East, South, and West.

I will not say such arguments are wholly justified,—I will not insist that there is no other side to the shield; but I do say that of the nine millions of Negroes in this nation, there is scarcely one out of the cradle to whom these arguments do not daily present themselves in the guise of terrible truth. I insist that the question of the future is how best to keep these millions from brooding over the wrongs of the past and the difficulties of the present, so that all their energies may be bent toward a cheerful striving and coöperation with their white neighbors toward a larger, juster, and fuller future. That one wise method of doing this lies in the closer knitting of the Negro to the great industrial possibilities of the South is a great truth. And this the common schools and the manual training and trade schools are working to accomplish. But these alone are not enough. The foundations of knowledge in this race, as in others, must be sunk deep in the college and university if we would build a solid, permanent structure. Internal problems of social advance must inevitably come,—problems of work and wages, of families and homes, of morals and the true valuing of the things of life; and all these and other inevitable problems of civilization the Negro must meet and solve largely for himself, by reason of his isolation; and can there be any possible solution other than by study and thought and an appeal to the rich experience of the past? Is there not, with such a group and in such a crisis, infinitely more danger to be apprehended from half-trained minds and shallow thinking than from over-education and over-refinement? Surely we have wit enough to found a Negro college so manned and equipped as to steer successfully between the dilettante and the fool. We shall hardly induce black men to believe that if their stomachs be full, it matters little about their brains. They already dimly perceive that the paths of peace winding between honest toil and dignified manhood call for the guidance of skilled thinkers, the loving, reverent comradeship between the black lowly and the black men emancipated by training and culture.

The function of the Negro college, then, is clear: it must maintain the standards of popular education, it must seek the social regeneration of the Negro, and it must help in the solution of problems of race contact and coöperation. And finally, beyond all this, it must develop men. Above our modern socialism, and out of the worship of the mass, must persist and evolve that higher individualism which the centres of culture protect; there must come a loftier respect for the sovereign human soul that seeks to know itself and the world about it; that seeks a freedom for expansion and self-development; that will love and hate and labor in its own way, untrammeled alike by old and new. Such souls aforetime have inspired and guided worlds, and if we be not wholly bewitched by our Rhinegold,* they shall again. Herein the longing of black men must have respect: the rich and bitter depth of their experience, the unknown treasures of their inner life, the strange rendings of nature they have seen, may give the world new points of view and make their loving, living, and doing precious to all human hearts. And to themselves in these the days that try their souls, the chance to soar in the dim blue air above the smoke is to their finer spirits boon and guerdon for what they lose on earth by being black.

I sit with Shakespeare* and he winces not. Across the color line I move arm in arm with Balzac and Dumas, where smiling men and welcoming women glide in gilded halls. From out the caves of evening that swing between the strong-limbed earth and the tracery of the stars, I summon Aristotle* and Aurelius* and what soul I will, and they come all graciously with no scorn nor condescension. So, wed with Truth, I dwell above the Veil. Is this the life you grudge us, O knightly America? Is this the life you long to change into the dull red hideousness of Georgia? Are you so afraid lest peering from this high Pisgah,* between Philistine* and Amalekite, we sight the Promised Land?

Chapter **VII**

Of the Black Belt

I am black but comely, O ye daughters of Jerusalem,
As the tents of Kedar, as the curtains of Solomon.
Look not upon me, because I am black,
Because the sun hath looked upon me:
My mother's children were angry with me;
They made me the keeper of the vineyards;
But mine own vineyard have I not kept.

THE SONG OF SOLOMON.

Out of the North the train thundered, and we woke to
see the crimson soil of Georgia stretching away bare
and monotonous right and left. Here and there lay
straggling, unlovely villages, and lean men loafed
leisurely at the depots; then again came the stretch of
pines and clay. Yet we did not nod, nor weary of the
scene; for this is historic ground. Right across our
track, three hundred and sixty years ago, wandered
the cavalcade of Hernando de Soto,* looking for gold

and the Great Sea; and he and his foot-sore captives disappeared yonder in the grim forests to the west. Here sits Atlanta, the city of a hundred hills, with something Western, something Southern, and something quite its own, in its busy life. Just this side Atlanta is the land of the Cherokees and to the southwest, not far from where Sam Hose* was crucified, you may stand on a spot which is to-day the centre of the Negro problem,—the centre of those nine million men who are America's dark heritage from slavery and the slave-trade.

Not only is Georgia thus the geographical focus of our Negro population, but in many other respects, both now and yesterday, the Negro problems have seemed to be centered in this State. No other State in the Union can count a million Negroes among its citizens,—a population as large as the slave population of the whole Union in 1800; no other State fought so long and strenuously to gather this host of Africans. Oglethorpe* thought slavery against law and gospel; but the circumstances which gave Georgia its first inhabitants were not calculated to furnish citizens over-nice in their ideas about rum and slaves. Despite the prohibitions of the trustees, these Georgians, like some of their descendants, proceeded to take the law into their own hands; and so pliant were the judges, and so flagrant the smuggling, and so earnest were the prayers of Whitefield,* that by the middle of the eighteenth century all restrictions were swept away, and the slave-trade went merrily on for fifty years and more.

Down in Darien,* where the Delegal riots took place some summers ago, there used to come a strong protest against slavery from the Scotch Highlanders; and the Moravians of Ebenezer* did not like the system. But not till the Haytian Terror of Toussaint* was the trade in men even checked; while the national statute of 1808* did not suffice to stop it. How the Africans poured in!—fifty thousand between 1790 and 1810, and then, from Virginia and from smugglers, two thousand a year for many years more. So the thirty thousand Negroes of Georgia in 1790 doubled in a decade,—were over a hundred thousand in 1810, had reached two hundred thousand in 1820, and half a million at the time of the war. Thus like a snake the black population writhed upward.

But we must hasten on our journey. This that we pass as we near Atlanta is the ancient land of the Cherokees,—that brave Indian nation which strove so long for its fatherland, until Fate and the United States Government drove them beyond the Mississippi. If you wish to ride with me you must come into the "Jim Crow Car." There will be no objection,—already four other white men, and a little white girl with her nurse, are in there. Usually the races are mixed in there; but the white coach is all white. Of course this car is not so good as the other, but it is fairly clean and comfortable. The discomfort lies chiefly in the hearts of those four black men yonder—and in mine.

We rumble south in quite a business-like way. The bare red clay and pines of Northern Georgia begin to disappear, and in their place appears a rich rolling land, luxuriant, and here and there well tilled. This is the land of the Creek Indians; and a hard time the Georgians had to seize it. The towns grow more frequent and more interesting, and brand-new cotton mills rise on every side. Below Macon the world grows darker; for now we approach the Black Belt,— that strange land of shadows, at which even slaves paled in the past, and whence come now only faint and half-intelligible murmurs to the world beyond. The "Jim Crow Car" grows larger and a shade better;

three rough field-hands and two or three white loafers accompany us, and the newsboy still spreads his wares at one end. The sun is setting, but we can see the great cotton country as we enter it,—the soil now dark and fertile, now thin and gray, with fruit-trees and dilapidated buildings,—all the way to Albany.

At Albany, in the heart of the Black Belt, we stop. Two hundred miles south of Atlanta, two hundred miles west of the Atlantic, and one hundred miles north of the Great Gulf lies Dougherty County, with ten thousand Negroes and two thousand whites. The Flint River winds down from Andersonville, and, turning suddenly at Albany, the county-seat, hurries on to join the Chattahoochee and the sea. Andrew Jackson knew the Flint well, and marched across it once to avenge the Indian Massacre at Fort Mims. That was in 1814, not long before the battle of New Orleans; and by the Creek treaty that followed this campaign, all Dougherty County, and much other rich land, was ceded to Georgia. Still, settlers fought shy of this land, for the Indians were all about, and they were unpleasant neighbors in those days. The panic of 1837,* which Jackson bequeathed to Van Buren, turned the planters from the impoverished lands of Virginia, the Carolinas, and east Georgia, toward the West. The Indians were removed to Indian Territory, and settlers poured into these coveted lands to retrieve their broken fortunes. For a radius of a hundred miles about Albany, stretched a great fertile land, luxuriant with forests of pine, oak, ash, hickory, and poplar; hot with the sun and damp with the rich black swamp-land; and here the corner-stone of the Cotton Kingdom was laid.

Albany is to-day a wide-streeted, placid, Southern town, with a broad sweep of stores and saloons, and flanking rows of homes,—whites usually to the north, and blacks to the south. Six days in the week the town looks decidedly too small for itself, and takes frequent and prolonged naps. But on Saturday suddenly the whole county disgorges itself upon the place, and a perfect flood of black peasantry pours through the streets, fills the stores, blocks the sidewalks, chokes the thoroughfares, and takes full possession of the town. They are black, sturdy, uncouth country folk, good-natured and simple, talkative to a degree, and yet far more silent and brooding than the crowds of the Rhine-pfalz,* or Naples, or Cracow. They drink considerable quantities of whiskey, but do not get very drunk; they talk and laugh loudly at times, but seldom quarrel or fight. They walk up and down the streets, meet and gossip with friends, stare at the shop windows, buy coffee, cheap candy, and clothes, and at dusk drive home—happy? well no, not exactly happy, but much happier than as though they had not come.

Thus Albany is a real capital,—a typical Southern county town, the centre of the life of ten thousand souls; their point of contact with the outer world, their centre of news and gossip, their market for buying and selling, borrowing and lending, their fountain of justice and law. Once upon a time we knew country life so well and city life so little, that we illustrated city life as that of a closely crowded country district. Now the world has well-nigh forgotten what the country is, and we must imagine a little city of black people scattered far and wide over three hundred lonesome square miles of land, without train or trolley, in the midst of cotton and corn, and wide patches of sand and gloomy soil.

It gets pretty hot in Southern Georgia in July,—a sort of dull, determined heat that seems quite independent of the sun; so it took us some days to muster courage enough to leave the porch and venture out on the long country roads, that we might see this unknown world. Finally we started. It was about ten in the morning, bright with a faint breeze, and we jogged leisurely southward in the valley of the Flint. We passed the scattered box-like cabins of the brickyard hands, and the long tenement-row facetiously called "The Ark," and were soon in the open country, and on the confines of the great plantations of other days. There is the "Joe Fields place"; a rough old fellow was he, and had killed many a "nigger" in his day. Twelve miles his plantation used to run,—a regular barony. It is nearly all gone now; only straggling bits belong to the family, and the rest has passed to Jews and Negroes. Even the bits which are left are heavily mortgaged, and, like the rest of the land, tilled by tenants. Here is one of them now,—a tall brown man, a hard worker and a hard drinker, illiterate, but versed in farmlore, as his nodding crops declare. This distressingly new broad house is his, and he has just moved out of yonder moss-grown cabin with its one square room.

From the curtains in Benton's house, down the road, a dark comely face is staring at the strangers; for passing carriages are not every-day occurrences here. Benton is an intelligent yellow man with a good-sized family, and manages a plantation blasted by the war and now the broken staff of the widow. He might be well-to-do, they say; but he carouses too much in Albany. And the half-desolate spirit of neglect born of the very soil seems to have settled on these acres. In times past there were cotton-gins and machinery here; but they have rotted away.

The whole land seems forlorn and forsaken. Here are the remnants of the vast plantations of the Sheldons, the Pellots, and the Rensons; but the souls of them are passed. The houses lie in half ruin, or have wholly disappeared; the fences have flown, and the families are wandering in the world. Strange vicissitudes have met these whilom masters. Yonder stretch the wide acres of Bildad Reasor; he died in war-time, but the upstart overseer hastened to wed the widow. Then he went, and his neighbors too, and now only the black tenant remains; but the shadow-hand of the master's grand-nephew or cousin or creditor stretches out of the gray distance to collect the rack-rent remorselessly, and so the land is uncared-for and poor. Only black tenants can stand such a system, and they only because they must. Ten miles we have ridden to-day and have seen no white face.

A resistless feeling of depression falls slowly upon us, despite the gaudy sunshine and the green cottonfields. This, then, is the Cotton Kingdom,—the shadow of a marvellous dream. And where is the King? Perhaps this is he,—the sweating ploughman, tilling his eighty acres with two lean mules, and fighting a hard battle with debt. So we sit musing, until, as we turn a corner on the sandy road, there comes a fairer scene suddenly in view,—a neat cottage snugly ensconced by the road, and near it a little store. A tall bronzed man rises from the porch as we hail him, and comes out to our carriage. He is six feet in height, with a sober face that smiles gravely. He walks too straight to be a tenant,—yes, he owns two hundred and forty acres. "The land is run down since the boom-days of eighteen hundred and fifty," he explains, and cotton is low. Three black tenants live on his place, and in his little store he keeps a small stock of tobacco, snuff, soap, and soda, for the neighborhood. Here is his gin-house with new machinery just installed. Three hundred bales of cotton went through it last year. Two children he has sent away to school. Yes, he says sadly, he is getting on, but cotton is down to four cents; I know how Debt sits staring at him.

Wherever the King may be, the parks and palaces of the Cotton Kingdom have not wholly disappeared. We plunge even now into great groves of oak and towering pine, with an undergrowth of myrtle and shrubbery. This was the "home-house" of the Thompsons,—slave-barons who drove their coach and four in the merry past. All is silence now, and ashes, and tangled weeds. The owner put his whole fortune into the rising cotton industry of the fifties, and with the falling prices of the eighties he packed up and stole away. Yonder is another grove, with unkempt lawn, great magnolias, and grass-grown paths. The Big House stands in half-ruin, its great front door staring blankly at the street, and the back part grotesquely restored for its black tenant. A shabby, well-built Negro he is, unlucky and irresolute. He digs hard to pay rent to the white girl who owns the remnant of the place. She married a policeman, and lives in Savannah.

Now and again we come to churches. Here is one now,—Shepherds, they call it,—a great whitewashed barn of a thing, perched on stilts of stone, and looking for all the world as though it were just resting here a moment and might be expected to waddle off down the road at almost any time. And yet it is the centre of a hundred cabin homes; and sometimes, of a Sunday, five hundred persons from far and near gather here and talk and eat and sing. There is a schoolhouse near,—a very airy, empty shed; but even this is an improvement, for usually the school is held in the church. The churches vary from log-huts to those like Shepherd's, and the schools from nothing to this little house that sits demurely on the county line. It is a tiny plank-house, perhaps ten by twenty, and has within a double row of rough unplaned benches, resting mostly on legs, sometimes on boxes. Opposite the door is a square home-made desk. In one corner are the ruins of a stove, and in the other a dim blackboard. It is the cheerfulest schoolhouse I have seen in Dougherty, save in town. Back of the schoolhouse is a lodgehouse two stories high and not quite finished. Societies meet there,—societies "to care for the sick and bury the dead"; and these societies grow and flourish.

We had come to the boundaries of Dougherty, and were about to turn west along the county-line, when all these sights were pointed out to us by a kindly old man, black, white-haired, and seventy. Forty-five years he had lived here, and now supports himself and his old wife by the help of the steer tethered yonder and the charity of his black neighbors. He shows us the farm of the Hills just across the county line in Baker,—a widow and two strapping sons, who raised ten bales (one need not add "cotton" down here) last year. There are fences and pigs and cows, and the soft-voiced, velvet-skinned young Memnon, who sauntered half-bashfully over to greet the strangers, is proud of his home. We turn now to the west along the county line. Great dismantled trunks of pines tower above the green cotton-fields, cracking their naked gnarled fingers toward the border of living forest beyond. There is little beauty in this region, only a sort of crude abandon that suggests power,—a naked grandeur, as it were. The houses are bare and straight; there are no hammocks or easy-chairs, and few flowers. So when, as here at Rawdon's, one sees a vine clinging to a little porch, and home-like windows peeping over the fences, one takes a long breath. I think I never before quite realized the place of the Fence in civilization. This is the Land of the Unfenced, where crouch on either hand scores of ugly one-room cabins, cheerless and dirty. Here lies the Negro problem in its naked dirt and penury. And here are no fences. But now and then the criss-cross rails or straight palings break into view, and then we know a touch of culture is near. Of course Harrison Gohagen,—a quiet yellow man, young, smooth-faced, and diligent,—of course he is lord of some hundred acres, and we expect to see a vision of well-kept rooms and fat beds and laughing children. For has he not fine fences? And those over yonder, why should they build fences on the rack-rented land? It will only increase their rent.

On we wind, through sand and pines and glimpses of old plantations, till there creeps into sight a cluster of buildings,—wood and brick, mills and houses, and scattered cabins. It seemed quite a village. As it came nearer and nearer, however, the aspect changed: the buildings were rotten, the bricks were falling out, the mills were silent, and the store was closed. Only in the cabins appeared now and then a bit of lazy life. I could imagine the place under some weird spell, and was half-minded to search out the princess. An old ragged black man, honest, simple, and improvident, told us the tale. The Wizard of the North—the Capitalist—had rushed down in the seventies to woo this coy dark soil. He bought a square mile or more, and for a time the field-hands sang, the gins groaned, and the mills buzzed. Then came a change. The agent's son embezzled the funds and ran off with them. Then the agent himself disappeared. Finally the new agent stole even the books, and the company in wrath closed its business and its houses, refused to sell, and let houses and furniture and machinery rust and rot. So the Waters-Loring plantation was stilled by the spell of dishonesty, and stands like some gaunt rebuke to a scarred land.

Somehow that plantation ended our day's journey; for I could not shake off the influence of that silent scene. Back toward town we glided, past the straight and thread-like pines, past a dark tree-dotted pond where the air was heavy with a dead sweet perfume. White slender-legged curlews flitted by us, and the garnet blooms of the cotton looked gay against the green and purple stalks. A peasant girl was hoeing in the field, white-turbaned and black-limbed. All this we saw, but the spell still lay upon us.

How curious a land is this,—how full of untold story, of tragedy and laughter, and the rich legacy of human life; shadowed with a tragic past, and big with future promise! This is the Black Belt of Georgia. Dougherty County is the west end of the Black Belt, and men once called it the Egypt of the Confederacy. It is full of historic interest. First there is the Swamp, to the west, where the Chickasawhatchee flows sullenly southward. The shadow of an old plantation lies at its edge, forlorn and dark. Then comes the pool; pendent gray moss and brackish waters appear, and forests filled with wildfowl. In one place the wood is on fire, smouldering in dull red anger; but nobody minds. Then the swamp grows beautiful; a raised road, built by chained Negro convicts, dips down into it, and forms a way walled and almost covered in living green. Spreading trees spring from a prodigal luxuriance of undergrowth; great dark green shadows fade into the black background, until all is one mass of tangled semi-tropical foliage, marvellous in its weird savage splendor. Once we crossed a black silent stream, where the sad trees and writhing creepers, all glinting fiery yellow and green, seemed like some vast cathedral,—some green Milan builded of wildwood. And as I crossed, I seemed to see again that fierce tragedy of seventy years ago. Osceola, the Indian-

Negro chieftain, had risen in the swamps of Florida, vowing vengeance. His war-cry reached the red Creeks of Dougherty, and their war-cry rang from the Chattahoochee to the sea. Men and women and children fled and fell before them as they swept into Dougherty. In yonder shadows a dark and hideously painted warrior glided stealthily on,—another and another, until three hundred had crept into the treacherous swamp. Then the false slime closing about them called the white men from the east. Waist-deep, they fought beneath the tall trees, until the war-cry was hushed and the Indians glided back into the west. Small wonder the wood is red.

Then came the black slaves. Day after day the clank of chained feet marching from Virginia and Carolina to Georgia was heard in these rich swamp lands. Day after day the songs of the callous, the wail of the motherless, and the muttered curses of the wretched echoed from the Flint to the Chickasawhatchee, until by 1860 there had risen in West Dougherty perhaps the richest slave kingdom the modern world ever knew. A hundred and fifty barons commanded the labor of nearly six thousand Negroes, held sway over farms with ninety thousand acres tilled land, valued even in times of cheap soil at three millions of dollars. Twenty thousand bales of ginned cotton went yearly to England, New and Old; and men that came there bankrupt made money and grew rich. In a single decade the cotton output increased four-fold and the value of lands was tripled. It was the heyday of the *nouveau riche,** and a life of careless extravagance among the masters. Four and six bobtailed thoroughbreds rolled their coaches to town; open hospitality and gay entertainment were the rule. Parks and groves were laid out, rich with flower and vine, and in the midst stood the low wide-halled "big house," with its porch and columns and great fireplaces.

And yet with all this there was something sordid, something forced,—a certain feverish unrest and recklessness; for was not all this show and tinsel built upon a groan? "This land was a little Hell," said a ragged, brown, and grave-faced man to me. We were seated near a roadside blacksmith-shop, and behind was the bare ruin of some master's home. "I've seen niggers drop dead in the furrow, but they were kicked aside, and the plough never stopped. Down in the guard-house, there's where the blood ran."

With such foundations a kingdom must in time sway and fall. The masters moved to Macon and Augusta, and left only the irresponsible overseers on the land. And the result is such ruin as this, the Lloyd "home-place":—great waving oaks, a spread of lawn, myrtles and chestnuts, all ragged and wild; a solitary gate-post standing where once was a castle entrance; an old rusty anvil lying amid rotting bellows and wood in the ruins of a blacksmith shop; a wide rambling old mansion, brown and dingy, filled now with the grandchildren of the slaves who once waited on its tables; while the family of the master has dwindled to two lone women, who live in Macon and feed hungrily off the remnants of an earldom. So we ride on, past phantom gates and falling homes,—past the once flourishing farms of the Smiths, the Gandys, and the Lagores,—and find all dilapidated and half ruined, even there where a solitary white woman, a relic of other days, sits alone in state among miles of Negroes and rides to town in her ancient coach each day.

This was indeed the Egypt of the Confederacy,—the rich granary whence potatoes and corn and cotton poured out to the famished and ragged Confederate troops as they battled for a cause lost long before 1861. Sheltered and secure, it became the place of refuge for families, wealth, and slaves. Yet even then the hard ruthless rape of the land began to tell. The red-clay sub-soil already had begun to peer above the loam. The harder the slaves were driven the more careless and fatal was their farming. Then came the revolution of war and Emancipation, the bewilderment of Reconstruction,—and now, what is the Egypt of the Confederacy, and what meaning has it for the nation's weal or woe?

It is a land of rapid contrasts and of curiously mingled hope and pain. Here sits a pretty blue-eyed quadroon hiding her bare feet; she was married only last week, and yonder in the field is her dark young husband, hoeing to support her, at thirty cents a day without board. Across the way is Gatesby, brown and tall, lord of two thousand acres shrewdly won and held. There is a store conducted by his black son, a blacksmith shop, and a ginnery. Five miles below here is a town owned and controlled by one white New Englander. He owns almost a Rhode Island county, with thousands of acres and hundreds of black laborers. Their cabins look better than most, and the farm, with machinery and fertilizers, is much more business-like than any in the county, although the manager drives hard bargains in wages. When now we turn and look five miles above, there on the edge of town are five houses of prostitutes,—two of blacks and three of whites; and in one of the houses of the whites a worthless black boy was harbored too openly two years ago; so he was hanged for rape. And here, too, is the high whitewashed fence of the "stockade," as the county prison is called; the white folks say it is ever full of black criminals,—the black folks say that only colored boys are sent to jail, and they not because they are guilty, but because the State needs criminals to eke out its income by their forced labor.

Immigrants are heirs of the slave baron in Dougherty; and as we ride westward, by wide stretching cornfields and stubby orchards of peach and pear, we see on all sides within the circle of dark forest a Land of Canaan.* Here and there are tales of projects for money-getting, born in the swift days of Reconstruction,—"improvement" companies, wine companies, mills and factories; most failed, and foreigners fell heir. It is a beautiful land, this Dougherty, west of the Flint. The forests are wonderful, the solemn pines have disappeared, and this is the "Oakey Woods," with its wealth of hickories, beeches, oaks and palmettos. But a pall of debt hangs over the beautiful land; the merchants are in debt to the wholesalers, the planters are in debt to the merchants, the tenants owe the planters, and laborers bow and bend beneath the burden of it all. Here and there a man has raised his head above these murky waters. We passed one fenced stock-farm with grass and grazing cattle, that looked very home-like after endless corn and cotton. Here and there are black free-holders: there is the gaunt dull-black Jackson, with his hundred acres. "I says, 'Look up! If you don't look up you can't get up,'" remarks Jackson, philosophically. And he's gotten up. Dark Carter's neat barns would do credit to New England. His master helped him to get a start, but when the black man died last fall the master's sons immediately laid claim to the estate. "And them white folks will get it, too," said my yellow gossip.

I turn from these well-tended acres with a comfortable feeling that the Negro is rising. Even then, however, the fields, as we proceed, begin to redden and the trees disappear. Rows of old cabins appear filled with renters and laborers,—cheerless, bare, and dirty, for the most part, although here and there the very age and decay makes the scene picturesque. A young black fellow greets us. He is twenty-two, and just married. Until last year he had good luck renting; then cotton fell, and the sheriff seized and sold all he had. So he moved here, where the rent is higher, the land poorer, and the owner inflexible; he rents a forty-dollar mule for twenty dollars a year. Poor lad!—a slave at twenty-two. This plantation, owned now by a foreigner, was a part of the famous Bolton estate. After the war it was for many years worked by gangs of Negro convicts,—and black convicts then were even more plentiful than now; it was a way of making Negroes work, and the question of guilt was a minor one. Hard tales of cruelty and mistreatment of the chained freemen are told, but the county authorities were deaf until the free-labor market was nearly ruined by wholesale migration. Then they took the convicts from the plantations, but not until one of the fairest regions of the "Oakey Woods" had been ruined and ravished into a red waste, out of which only a Yankee or an immigrant could squeeze more blood from debt-cursed tenants.

No wonder that Luke Black, slow, dull, and discouraged, shuffles to our carriage and talks hopelessly. Why should he strive? Every year finds him deeper in debt. How strange that Georgia, the world-heralded refuge of poor debtors, should bind her own to sloth and misfortune as ruthlessly as ever England did! The poor land groans with its birth-pains, and brings forth scarcely a hundred pounds of cotton to the acre, where fifty years ago it yielded eight times as much. Of his meagre yield the tenant pays from a quarter to a third in rent, and most of the rest in interest on food and supplies bought on credit. Twenty years yonder sunken-cheeked, old black man has labored under that system, and now, turned day-laborer, is supporting his wife and boarding himself on his wages of a dollar and a half a week, received only part of the year.

The Bolton convict farm formerly included the neighboring plantation. Here it was that the convicts were lodged in the great log prison still standing. A dismal place it still remains, with rows of ugly huts filled with surly ignorant tenants. "What rent do you pay here?" I inquired. "I don't know,—what is it, Sam?" "All we make," answered Sam. It is a depressing place,—bare, unshaded, with no charm of past association, only a memory of forced human toil,—now, then, and before the war. They are not happy, these black men whom we meet throughout this region. There is little of the joyous abandon and playfulness which we are wont to associate with the plantation Negro. At best, the natural good-nature is edged with complaint or has changed into sullenness and gloom. And now and then it blazes forth in veiled but hot anger. I remember one big red-eyed black whom we met by the roadside. Forty-five years he had labored on this farm, beginning with nothing, and still having nothing. To be sure, he had given four children a common-school training, and perhaps if the new fence-law had not allowed unfenced crops in West Dougherty he might have raised a little stock and kept ahead. As it is, he is hopelessly in debt, disappointed, and embittered. He stopped us to inquire after the black boy in Albany, whom it was said a policeman had shot and killed for loud talking on the sidewalk. And then he said slowly: "Let a white man touch me, and he dies; I don't boast this,—I don't say it around loud, or before the children,—but I mean it. I've seen them whip my father and my old mother in them cotton-rows till the blood ran; by—" and we passed on.

Now Sears, whom we met next lolling under the chubby oak-trees, was of quite different fibre. Happy?—Well, yes; he laughed and flipped pebbles, and thought the world was as it was. He had worked here twelve years and has nothing but a mortgaged mule. Children? Yes, seven; but they hadn't been to school this year,—couldn't afford books and clothes, and couldn't spare their work. There go part of them to the fields now,—three big boys astride mules, and a strapping girl with bare brown legs. Careless ignorance and laziness here, fierce hate and vindictiveness there;—these are the extremes of the Negro problem which we met that day, and we scarce knew which we preferred.

Here and there we meet distinct characters quite out of the ordinary. One came out of a piece of newly cleared ground, making a wide detour to avoid the snakes. He was an old, hollow-cheeked man, with a drawn and characterful brown face. He had a sort of self-contained quaintness and rough humor impossible to describe; a certain cynical earnestness that puzzled one. "The niggers were jealous of me over on the other place," he said, "and so me and the old woman begged this piece of woods, and I cleared it up myself. Made nothing for two years, but I reckon I've got a crop now." The cotton looked tall and rich, and we praised it. He curtsied low, and then bowed almost to the ground, with an imperturbable gravity that seemed almost suspicious. Then he continued, "My mule died last week,"—a calamity in this land equal to a devastating fire in town,—"but a white man loaned me another." Then he added, eyeing us, "Oh, I gets along with white folks." We turned the conversation. "Bears? deer?" he answered, "well, I should say there were," and he let fly a string of brave oaths, as he told hunting-tales of the swamp. We left him standing still in the middle of the road looking after us, and yet apparently not noticing us.

The Whistle place, which includes his bit of land, was bought soon after the war by an English syndicate, the "Dixie Cotton and Corn Company." A marvellous deal of style their factor put on, with his servants and coach-and-six; so much so that the concern soon landed in inextricable bankruptcy. Nobody lives in the old house now, but a man comes each winter out of the North and collects his high rents. I know not which are the more touching,—such old empty houses, or the homes of the masters' sons. Sad and bitter tales lie hidden back of those white doors,—tales of poverty, of struggle, of disappointment. A revolution such as that of '63 is a terrible thing; they that rose rich in the morning often slept in paupers' beds. Beggars and vulgar speculators rose to rule over them, and their children went astray. See yonder sad-colored house, with its cabins and fences and glad crops! It is not glad within; last month the prodigal son of the struggling father wrote home from the city for money. Money! Where was it to come from? And so the son rose in the night and killed his baby, and killed his wife, and shot himself dead. And the world passed on.

I remember wheeling around a bend in the road beside a graceful bit of forest and a singing brook. A long low house faced us, with porch and flying pillars, great oaken door, and a broad lawn shining in the evening sun. But the window-panes were gone, the pillars were worm-eaten, and the moss-grown roof was falling in. Half curiously I peered through the unhinged door, and saw where, on the wall across the hall, was written in once gay letters a faded "Welcome."

Quite a contrast to the southwestern part of Dougherty County is the northwest. Soberly timbered in oak and pine, it has none of that half-tropical luxuriance of the southwest. Then, too, there are fewer signs of a romantic past, and more of systematic modern land-grabbing and money-getting. White people are more in evidence here, and farmer and hired labor replace to some extent the absentee landlord and rack-rented tenant. The crops have neither the luxuriance of the richer land nor the signs of neglect so often seen, and there were fences and meadows here and there. Most of this land was poor, and beneath the notice of the slave-baron, before the war. Since then his poor relations and foreign immigrants have seized it. The returns of the farmer are too small to allow much for wages, and yet he will not sell off small farms. There is the Negro Sanford; he has worked fourteen years as overseer on the Ladson place, and "paid out enough for fertilizers to have bought a farm," but the owner will not sell off a few acres.

Two children—a boy and a girl—are hoeing sturdily in the fields on the farm where Corliss works. He is smooth-faced and brown, and is fencing up his pigs. He used to run a successful cotton-gin, but the Cotton Seed Oil Trust has forced the price of ginning so low that he says it hardly pays him. He points out a stately old house over the way as the home of "Pa Willis." We eagerly ride over, for "Pa Willis" was the tall and powerful black Moses who led the Negroes for a generation, and led them well. He was a Baptist preacher, and when he died, two thousand black people followed him to the grave; and now they preach his funeral sermon each year. His widow lives here,—a weazened, sharp-featured little woman, who curtsied quaintly as we greeted her. Further on lives Jack Delson, the most prosperous Negro farmer in the county. It is a joy to meet him,—a great broad-shouldered, handsome black man, intelligent and jovial. Six hundred and fifty acres he owns, and has eleven black tenants. A neat and tidy home nestled in a flower-garden, and a little store stands beside it.

We pass the Munson place, where a plucky white widow is renting and struggling; and the eleven hundred acres of the Sennet plantation, with its Negro overseer. Then the character of the farms begins to change. Nearly all the lands belong to Russian Jews; the overseers are white, and the cabins are bare board-houses scattered here and there. The rents are high, and day-laborers and "contract" hands abound. It is a keen, hard struggle for living here, and few have time to talk. Tired with the long ride, we gladly drive into Gillonsville. It is a silent cluster of farmhouses standing on the crossroads, with one of its stores closed and the other kept by a Negro preacher. They tell great tales of busy times at Gillonsville before all the railroads came to Albany; now it is chiefly a memory. Riding down the street, we stop at the preacher's and seat ourselves before the door. It was one of those scenes one cannot soon forget:—a wide, low, little house, whose motherly roof reached over and sheltered a snug little porch. There we sat, after the long hot drive, drinking cool water,—the talkative little storekeeper who is my daily companion; the silent old black woman patching pantaloons and saying never a word; the ragged picture of helpless misfortune who called in just to see the preacher; and finally the neat matronly preacher's wife, plump, yellow, and intelligent. "Own land?" said the wife; "well, only this house." Then she added quietly, "We did buy seven hundred acres across up yonder, and paid for it; but they cheated us out of it. Sells was the owner." "Sells!" echoed the ragged misfortune, who was leaning against the balustrade and listening, "he's a regular cheat. I worked for him thirty-seven days this spring, and he paid me in cardboard checks which were to be cashed at the end of the month. But he never cashed them,—kept putting me off. Then the sheriff came and took my mule and corn and furniture—" "Furniture? But furniture is exempt from seizure by law." "Well, he took it just the same," said the hard-faced man.

Chapter VIII

Of the Quest of the Golden Fleece

But the Brute said in his breast, "Till the mills I grind have
ceased,
The riches shall be dust of dust, dry ashes be the feast!

"On the strong and cunning few
Cynic favors I will strew;
I will stuff their maw with overplus until their spirit dies;
From the patient and the low
I will take the joys they know;
They shall hunger after vanities and still an-hungered
go.
Madness shall be on the people, ghastly jealousies arise;
Brother's blood shall cry on brother up the dead and empty
skies."

WILLIAM VAUGHN MOODY.

Have you ever seen a cotton-field white with the
harvest,—its golden fleece hovering above the black
earth like a silvery cloud edged with dark green, its
bold white signals waving like the foam of billows
from Carolina to Texas across that Black and human

Sea? I have sometimes half suspected that here the winged ram Chrysomallus* left that Fleece after which Jason and his Argonauts went vaguely wandering into the shadowy East three thousand years ago; and certainly one might frame a pretty and not far-fetched analogy of witchery and dragon's teeth, and blood and armed men, between the ancient and the modern quest of the Golden Fleece in the Black Sea.

And now the golden fleece is found; not only found, but, in its birthplace, woven. For the hum of the cotton-mills is the newest and most significant thing in the New South to-day. All through the Carolinas and Georgia, away down to Mexico, rise these gaunt red buildings, bare and homely, and yet so busy and noisy withal that they scarce seem to belong to the slow and sleepy land. Perhaps they sprang from dragons' teeth. So the Cotton Kingdom still lives; the world still bows beneath her sceptre. Even the markets that once defied the *parvenu** have crept one by one across the seas, and then slowly and reluctantly, but surely, have started toward the Black Belt.

To be sure, there are those who wag their heads knowingly and tell us that the capital of the Cotton Kingdom has moved from the Black to the White Belt,—that the Negro of to-day raises not more than half of the cotton crop. Such men forget that the cotton crop has doubled, and more than doubled, since the era of slavery, and that, even granting their contention, the Negro is still supreme in a Cotton Kingdom larger than that on which the Confederacy builded its hopes. So the Negro forms to-day one of the chief figures in a great world-industry; and this, for its own sake, and in the light of historic interest, makes the field-hands of the cotton country worth studying.

We seldom study the condition of the Negro to-day honestly and carefully. It is so much easier to assume that we know it all. Or perhaps, having already reached conclusions in our own minds, we are loth to have them disturbed by facts. And yet how little we really know of these millions,—of their daily lives and longings, of their homely joys and sorrows, of their real shortcomings and the meaning of their crimes! All this we can only learn by intimate contact with the masses, and not by wholesale arguments covering millions separate in time and space, and differing widely in training and culture. To-day, then, my reader, let us turn our faces to the Black Belt of Georgia and seek simply to know the condition of the black farm-laborers of one county there.

Here in 1890 lived ten thousand Negroes and two thousand whites. The country is rich, yet the people are poor. The keynote of the Black Belt is debt; not commercial credit, but debt in the sense of continued inability on the part of the mass of the population to make income cover expense. This is the direct heritage of the South from the wasteful economies of the slave régime; but it was emphasized and brought to a crisis by the Emancipation of the slaves. In 1860, Dougherty County had six thousand slaves, worth at least two and a half millions of dollars; its farms were estimated at three millions,—making five and a half millions of property, the value of which depended largely on the slave system, and on the speculative demand for land once marvellously rich but already partially devitalized by careless and exhaustive culture. The war then meant a financial crash; in place of the five and a half millions of 1860, there remained in 1870 only farms valued at less than two millions. With this came increased competition in cotton culture from the rich lands of Texas; a steady fall in the normal price of cotton followed, from about fourteen cents a pound in 1860 until it reached four cents in 1898. Such a financial revolution was it that involved the owners of the cotton-belt in debt. And if things went ill with the master, how fared it with the man?

The plantations of Dougherty County in slavery days were not as imposing and aristocratic as those of Virginia. The Big House was smaller and usually one-storied, and sat very near the slave cabins. Sometimes these cabins stretched off on either side like wings; sometimes only on one side, forming a double row, or edging the road that turned into the plantation from the main thoroughfare. The form and disposition of the laborers' cabins throughout the Black Belt is to-day the same as in slavery days. Some live in the self-same cabins, others in cabins rebuilt on the sites of the old. All are sprinkled in little groups over the face of the land, centering about some dilapidated Big House where the head-tenant or agent lives. The general character and arrangement of these dwellings remains on the whole unaltered. There were in the county, outside the corporate town of Albany, about fifteen hundred Negro families in 1898. Out of all these, only a single family occupied a house with seven rooms; only fourteen have five rooms or more. The mass live in one- and two-room homes.

The size and arrangements of a people's homes are no unfair index of their condition. If, then, we inquire more carefully into these Negro homes, we find much that is unsatisfactory. All over the face of the land is the one-room cabin,—now standing in the shadow of the Big House, now staring at the dusty road, now rising dark and sombre amid the green of the cotton-fields. It is nearly always old and bare, built of rough boards, and neither plastered nor ceiled. Light and ventilation are supplied by the single door and by the square hole in the wall with its wooden shutter. There is no glass, porch, or ornamentation without. Within is a fireplace, black and smoky, and usually unsteady with age. A bed or two, a table, a wooden chest, and a few chairs compose the furniture; while a stray show-bill or a newspaper makes up the decorations for the walls. Now and then one may find such a cabin kept scrupulously neat, with merry steaming fireplaces and hospitable door; but the majority are dirty and dilapidated, smelling of eating and sleeping, poorly ventilated, and anything but homes.

Above all, the cabins are crowded. We have come to associate crowding with homes in cities almost exclusively. This is primarily because we have so little accurate knowledge of country life. Here in Dougherty County one may find families of eight and ten occupying one or two rooms, and for every ten rooms of house accommodation for the Negroes there are twenty-five persons. The worst tenement abominations of New York do not have above twenty-two persons for every ten rooms. Of course, one small, close room in a city, without a yard, is in many respects worse than the larger single country room. In other respects it is better; it has glass windows, a decent chimney, and a trustworthy floor. The single great advantage of the Negro peasant is that he may spend most of his life outside his hovel, in the open fields.

There are four chief causes of these wretched homes: First, long custom born of slavery has assigned such homes to Negroes; white laborers would be offered better accommodations, and might, for that and similar reasons, give better work. Secondly, the Negroes, used to such accommodations, do not as a rule demand better; they do not know what better houses mean. Thirdly, the landlords as a class have not yet come to realize that it is a good business investment to raise the standard of living among labor by slow and judicious methods; that a Negro laborer who demands three rooms and fifty cents a day would give more efficient work and leave a larger profit than a discouraged toiler herding his family in one room and working for thirty cents. Lastly, among such conditions of life there are few incentives to make the laborer become a better farmer. If he is ambitious, he moves to town or tries other labor; as a tenant-farmer his outlook is almost hopeless, and following it as a makeshift, he takes the house that is given him without protest.

In such homes, then, these Negro peasants live. The families are both small and large; there are many single tenants,—widows and bachelors, and remnants of broken groups. The system of labor and the size of the houses both tend to the breaking up of family groups: the grown children go away as contract hands or migrate to town, the sister goes into service; and so one finds many families with hosts of babies, and many newly married couples, but comparatively few families with half-grown and grown sons and daughters. The average size of Negro families has undoubtedly decreased since the war, primarily from economic stress. In Russia over a third of the bridegrooms and over half the brides are under twenty; the same was true of the ante-bellum* Negroes. To-day, however, very few of the boys and less than a fifth of the Negro girls under twenty are married. The young men marry between the ages of twenty-five and thirty-five; the young women between twenty and thirty. Such postponement is due to the difficulty of earning sufficient to rear and support a family; and it undoubtedly leads, in the country districts, to sexual immorality. The form of this immorality, however, is very seldom that of prostitution, and less frequently that of illegitimacy than one would imagine. Rather, it takes the form of separation and desertion after a family group has been formed. The number of separated persons is thirty-five to the thousand,—a very large number. It would of course be unfair to compare this number with divorce statistics, for many of these separated women are in reality widowed, were the truth known, and in other cases the separation is not permanent. Nevertheless, here lies the seat of greatest moral danger. There is little or no prostitution among these Negroes, and over three-forths of the families, as found by house-to-house investigation, deserve to be classed as decent people with considerable regard for female chastity. To be sure, the ideas of the mass would not suit New England, and there are many loose habits and notions. Yet the rate of illegitimacy is undoubtedly lower than in Austria or Italy, and the women as a class are modest. The plague-spot in sexual relations is easy marriage and easy separation. This is no sudden development, nor the fruit of Emancipation. It is the plain heritage from slavery. In those days Sam, with his master's consent, "took up" with Mary. No ceremony was necessary, and in the busy life of the great plantations of the Black Belt it was usually dispensed with. If now the master needed Sam's work in another plantation or in another part of the same plantation, or if he took a notion to sell the slave, Sam's married life with Mary was usually unceremoniously broken, and then it was clearly to the master's interest to have both of them take new mates. This widespread custom of two centuries has not been eradicated in thirty years. To-day Sam's grandson "takes up" with a woman without license or ceremony; they live together decently and honestly, and are, to all intents and purposes, man and wife. Sometimes these unions are never broken until death; but in too many cases family quarrels, a roving spirit, a rival suitor, or perhaps more frequently the hopeless battle to support a family, lead to separation, and a broken household is the result. The Negro church has done much to stop this practice, and now most marriage ceremonies are performed by the pastors. Nevertheless, the evil is still deep seated, and only a general raising of the standard of living will finally cure it.

Looking now at the county black population as a whole, it is fair to characterize it as poor and ignorant. Perhaps ten per cent compose the well-to-do and the best of the laborers, while at least nine per cent are thoroughly lewd and vicious. The rest, over eighty per cent, are poor and ignorant, fairly honest and well meaning, plodding, and to a degree shiftless, with some but not great sexual looseness. Such class lines are by no means fixed; they vary, one might almost say, with the price of cotton. The degree of ignorance cannot easily be expressed. We may say, for instance, that nearly two-thirds of them cannot read or write. This but partially expresses the fact. They are ignorant of the world about them, of modern economic organization, of the function of government, of individual worth and possibilities,— of nearly all those things which slavery in self-defence had to keep them from learning. Much that the white boy imbibes from his earliest social atmosphere forms the puzzling problems of the black boy's mature years. America is not another world for Opportunity to *all* her sons.

It is easy for us to lose ourselves in details in endeavoring to grasp and comprehend the real condition of a mass of human beings. We often forget that each unit in the mass is a throbbing human soul. Ignorant it may be, and poverty stricken, black and curious in limb and ways and thought; and yet it loves and hates, it toils and tires, it laughs and weeps its bitter tears, and looks in vague and awful longing at the grim horizon of its life,—all this, even as you and I. These black thousands are not in reality lazy; they are improvident and careless; they insist on breaking the monotony of toil with a glimpse at the great town-world on Saturday; they have their loafers and their rascals; but the great mass of them work continuously and faithfully for a return, and under circumstances that would call forth equal voluntary effort from few if any other modern laboring class. Over eighty-eight per cent of them—men, women, and children—are farmers. Indeed, this is almost the only industry. Most of the children get their schooling after the "crops are laid by," and very few there are that stay in school after the spring work has begun. Child-labor is to be found here in some of its worst phases, as fostering ignorance and stunting physical development. With the grown men of the county there is little variety in work: thirteen hundred are farmers, and two hundred are laborers, teamsters, etc., including twenty-four artisans, ten merchants, twenty-one preachers, and four teachers. This narrowness of life reaches its maximum among the women: thirteen hundred and fifty of these are farm laborers, one hundred are servants and washerwomen, leaving sixty-five housewives, eight teachers, and six seamstresses.

Among this people there is no leisure class. We often forget that in the United States over half the youth and adults are not in the world earning incomes, but are making homes, learning of the world, or resting after the heat of the strife. But here ninety-six per cent are toiling; no one with leisure to turn the bare and cheerless cabin into a home, no old folks to sit beside the fire and hand down traditions of the past; little of careless happy childhood and dreaming youth. The dull monotony of daily toil is broken only by the gayety of the thoughtless and the Saturday trip to town. The toil, like all farm toil, is monotonous, and here there are little machinery and few tools to relieve its burdensome drudgery. But with all this, it is work in the pure open air, and this is something in a day when fresh air is scarce.

The land on the whole is still fertile, despite long abuse. For nine or ten months in succession the crops will come if asked: garden vegetables in April, grain in May, melons in June and July, hay in August, sweet potatoes in September, and cotton from then to Christmas. And yet on two-thirds of the land there is but one crop, and that leaves the toilers in debt. Why is this?

Away down the Baysan road, where the broad flat fields are flanked by great oak forests, is a plantation; many thousands of acres it used to run, here and there, and beyond the great wood. Thirteen hundred human beings here obeyed the call of one,—were his in body, and largely in soul. One of them lives there yet,—a short, stocky man, his dull-brown face seamed and drawn, and his tightly curled hair gray-white. The crops? Just tolerable, he said; just tolerable. Getting on? No—he wasn't getting on at all. Smith of Albany "furnishes" him, and his rent is eight hundred pounds of cotton. Can't make anything at that. Why didn't he buy land! Humph! Takes money to buy land. And he turns away. Free! The most piteous thing amid all the black ruin of war-time, amid the broken fortunes of the masters, the blighted hopes of mothers and maidens, and the fall of an empire,—the most piteous thing amid all this was the black freedman who threw down his hoe because the world called him free. What did such a mockery of freedom mean? Not a cent of money, not an inch of land, not a mouthful of victuals,—not even ownership of the rags on his back. Free! On Saturday, once or twice a month, the old master, before the war, used to dole out bacon and meal to his Negroes. And after the first flush of freedom wore off, and his true helplessness dawned on the freedman, he came back and picked up his hoe, and old master still doled out his bacon and meal. The legal form of service was theoretically far different; in practice, task-work or "cropping" was substituted for daily toil in gangs; and the slave gradually became a metayer, or tenant on shares, in name, but a laborer with indeterminate wages in fact.

Still the price of cotton fell, and gradually the landlords deserted their plantations, and the reign of the merchant began. The merchant of the Black Belt is a contractor, and part despot. His store, which used most frequently to stand at the cross-roads and become the centre of a weekly village, has now moved to town; and thither the Negro tenant follows him. The merchant keeps everything,—clothes and shoes, coffee and sugar, pork and meal, canned and dried goods, wagons and ploughs, seed and fertilizer,—and what he has not in stock he can give you an order for at the store across the way. Here, then, comes the tenant, Sam Scott, after he has contracted with some absent landlord's agent for hiring forty acres of land; he fingers his hat nervously until the merchant finishes his morning chat with Colonel Saunders, and calls out, "Well, Sam, what do you want?" Sam wants him to "furnish" him,—i.e., to advance him food and clothing for the year, and perhaps seed and tools, until his crop is raised and sold. If Sam seems a favorable subject, he and the merchant go to a lawyer, and Sam executes a chattel mortgage on his mule and wagon in return for seed and a week's rations. As soon as the green cotton-leaves appear above the ground, another mortgage is given on the "crop." Every Saturday, or at longer intervals, Sam calls upon the merchant for his "rations"; a family of five usually gets about thirty pounds of fat side-pork and a couple of bushels of cornmeal a month. Besides this, clothing and shoes must be furnished; if Sam or his family is sick, there are orders on the druggist and doctor; if the mule wants shoeing, an order on the blacksmith, etc. If Sam is a hard worker and crops promise well, he is often encouraged to buy more,—sugar, extra clothes, perhaps a buggy. But he is seldom encouraged to save. When cotton rose to ten cents last fall, the shrewd merchants of Dougherty County sold a thousand buggies in one season, mostly to black men.

The security offered for such transactions—a crop and chattel mortgage—may at first seem slight. And, indeed, the merchants tell many a true tale of shiftlessness and cheating; of cotton picked at night, mules disappearing, and tenants absconding. But on the whole the merchant of the Black Belt is the most prosperous man in the section. So skilfully and so closely has he drawn the bonds of the law about the tenant, that the black man has often simply to choose between pauperism and crime; he "waives" all homestead exemptions in his contract; he cannot touch his own mortgaged crop, which the laws put almost in the full control of the land-owner and of the merchant. When the crop is growing the merchant watches it like a hawk; as soon as it is ready for market he takes possession of it, sells it, pays the landowner his rent, subtracts his bill for supplies, and if, as sometimes happens, there is anything left, he hands it over to the black serf for his Christmas celebration.

The direct result of this system is an all-cotton scheme of agriculture and the continued bankruptcy of the tenant. The currency of the Black Belt is cotton. It is a crop always salable for ready money, not usually subject to great yearly fluctuations in price, and one which the Negroes know how to raise. The landlord therefore demands his rent in cotton, and the merchant will accept mortgages on no other crop. There is no use asking the black tenant, then, to diversify his crops,—he cannot under this system. Moreover, the system is bound to bankrupt the tenant. I remember once meeting a little one-mule wagon on the River road. A young black fellow sat in it driving listlessly, his elbows on his knees. His dark-faced wife sat beside him, stolid, silent.

"Hello!" cried my driver,—he has a most imprudent way of addressing these people, though they seem used to it,—"what have you got there?"

"Meat and meal," answered the man, stopping. The meat lay uncovered in the bottom of the wagon,—a great thin side of fat pork covered with salt; the meal was in a white bushel bag.

"What did you pay for that meat?"

"Ten cents a pound." It could have been bought for six or seven cents cash.

"And the meal?"

"Two dollars." One dollar and ten cents is the cash price in town. Here was a man paying five dollars for goods which he could have bought for three dollars cash, and raised for one dollar or one dollar and a half.

Yet it is not wholly his fault. The Negro farmer

started behind,—started in debt. This was not his choosing, but the crime of this happy-go-lucky nation which goes blundering along with its Reconstruction tragedies, its Spanish war interludes and Philippine matinees, just as though God really were dead. Once in debt, it is no easy matter for a whole race to emerge.

In the year of low-priced cotton, 1898, out of three hundred tenant families one hundred and seventy-five ended their year's work in debt to the extent of fourteen thousand dollars; fifty cleared nothing, and the remaining seventy-five made a total profit of sixteen hundred dollars. The net indebtedness of the black tenant families of the whole county must have been at least sixty thousand dollars. In a more prosperous year the situation is far better; but on the average the majority of tenants end the year even, or in debt, which means that they work for board and clothes. Such an economic organization is radically wrong. Whose is the blame?

The underlying causes of this situation are complicated but discernible. And one of the chief, outside the carelessness of the nation in letting the slave start with nothing, is the widespread opinion among the merchants and employers of the Black Belt that only by the slavery of debt can the Negro be kept at work. Without doubt, some pressure was necessary at the beginning of the free-labor system to keep the listless and lazy at work; and even to-day the mass of the Negro laborers need stricter guardianship than most Northern laborers. Behind this honest and widespread opinion dishonesty and cheating of the ignorant laborers have a good chance to take refuge. And to all this must be added the obvious fact that a slave ancestry and a system of unrequited toil has not improved the efficiency or temper of the mass of black laborers. Nor is this peculiar to Sambo; it has in history been just as true of John and Hans, of Jacques and Pat, of all ground-down peasantries. Such is the situation of the mass of the Negroes in the Black Belt to-day; and they are thinking about it. Crime, and a cheap and dangerous socialism, are the inevitable results of this pondering. I see now that ragged black man sitting on a log, aimlessly whittling a stick. He muttered to me with the murmur of many ages, when he said: "White man sit down whole year; Nigger work day and night and make crop; Nigger hardly gits bread and meat; white man sittin' down gits all. *It's wrong.*" And what do the better classes of Negroes do to improve their situation? One of two things: if any way possible, they buy land; if not, they migrate to town. Just as centuries ago it was no easy thing for the serf to escape into the freedom of town-life, even so to-day there are hindrances laid in the way of county laborers. In considerable parts of all the Gulf States, and especially in Mississippi, Louisiana, and Arkansas, the Negroes on the plantations in the back-country districts are still held at forced labor practically without wages. Especially is this true in districts where the farmers are composed of the more ignorant class of poor whites, and the Negroes are beyond the reach of schools and intercourse with their advancing fellows. If such a peon should run away, the sheriff, elected by white suffrage, can usually be depended on to catch the fugitive, return him, and ask no questions. If he escape to another country, a charge of petty thieving, easily true, can be depended upon to secure his return. Even if some unduly officious person insist upon a trial, neighborly comity will probably make his conviction sure, and then the labor due the county can easily be bought by the master. Such a system is impossible in the more civilized parts of the South, or near the large towns and cities; but in those vast stretches of land beyond the telegraph and the newspaper the spirit of the Thirteenth Amendment is sadly broken. This represents the lowest economic depths of the black American peasant; and in a study of the rise and condition of the Negro freeholder we must trace his economic progress from the modern serfdom.

Even in the better-ordered country districts of the South the free movement of agricultural laborers is hindered by the migration-agent laws. The "Associated Press" recently informed the world of the arrest of a young white man in Southern Georgia who represented the "Atlantic Naval Supplies Company," and who "was caught in the act of enticing hands from the turpentine farm of Mr. John Greer." The crime for which this young man was arrested is taxed five hundred dollars for each county in which the employment agent proposes to gather laborers for work outside the State. Thus the Negroes' ignorance of the labor-market outside his own vicinity is increased rather than diminished by the laws of nearly every Southern State.

Similar to such measures is the unwritten law of the back districts and small towns of the South, that the character of all Negroes unknown to the mass of the community must be vouched for by some white man. This is really a revival of the old Roman idea of the patron under whose protection the new-made freedman was put. In many instances this system has been of great good to the Negro, and very often under the protection and guidance of the former master's family, or other white friends, the freedman progressed in wealth and morality. But the same system has in other cases resulted in the refusal of whole communities to recognize the right of a Negro to change his habitation and to be master of his own fortunes. A black stranger in Baker County, Georgia, for instance, is liable to be stopped anywhere on the public highway and made to state his business to the satisfaction of any white interrogator. If he fails to give a suitable answer, or seems too independent or "sassy," he may be arrested or summarily driven away.

Thus it is that in the country districts of the South, by written or unwritten law, peonage, hindrances to the migration of labor, and a system of white patronage exists over large areas. Besides this, the chance for lawless oppression and illegal exactions is vastly greater in the country than in the city, and nearly all the more serious race disturbances of the last decade have arisen from disputes in the county between master and man,—as, for instance, the Sam Hose affair. As a result of such a situation, there arose, first, the Black Belt; and, second, the Migration to Town. The Black Belt was not, as many assumed, a movement toward fields of labor under more genial climatic conditions; it was primarily a huddling for self-protection,—a massing of the black population for mutual defence in order to secure the peace and tranquillity necessary to economic advance. This movement took place between Emancipation and 1880, and only partially accomplished the desired results. The rush to town since 1880 is the counter-movement of men disappointed in the economic opportunities of the Black Belt.

In Dougherty County, Georgia, one can see easily the results of this experiment in huddling for protection. Only ten per cent of the adult population was born in the county, and yet the blacks outnumber the whites four or five to one. There is undoubtedly a security to the blacks in their very numbers,—a personal freedom from arbitrary treatment, which makes hundreds of laborers cling to Dougherty in spite of low wages and economic distress. But a change is coming, and slowly but surely even here the agricultural laborers are drifting to town and leaving the broad acres behind. Why is this? Why do not the Negroes become land-owners, and build up the black landed peasantry, which has for a generation and more been the dream of philanthropist and statesman?

To the car-window sociologist, to the man who seeks to understand and know the South by devoting the few leisure hours of a holiday trip to unravelling the snarl of centuries,—to such men very often the whole trouble with the black field-hand may be summed up by Aunt Ophelia's word, "Shiftless!" They have noted repeatedly scenes like one I saw last summer. We were riding along the highroad to town at the close of a long hot day. A couple of young black fellows passed us in a muleteam, with several bushels of loose corn in the ear. One was driving, listlessly bent forward, his elbows on his knees,—a happy-go-lucky, careless picture of irresponsibility. The other was fast asleep in the bottom of the wagon. As we passed we noticed an ear of corn fall from the wagon. They never saw it,—not they. A rod farther on we noted another ear on the ground; and between that creeping mule and town we counted twenty-six ears of corn. Shiftless? Yes, the personification of shiftlessness. And yet follow those boys: they are not lazy; to-morrow morning they'll be up with the sun; they work hard when they do work, and they work willingly. They have no sordid, selfish, money-getting ways, but rather a fine disdain for mere cash. They'll loaf before your face and work behind your back with good-natured honesty. They'll steal a watermelon, and hand you back your lost purse intact. Their great defect as laborers lies in their lack of incentive beyond the mere pleasure of physical exertion. They are careless because they have not found that it pays to be careful; they are improvident because the improvident ones of their acquaintance get on about as well as the provident. Above all, they cannot see why they should take unusual pains to make the white man's land better, or to fatten his mule, or save his corn. On the other hand, the white land-owner argues that any attempt to improve these laborers by increased responsibility, or higher wages, or better homes, or land of their own, would be sure to result in failure. He shows his Northern visitor the scarred and wretched land; the ruined mansions, the wornout soil and mortgaged acres, and says, This is Negro freedom!

Now it happens that both master and man have just enough argument on their respective sides to make it difficult for them to understand each other. The Negro dimly personifies in the white man all his ills and misfortunes; if he is poor, it is because the white man seizes the fruit of his toil; if he is ignorant, it is because the white man gives him neither time nor facilities to learn; and, indeed, if any misfortune happens to him, it is because of some hidden machinations of "white folks." On the other hand, the masters and the masters' sons have never been able to see why the Negro, instead of settling down to be day-laborers for bread and clothes, are infected with a silly desire to rise in the world, and why they are sulky, dissatisfied, and careless, where their fathers were happy and dumb and faithful. "Why, you niggers have an easier time than I do," said a puzzled Albany merchant to his black customer. "Yes," he replied, "and so does yo' hogs."

Taking, then, the dissatisfied and shiftless fieldhand as a starting-point, let us inquire how the black thousands of Dougherty have struggled from him up toward their ideal, and what that ideal is. All social struggle is evidenced by the rise, first of economic, then of social classes, among a homogeneous population. To-day the following economic classes are plainly differentiated among these Negroes.

A "submerged tenth" of croppers, with a few paupers; forty per cent who are metayers and thirty-nine per cent of semi-metayers and wage-laborers. There are left five per cent of money-renters and six per cent of freeholders,—the "Upper Ten" of the land. The croppers are entirely without capital, even in the limited sense of food or money to keep them from seed-time to harvest. All they furnish is their labor; the land-owner furnishes land, stock, tools, seed, and house; and at the end of the year the laborer gets from a third to a half of the crop. Out of his share, however, comes pay and interest for food and clothing advanced him during the year. Thus we have a laborer without capital and without wages, and an employer whose capital is largely his employees' wages. It is an unsatisfactory arrangement, both for hirer and hired, and is usually in vogue on poor land with hard-pressed owners.

Above the croppers come the great mass of the black population who work the land on their own responsibility, paying rent in cotton and supported by the crop-mortgage system. After the war this system was attractive to the freedmen on account of its larger freedom and its possibility for making a surplus. But with the carrying out of the crop-lien system, the deterioration of the land, and the slavery of debt, the position of the metayers has sunk to a dead level of practically unrewarded toil. Formerly all tenants had some capital, and often considerable; but absentee landlordism, rising rack-rent, and falling cotton have stripped them well-nigh of all, and probably not over half of them to-day own their mules. The change from cropper to tenant was accomplished by fixing the rent. If, now, the rent fixed was reasonable, this was an incentive to the tenant to strive. On the other hand, if the rent was too high, or if the land deteriorated, the result was to discourage and check the efforts of the black peasantry. There is no doubt that the latter case is true; that in Dougherty County every economic advantage of the price of cotton in market and of the strivings of the tenant has been taken advantage of by the landlords and merchants, and swallowed up in rent and interest. If cotton rose in price, the rent rose even higher; if cotton fell, the rent remained or followed reluctantly. If the tenant worked hard and raised a large crop, his rent was raised the next year; if that year the crop failed, his corn was confiscated and his mule sold for debt. There were, of course, exceptions to this,—cases of personal kindness and forbearance; but in the vast majority of cases the rule was to extract the uttermost farthing from the mass of the black farm laborers.

The average metayer pays from twenty to thirty per cent of his crop in rent. The result of such rack-rent can only be evil,—abuse and neglect of the soil, deterioration in the character of the laborers, and a widespread sense of injustice. "Wherever the country is poor," cried Arthur Young, "it is in the hands of metayers," and "their condition is more wretched than that of day-laborers." He was talking of Italy a century ago; but he might have been talking of Dougherty County to-day. And especially is that true to-day which he declares was true in France before the Revolution: "The metayers are considered as little better than menial servants, removable at pleasure, and obliged to conform in all things to the will of the landlords." On this low plane half the black population of Dougherty County—perhaps more than half the black millions of this land—are to-day struggling.

A degree above these we may place those laborers who receive money wages for their work. Some receive a house with perhaps a garden-spot; then supplies of food and clothing are advanced, and certain fixed wages are given at the end of the year, varying from thirty to sixty dollars, out of which the supplies must be paid for, with interest. About eighteen per cent of the population belong to this class of semi-metayers, while twenty-two per cent are laborers paid by the month or year, and are either "furnished" by their own savings or perhaps more usually by some merchant who takes his chances of payment. Such laborers receive from thirty-five to fifty cents a day during the working season. They are usually young unmarried persons, some being women; and when they marry they sink to the class of metayers, or, more seldom, become renters.

The renters for fixed money rentals are the first of the emerging classes, and form five per cent of the families. The sole advantage of this small class is their freedom to choose their crops, and the increased responsibility which comes through having money transactions. While some of the renters differ little in condition from the metayers, yet on the whole they are more intelligent and responsible persons, and are the ones who eventually become land-owners. Their better character and greater shrewdness enable them to gain, perhaps to demand, better terms in rents; rented farms, varying from forty to a hundred acres, bear an average rental of about fifty-four dollars a year. The men who conduct such farms do not long remain renters; either they sink to metayers, or with a successful series of harvests rise to be land-owners.

In 1870 the tax-books of Dougherty report no Negroes as landholders. If there were any such at that time,—and there may have been a few,—their land was probably held in the name of some white patron,—a method not uncommon during slavery. In 1875 ownership of land had begun with seven hundred and fifty acres; ten years later this had increased to over sixty-five hundred acres, to nine thousand acres in 1890 and ten thousand in 1900. The total assessed property has in this same period risen from eighty thousand dollars in 1875 to two hundred and forty thousand dollars in 1900.

Two circumstances complicate this development and make it in some respects difficult to be sure of the real tendencies; they are the panic of 1893, and the low price of cotton in 1898. Besides this, the system of assessing property in the country districts of Georgia is somewhat antiquated and of uncertain statistical value; there are no assessors, and each man makes a sworn return to a tax-receiver. Thus public opinion plays a large part, and the returns vary strangely from year to year. Certainly these figures show the small amount of accumulated capital among the Negroes, and the consequent large dependence of their property on temporary prosperity. They have little to tide over a few years of economic depression, and are at the mercy of the cotton-market far more than the whites. And thus the land-owners, despite their marvellous efforts, are really a transient class, continually being depleted by those who fall back into the class of renters or metayers, and augmented by newcomers from the masses. Of one hundred land-owners in 1898, half had bought their land since 1893, a fourth between 1890 and 1893, a fifth between 1884 and 1890, and the rest between 1870 and 1884. In all, one hundred and eighty-five Negroes have owned land in this county since 1875.

If all the black land-owners who had ever held land here had kept it or left it in the hands of black men, the Negroes would have owned nearer thirty thousand acres than the fifteen thousand they now hold. And yet these fifteen thousand acres are a creditable showing,—a proof of no little weight of the worth and ability of the Negro people. If they had been given an economic start at Emancipation, if they had been in an enlightened and rich community which really desired their best good, then we might perhaps call such a result small or even insignificant. But for a few thousand poor ignorant field-hands, in the face of poverty, a falling market, and social stress, to save and capitalize two hundred thousand dollars in a generation has meant a tremendous effort. The rise of a nation, the pressing forward of a social class, means a bitter struggle, a hard and soul-sickening battle with the world such as few of the more favored classes know or appreciate.

Out of the hard economic conditions of this portion of the Black Belt, only six per cent of the population have succeeded in emerging into peasant proprietorship; and these are not all firmly fixed, but grow and shrink in number with the wavering of the cotton-market. Fully ninety-four per cent have struggled for land and failed, and half of them sit in hopeless serfdom. For these there is one other avenue of escape toward which they have turned in increasing numbers, namely, migration to town. A glance at the distribution of land among the black owners curiously reveals this fact. In 1898 the holdings were as follows: Under forty acres, forty-nine families; forty to two hundred and fifty acres, seventeen families; two hundred and fifty to one thousand acres, thirteen families; one thousand or more acres, two families. Now in 1890 there were forty-four holdings, but only nine of these were under forty acres. The great increase of holdings, then, has come in the buying of small homesteads near town, where their owners really share in the town life; this is a part of the rush to town. And for every land-owner who has thus hurried away from the narrow and hard conditions of country life, how many field-hands, how many tenants, how many ruined renters, have joined that long procession? Is it not strange compensation? The sin of the country districts is visited on the town, and the social sores of city life to-day may, here in Dougherty County, and perhaps in many places near and far, look for their final healing without the city walls.

Chapter

Of the Sons of Master and Man

Life treads on life, and heart on heart;
We press too close in church and mart
To keep a dream or grave apart.

MRS. BROWNING.

The world-old phenomenon of the contact of diverse races of men is to have new exemplification during the new century. Indeed, the characteristic of our age is the contact of European civilization with the world's undeveloped peoples. Whatever we may say of the results of such contact in the past, it certainly forms a chapter in human action not pleasant to look back upon. War, murder, slavery, extermination, and debauchery,—this has again and again been the result of carrying civilization and the blessed gospel to the isles of the sea and the heathen without the law. Nor does it altogether satisfy the conscience of the modern world to be told complacently that all this has been right and proper, the fated triumph of strength over weakness, of righteousness over evil, of superiors over inferiors. It would certainly be soothing if one could readily believe all this; and yet there are too many ugly facts for everything to be thus easily explained away. We feel and know that there are many delicate differences in race psychology, numberless changes that our crude social measurements are not yet able to follow minutely, which explain much of history and social development. At the same time, too, we know that these considerations have never adequately explained or excused the triumph of brute force and cunning over weakness and innocence.

It is, then, the strife of all honorable men of the twentieth century to see that in the future competition of races the survival of the fittest shall mean the triumph of the good, the beautiful, and the true; that we may be able to preserve for future civilization all that is really fine and noble and strong, and not continue to put a premium on greed and impudence and cruelty. To bring this hope to fruition, we are compelled daily to turn more and more to a conscientious study of the phenomena of race-contact,—to a study frank and fair, and not falsified and colored by our wishes or our fears. And we have in the South as fine a field for such a study as the world affords,—a field, to be sure, which the average American scientist deems somewhat beneath his dignity, and which the average man who is not a scientist knows all about, but nevertheless a line of study which by reason of the enormous race complications with which God seems about to punish this nation must increasingly claim our sober attention, study, and thought, we must ask, what are the actual relations of whites and blacks in the South? and we must be answered, not by apology or fault-finding, but by a plain, unvarnished tale.

In the civilized life of to-day the contact of men and their relations to each other fall in a few main lines of action and communication: there is, first, the physical proximity of home and dwelling-places, the way in which neighborhoods group themselves, and the contiguity of neighborhoods. Secondly, and in our age chiefest, there are the economic relations,—the methods by which individuals coöperate for earning a living, for the mutual satisfaction of wants, for the production of wealth. Next, there are the political relations, the coöperation in social control, in group government, in laying and paying the burden of taxation. In the fourth place there are the less tangible but highly important forms of intellectual contact and commerce, the interchange of ideas through conversation and conference, through periodicals and libraries; and, above all, the gradual formation for each community of that curious *tertium quid** which we call public opinion. Closely allied with this come the various forms of social contact in everyday life, in travel, in theatres, in house gatherings, in marrying and giving in marriage. Finally, there are the varying forms of religious enterprise, of moral teaching and benevolent endeavor. These are the principle ways in which men living in the same communities are brought into contact with each other. It is my present task, therefore, to indicate, from my point of view, how the black race in the South meet and mingle with the whites in these matters of everyday life.

First, as to physical dwelling. It is usually possible to draw in nearly every Southern community a physical color-line on the map, on the one side of which whites dwell and on the other Negroes. The winding and intricacy of the geographical color-line varies, of course, in different communities. I know some towns where a straight line drawn through the middle of the main street separates nine-tenths of the whites from nine-tenths of the blacks. In other towns the older settlement of whites has been encircled by a broad band of blacks; in still other cases little settlements or nuclei of blacks have sprung up amid surrounding whites. Usually in cities each street has its distinctive color, and only now and then do the colors meet in close proximity. Even in the country something of this segregation is manifest in the smaller areas, and of course in the larger phenomena of the Black Belt.

All this segregation by color is largely independent of that natural clustering by social grades common to all communities. A Negro slum may be in dangerous proximity to a white residence quarter, while it is quite common to find a white slum planted in the heart of a respectable Negro district. One thing, however, seldom occurs: the best of the whites and the best of the Negroes almost never live in anything like close proximity. It thus happens that in nearly every Southern town and city, both whites and blacks see commonly the worst of each other. This is a vast change from the situation in the past, when, through the close contact of master and house-servant in the patriarchal big house, one found the best of both races in close contact and sympathy, while at the same time the squalor and dull round of toil among the field-hands was removed from the sight and hearing of the family. One can easily see how a person who saw slavery thus from his father's parlors, and sees freedom on the streets of a great city, fails to grasp or comprehend the whole of the new picture. On the other hand, the settled belief of the mass of the Negroes that the Southern white people do not have the black man's best interests at heart has been intensified in later years by this continual daily contact of the better class of blacks with the worst representatives of the white race.

Coming now to the economic relations of the races, we are on ground made familiar by study, much discussion, and no little philanthropic effort. And yet with all this there are many essential elements in the coöperation of Negroes and whites for work and wealth that are too readily overlooked or not thoroughly understood. The average American can easily conceive of a rich land awaiting development and filled with black laborers. To him the Southern problem is simply that of making efficient workingmen out of this material, by giving them the requisite technical skill and the help of invested capital. The problem, however is by no means as simple as this, from the obvious fact that these workingmen have been trained for centuries as slaves. They exhibit, therefore, all the advantages and defects of such training; they are willing and good-natured, but not self-reliant, provident, or careful. If now the economic development of the South is to be pushed to the verge of exploitation, as seems probable, then we have a mass of workingmen thrown into relentless competition with the workingmen of the world, but handicapped by a training the very opposite to that of the modern self-reliant democratic laborer. What the black laborer needs is careful personal guidance, group leadership of men with hearts in their bosoms, to train them to foresight, carefulness, and honesty. Nor does it require any fine-spun theories of racial differences to prove the necessity of such group training after the brains of the race have been knocked out by two hundred and fifty years of assiduous education in submission, carelessness, and stealing. After Emancipation, it was the plain duty of some one to assume this group leadership and training of the Negro laborer. I will not stop here to inquire whose duty it was—whether that of the white ex-master who had profited by unpaid toil, or the Northern philanthropist whose persistence brought on the crisis, or the National Government whose edict freed the bondmen; I will not stop to ask whose duty it was, but I insist it was the duty of some one to see that these workingmen were not left alone and unguided, without capital, without land, without skill, without economic organization, without even the bald protection of law, order, and decency,—left in a great land, not to settle down to slow and careful internal development, but destined to be thrown almost immediately into relentless and sharp competition with the best of modern workingmen under an economic system where every participant is fighting for himself, and too often utterly regardless of the rights or welfare of his neighbor.

For we must never forget that the economic system of the South to-day which has succeeded the old regime is not the same system as that of the old industrial North, of England, or of France, with their trade-unions, their restrictive laws, their written and unwritten commercial customs, and their long experience. It is, rather, a copy of that England of the early nineteenth century, before the factory acts,—the England that wrung pity from thinkers and fired the wrath of Carlyle.* The rod of empire that passed from the hands of Southern gentlemen in 1865, partly by force, partly by their own petulance, has never returned to them. Rather it has passed to those men who have come to take charge of the industrial exploitation of the New South,—the sons of poor whites fired with a new thirst for wealth and power, thrifty and avaricious Yankees, and unscrupulous immigrants. Into the hands of these men the Southern laborers, white and black, have fallen; and this to their sorrow. For the laborers as such, there is in these new captains of industry neither love nor hate, neither sympathy nor romance; it is a cold question of dollars and dividends. Under such a system all labor is bound to suffer. Even the white laborers are not yet intelligent, thrifty, and well trained enough to maintain themselves against the powerful inroads of organized capital. The results among them, even, are long hours of toil, low wages, child labor, and lack of protection against usury and cheating. But among the black laborers all this is aggravated, first, by a race prejudice which varies from a doubt and distrust among the best element of whites to a frenzied hatred among the worst; and, secondly, it is aggravated, as I have said before, by the wretched economic heritage of the freedmen from slavery. With this training it is difficult for the freedman to learn to grasp the opportunities already opened to him, and the new opportunities are seldom given him, but go by favor to the whites.

Left by the best elements of the South with little protection or oversight, he has been made in law and custom the victim of the worst and most unscrupulous men in each community. The crop-lien system which is depopulating the fields of the South is not simply the result of shiftlessness on the part of Negroes, but is also the result of cunningly devised laws as to mortgages, liens, and misdemeanors, which can be made by conscienceless men to entrap and snare the unwary until escape is impossible, further toil a farce, and protest a crime. I have seen, in the Black Belt of Georgia, an ignorant, honest Negro buy and pay for a farm in installments three separate times, and then in the face of law and decency the enterprising American who sold it to him pocketed the money and deed and left the black man landless, to labor on his own land at thirty cents a day. I have seen a black farmer fall in debt to a white storekeeper, and that storekeeper go to his farm and strip it of every single marketable article,—mules, ploughs, stored crops, tools, furniture, bedding, clocks, looking-glass,—and all this without a sheriff or officer, in the face of the law for homestead exemptions, and without rendering to a single responsible person any account or reckoning. And such proceedings can happen, and will happen, in any community where a class of ignorant toilers are placed by custom and race-prejudice beyond the pale of sympathy and race-brotherhood. So long as the best elements of a community do not feel in duty bound to protect and train and care for the weaker members of their group, they leave them to be preyed upon by these swindlers and rascals.

This unfortunate economic situation does not mean the hindrance of all advance in the black South, or the absence of a class of black landlords and mechanics who, in spite of disadvantages, are accumulating property and making good citizens. But it does mean that this class is not nearly so large as a fairer economic system might easily make it, that those who survive in the competition are handicapped so as to accomplish much less than they deserve to, and that, above all, the *personnel* of the successful class is left to chance and accident, and not to any intelligent culling or reasonable methods of selection. As a remedy for this, there is but one possible procedure. We must accept some of the race prejudice in the South as a fact,—deplorable in its intensity, unfortunate in results, and dangerous for the future, but nevertheless a hard fact which only time can efface. We cannot hope, then, in this generation, or for several generations, that the mass of the whites can be brought to assume that close sympathetic and self-sacrificing leadership of the blacks which their present situation so eloquently demands. Such leadership, such social teaching and example, must come from the blacks themselves. For some time men doubted as to whether the Negro could develop such leaders; but to-day no one seriously disputes the capability of individual Negroes to assimilate the culture and common sense of modern civilization, and to pass it on, to some extent at least, to their fellows. If this is true, then here is the path out of the economic situation, and here is the imperative demand for trained Negro leaders of character and intelligence,— men of skill, men of light and leading, college-bred men, black captains of industry, and missionaries of culture; men who thoroughly comprehend and know modern civilization, and can take hold of Negro communities and raise and train them by force of precept and example, deep sympathy, and the inspiration of common blood and ideals. But if such men are to be effective they must have some power,— they must be backed by the best public opinion of these communities, and able to wield for their objects and aims such weapons as the experience of the world has taught are indispensable to human progress.

Of such weapons the greatest, perhaps, in the modern world is the power of the ballot; and this brings me to a consideration of the third form of contact between whites and blacks in the South,— political activity.

In the attitude of the American mind toward Negro suffrage can be traced with unusual accuracy the prevalent conceptions of government. In the fifties we were near enough the echoes of the French Revolution to believe pretty thoroughly in universal suffrage. We argued, as we thought then rather logically, that no social class was so good, so true, and so disinterested as to be trusted wholly with the political destiny of its neighbors; that in every state the best arbiters of their own welfare are the persons directly affected; consequently that it is only by arming every hand with a ballot,—with the right to have a voice in the policy of the state,—that the greatest good to the greatest number could be attained. To be sure, there were objections to these arguments, but we thought we had answered them tersely and convincingly; if some one complained of the ignorance of voters, we answered, "Educate them." If another complained of their venality, we replied, "Disfranchise them or put them in jail." And, finally, to the men who feared demagogues and the natural perversity of some human beings we insisted that time and bitter experience would teach the most hardheaded. It was at this time that the question of Negro suffrage in the South was raised. Here was a defenceless people suddenly made free. How were they to be protected from those who did not believe in their freedom and were determined to thwart it? Not by force, said the North; not by government guardianship, said the South; then by the ballot, the sole and legitimate defence of a free people, said the Common Sense of the Nation. No one thought, at the time, that the ex-slaves could use the ballot intelligently or very effectively; but they did think that the possession of so great power by a great class in the nation would compel their fellows to educate this class to its intelligent use.

Meantime, new thoughts came to the nation: the inevitable period of moral retrogression and political trickery that ever follows in the wake of war overtook us. So flagrant became the political scandals that reputable men began to leave politics alone, and politics consequently became disreputable. Men began to pride themselves on having nothing to do with their own government, and to agree tacitly with those who regarded public office as a private perquisite. In this state of mind it became easy to wink at the suppression of the Negro vote in the South, and to advise self-respecting Negroes to leave politics entirely alone. The decent and reputable citizens of the North who neglected their own civic duties grew hilarious over the exaggerated importance with which the Negro regarded the franchise. Thus it easily happened that more and more the better class of Negroes followed the advice from abroad and the pressure from home, and took no further interest in politics, leaving to the careless and the venal of their race the exercise of their rights as voters. The black vote that still remained was not trained and educated, but further debauched by open and unblushing bribery, or force and fraud; until the Negro voter was thoroughly inoculated with the idea that politics was a method of private gain by disreputable means.

And finally, now, to-day, when we are awakening to the fact that the perpetuity of republican institutions on this continent depends on the purification of the ballot, the civic training of voters, and the raising of voting to the plane of a solemn duty which a patriotic citizen neglects to his peril and to the peril of his children's children,—in this day, when we are striving for a renaissance of civic virtue, what are we going to say to the black voter of the South? Are we going to tell him still that politics is a disreputable and useless form of human activity? Are we going to induce the best class of Negroes to take less and less interest in government, and to give up their right to take such an interest, without a protest? I am not saying a word against all legitimate efforts to purge the ballot of ignorance, pauperism, and crime. But few have pretended that the present movement for disfranchisement in the South is for such a purpose; it has been plainly and frankly declared in nearly every case that the object of the disfranchising laws is the elimination of the black man from politics.

Now, is this a minor matter which has no influence on the main question of the industrial and intellectual development of the Negro? Can we establish a mass of black laborers and artisans and landholders in the South who, by law and public opinion, have absolutely no voice in shaping the laws under which they live and work? Can the modern organization of industry, assuming as it does free democratic government and the power and ability of the laboring classes to compel respect for their welfare,—can this system be carried out in the South when half its laboring force is voiceless in the public councils and powerless in its own defence? To-day the black man of the South has almost nothing to say as to how much he shall be taxed, or how those taxes shall be expended; as to who shall execute the laws, and how they shall do it; as to who shall make the laws, and how they shall be made. It is pitiable that frantic efforts must be made at critical times to get law-makers in some States even to listen to the respectful presentation of the black man's side of a current controversy. Daily the Negro is coming more and more to look upon law and justice, not as protecting safeguards, but as sources of humiliation and oppression. The laws are made by men who have little interest in him; they are executed by men who have absolutely no motive for treating the black people with courtesy or consideration; and, finally, the accused law-breaker is tried, not by his peers, but too often by men who would rather punish ten innocent Negroes than let one guilty one escape.

I should be the last one to deny the patent

weaknesses and shortcomings of the Negro people; I should be the last to withhold sympathy from the white South in its efforts to solve its intricate social problems. I freely acknowledged that it is possible, and sometimes best, that a partially undeveloped people should be ruled by the best of their stronger and better neighbors for their own good, until such time as they can start and fight the world's battles alone. I have already pointed out how sorely in need of such economic and spiritual guidance the emancipated Negro was, and I am quite willing to admit that if the representatives of the best white Southern public opinion were the ruling and guiding powers in the South to-day the conditions indicated would be fairly well fulfilled. But the point I have insisted upon and now emphasize again, is that the best opinion of the South to-day is not the ruling opinion. That to leave the Negro helpless and without a ballot to-day is to leave him, not to the guidance of the best, but rather to the exploitation and debauchment of the worst; that this is no truer of the South than of the North,—of the North than of Europe: in any land, in any country under modern free competition, to lay any class of weak and despised people, be they white, black, or blue, at the political mercy of their stronger, richer, and more resourceful fellows, is a temptation which human nature seldom has withstood and seldom will withstand.

Moreover, the political status of the Negro in the South is closely connected with the question of Negro crime. There can be no doubt that crime among Negroes has sensibly increased in the last thirty years, and that there has appeared in the slums of great cities a distinct criminal class among the blacks. In explaining this unfortunate development, we must note two things: (1) that the inevitable result of Emancipation was to increase crime and criminals, and (2) that the police system of the South was primarily designed to control slaves. As to the first point, we must not forget that under a strict slave system there can scarcely be such a thing as crime. But when these variously constituted human particles are suddenly thrown broadcast on the sea of life, some swim, some sink, and some hang suspended, to be forced up or down by the chance currents of a busy hurrying world. So great an economic and social revolution as swept the South in '63 meant a weeding out among the Negroes of the incompetents and vicious, the beginning of a differentiation of social grades. Now a rising group of people are not lifted bodily from the ground like an inert solid mass, but rather stretch upward like a living plant with its roots still clinging in the mould. The appearance, therefore, of the Negro criminal was a phenomenon to be awaited; and while it causes anxiety, it should not occasion surprise.

Here again the hope for the future depended peculiarly on careful and delicate dealing with these criminals. Their offences at first were those of laziness, carelessness, and impulse, rather than of malignity or ungoverned viciousness. Such misdemeanors needed discriminating treatment, firm but reformatory, with no hint of injustice, and full proof of guilt. For such dealing with criminals, white or black, the South had no machinery, no adequate jails or reformatories; its police system was arranged to deal with blacks alone, and tacitly assumed that every white man was *ipso facto** a member of that police. Thus grew up a double system of justice, which erred on the white side by undue leniency and the practical immunity of red-handed criminals, and erred on the black side by undue severity, injustice, and lack of discrimination. For, as I have said, the police system of the South was originally designed to keep track of all Negroes, not simply of criminals; and when the Negroes were freed and the whole South was convinced of the impossibility of free Negro labor, the first and almost universal device was to use the courts as a means of reënslaving the blacks. It was not then a question of crime, but rather one of color, that settled a man's conviction on almost any charge. Thus Negroes came to look upon courts as instruments of injustice and oppression, and upon those convicted in them as martyrs and victims.

When, now, the real Negro criminal appeared, and instead of petty stealing and vagrancy we began to have highway robbery, burglary, murder, and rape, there was a curious effect on both sides the color-line: the Negroes refused to believe the evidence of white witnesses or the fairness of white juries, so that the greatest deterrent to crime, the public opinion of one's own social caste, was lost, and the criminal was looked upon as crucified rather than hanged. On the other hand, the whites, used to being careless as to the guilt or innocence of accused Negroes, were swept in moments of passion beyond law, reason, and decency. Such a situation is bound to increase crime, and has increased it. To natural viciousness and vagrancy are being daily added motives of revolt and revenge which stir up all the latent savagery of both races and make peaceful attention to economic development often impossible.

But the chief problem in any community cursed with crime is not the punishment of the criminals, but the preventing of the young from being trained to crime. And here again the peculiar conditions of the South have prevented proper precautions. I have seen twelve-year-old boys working in chains on the public streets of Atlanta, directly in front of the schools, in company with old and hardened criminals; and this indiscriminate mingling of men and women and children makes the chain-gangs perfect schools of crime and debauchery. The struggle for reformatories, which has gone on in Virginia, Georgia, and other States, is the one encouraging sign of the awakening of some communities to the suicidal results of this policy.

It is the public schools, however, which can be made, outside the homes, the greatest means of training decent self-respecting citizens. We have been so hotly engaged recently in discussing trade-schools and the higher education that the pitiable plight of the public-school system in the South has almost dropped from view. Of every five dollars spent for public education in the State of Georgia, the white schools get four dollars and the Negro one dollar; and even then the white public-school system, save in the cities, is bad and cries for reform. If this is true of the whites, what of the blacks? I am becoming more and more convinced, as I look upon the system of common-school training in the South, that the national government must soon step in and aid popular education in some way. To-day it has been only by the most strenuous efforts on the part of the thinking men of the South that the Negro's share of the school fund has not been cut down to a pittance in some half-dozen States; and that movement not only is not dead, but in many communities is gaining strength. What in the name of reason does this nation expect of a people, poorly trained and hard pressed in severe economic competition, without political rights, and with ludicrously inadequate common-school facilities? What can it expect but crime and listlessness, offset here and there by the dogged struggles of the fortunate and more determined who are themselves buoyed by the hope that in due time the country will come to its senses?

I have thus far sought to make clear the physical, economic, and political relations of the Negroes and whites in the South, as I have conceived them, including, for the reasons set forth, crime and education. But after all that has been said on these more tangible matters of human contact, there still remains a part essential to a proper description of the South which it is difficult to describe or fix in terms easily understood by strangers. It is, in fine, the atmosphere of the land, the thought and feeling, the thousand and one little actions which go to make up life. In any community or nation it is these little things which are most elusive to the grasp and yet most essential to any clear conception of the group life taken as a whole. What is thus true of all communities is peculiarly true of the South, where, outside of written history and outside of printed law, there has been going on for a generation as deep a storm and stress of human souls, as intense a ferment of feeling, as intricate a writhing of spirit, as ever a people experienced. Within and without the sombre veil of color vast social forces have been at work,—efforts for human betterment, movements toward disintegration and despair, tragedies and comedies in social and economic life, and a swaying and lifting and sinking of human hearts which have made this land a land of mingled sorrow and joy, of change and excitement and unrest.

The centre of this spiritual turmoil has ever been the millions of black freedmen and their sons, whose destiny is so fatefully bound up with that of the nation. And yet the casual observer visiting the South sees at first little of this. He notes the growing frequency of dark faces as he rides along,—but otherwise the days slip lazily on, the sun shines, and this little world seems as happy and contented as other worlds he has visited. Indeed, on the question of questions—the Negro problem—he hears so little that there almost seems to be a conspiracy of silence; the morning papers seldom mention it, and then usually in a far-fetched academic way, and indeed almost every one seems to forget and ignore the darker half of the land, until the astonished visitor is inclined to ask if after all there is any problem here. But if he lingers long enough there comes the awakening: perhaps in a sudden whirl of passion which leaves him gasping at its bitter intensity; more likely in a gradually dawning sense of things he had not at first noticed. Slowly but surely his eyes begin to catch the shadows of the color-line: here he meets crowds of Negroes and whites; then he is suddenly aware that he cannot discover a single dark face; or again at the close of a day's wandering he may find himself in some strange assembly, where all faces are tinged brown or black, and where he has the vague, uncomfortable feeling of the stranger. He realizes at last that silently, resistlessly, the world about flows by him in two great streams: they ripple on in the same sunshine, they approach and mingle their waters in seeming carelessness,—then they divide and flow wide apart. It is done quietly; no mistakes are made, or if one occurs, the swift arm of the law and of public opinion swings down for a moment, as when the other day a black man and a white woman were arrested for talking together on Whitehall Street in Atlanta.

Now if one notices carefully one will see that between these two worlds, despite much physical contact and daily intermingling, there is almost no community of intellectual life or point of transference where the thoughts and feelings of one race can come into direct contact and sympathy with the thoughts and feelings of the other. Before and directly after the war, when all the best of the Negroes were domestic servants in the best of the white families, there were bonds of intimacy, affection, and sometimes blood relationship, between the races. They lived in the same home, shared in the family life, often attended the same church, and talked and conversed with each other. But the increasing civilization of the Negro since then has naturally meant the development of higher classes: there are increasing numbers of ministers, teachers, physicians, merchants, mechanics, and independent farmers, who by nature and training are the aristocracy and leaders of the blacks. Between them, however, and the best element of the whites, there is little or no intellectual commerce. They go to separate churches, they live in separate sections, they are strictly separated in all public gatherings, they travel separately, and they are beginning to read different papers and books. To most libraries, lectures, concerts, and museums, Negroes are either not admitted at all, or on terms peculiarly galling to the pride of the very classes who might otherwise be attracted. The daily paper chronicles the doings of the black world from afar with no great regard for accuracy; and so on, throughout the category of means for intellectual communication,—schools, conferences, efforts for social betterment, and the like,—it is usually true that the very representatives of the two races, who for mutual benefit and the welfare of the land ought to be in complete understanding and sympathy, are so far strangers that one side thinks all whites are narrow and prejudiced, and the other thinks educated Negroes dangerous and insolent. Moreover, in a land where the tyranny of public opinion and the intolerance of criticism is for obvious historical reasons so strong as in the South, such a situation is extremely difficult to correct. The white man, as well as the Negro, is bound and barred by the color-line, and many a scheme of friendliness and philanthropy, of broad-minded sympathy and generous fellowship between the two has dropped still-born because some busybody has forced the color-question to the front and brought the tremendous force of unwritten law against the innovators.

It is hardly necessary for me to add very much in regard to the social contact between the races. Nothing has come to replace that finer sympathy and love between some masters and house servants which the radical and more uncompromising drawing of the color-line in recent years has caused almost completely to disappear. In a world where it means so much to take a man by the hand and sit beside him, to look frankly into his eyes and feel his heart beating with red blood; in a world where a social cigar or a cup of tea together means more than legislative halls and magazine articles and speeches,—one can imagine the consequences of the almost utter absence of such social amenities between estranged races, whose separation extends even to parks and streetcars.

Here there can be none of that social going down to the people,—the opening of heart and hand of the best to the worst, in generous acknowledgment of a common humanity and a common destiny. On the other hand, in matters of simple almsgiving, where there can be no question of social contact, and in the succor of the aged and sick, the South, as if stirred by a feeling of its unfortunate limitations, is generous to a fault. The black beggar is never turned away without a good deal more than a crust, and a call for help for the unfortunate meets quick response. I remember, one cold winter, in Atlanta, when I refrained from contributing to a public relief fund lest Negroes should be discriminated against, I afterward inquired of a friend: "Were any black people receiving aid?" "Why," said he, "they were *all* black."

And yet this does not touch the kernel of the problem. Human advancement is not a mere question of almsgiving, but rather of sympathy and coöperation among classes who would scorn charity. And here is a land where, in the higher walks of life, in all the higher striving for the good and noble and true, the color-line comes to separate natural friends and coworkers; while at the bottom of the social group, in the saloon, the gambling-hell, and the brothel, that same line wavers and disappears.

I have sought to paint an average picture of real relations between the sons of master and man in the South. I have not glossed over matters for policy's sake, for I fear we have already gone too far in that sort of thing. On the other hand, I have sincerely sought to let no unfair exaggerations creep in. I do not doubt that in some Southern communities conditions are better than those I have indicated; while I am no less certain that in other communities they are far worse.

Nor does the paradox and danger of this situation fail to interest and perplex the best conscience of the South. Deeply religious and intensely democratic as are the mass of the whites, they feel acutely the false position in which the Negro problems place them. Such an essentially honest-hearted and generous people cannot cite the caste-levelling precepts of Christianity, or believe in equality of opportunity for all men, without coming to feel more and more with each generation that the present drawing of the color-line is a flat contradiction to their beliefs and professions. But just as often as they come to this point, the present social condition of the Negro stands as a menace and a portent before even the most open-minded: if there were nothing to charge against the Negro but his blackness or other physical peculiarities, they argue, the problem would be comparatively simple; but what can we say to his ignorance, shiftlessness, poverty, and crime? can a self-respecting group hold anything but the least possible fellowship with such persons and survive? and shall we let a mawkish sentiment sweep away the culture of our fathers or the hope of our children? The argument so put is of great strength, but it is not a whit stronger than the argument of thinking Negroes: granted, they reply, that the condition of our masses is bad; there is certainly on the one hand adequate historical cause for this, and unmistakable evidence that no small number have, in spite of tremendous disadvantages, risen to the level of American civilization. And when, by proscription and prejudice, these same Negroes are classed with and treated like the lowest of their people, simply *because* they are Negroes, such a policy not only discourages thrift and intelligence among black men, but puts a direct premium on the very things you complain of,— inefficiency and crime. Draw lines of crime, of incompetency, of vice, as tightly and uncompromisingly as you will, for these things must be proscribed; but a color-line not only does not accomplish this purpose, but thwarts it.

In the face of two such arguments, the future of the South depends on the ability of the representatives of these opposing views to see and appreciate and sympathize with each other's position,—for the Negro to realize more deeply than he does at present the need of uplifting the masses of his people, for the white people to realize more vividly than they have yet done the deadening and disastrous effect of a color-prejudice that classes Phillis Wheatley* and Sam Hose in the same despised class.

It is not enough for the Negroes to declare that color-prejudice is the sole cause of their social condition, nor for the white South to reply that their social condition is the main cause of prejudice. They both act as reciprocal cause and effect, and a change in neither alone will bring the desired effect. Both must change, or neither can improve to any great extent. The Negro cannot stand the present reactionary tendencies and unreasoning drawing of the color-line indefinitely without discouragement and retrogression. And the condition of the Negro is ever the excuse for further discrimination. Only by a union of intelligence and sympathy across the color-line in this critical period of the Republic shall justice and right triumph,

> "That mind and soul according well,
> May make one music as before,
> But vaster."

Of the Faith of the Fathers

Dim face of Beauty haunting all the world,
　　Fair face of Beauty all too fair to see,
Where the lost stars adown the heavens are hurled,—
　　　　There, there alone for thee
　　　　May white peace be.

Beauty, sad face of Beauty, Mystery, Wonder,
　　What are these dreams to foolish babbling men
Who cry with little noises 'neath the thunder
　　　　Of Ages ground to sand,
　　　　To a little sand.

　　　　　　　　　　　　Fiona Macleod.

It was out in the country, far from home, far from my foster home, on a dark Sunday night. The road wandered from our rambling log-house up the stony bed of a creek, past wheat and corn, until we could hear dimly across the fields a rhythmic cadence of song,—soft, thrilling, powerful, that swelled and died sorrowfully in our ears. I was a country schoolteacher then, fresh from the East, and had never seen a Southern Negro revival. To be sure, we in Berkshire were not perhaps as stiff and formal as they in Suffolk of olden time; yet we were very quiet and subdued, and I know not what would have happened those clear Sabbath mornings had some one punctuated the sermon with a wild scream, or interrupted the long prayer with a loud Amen! And so most striking to me, as I approached the village and the little plain church perched aloft, was the air of intense excitement that possessed that mass of black folk. A sort of suppressed terror hung in the air and seemed to seize us,—a pythian madness, a demoniac possession, that lent terrible reality to song and word. The black and massive form of the preacher swayed and quivered as the words crowded to his lips and flew at us in singular eloquence. The people moaned and fluttered, and then the gaunt-cheeked brown woman beside me suddenly leaped straight into the air and shrieked like a lost soul, while round about came wail and groan and outcry, and a scene of human passion such as I had never conceived before.

Those who have not thus witnessed the frenzy of a Negro revival in the untouched backwoods of the South can but dimly realize the religious feeling of the slave; as described, such scenes appear grotesque and funny, but as seen they are awful. Three things characterized this religion of the slave,—the Preacher, the Music, and the Frenzy. The Preacher is the most unique personality developed by the Negro on American soil. A leader, a politician, an orator, a "boss," an intriguer, an idealist,—all these he is, and ever, too, the centre of a group of men, now twenty, now a thousand in number. The combination of a certain adroitness with deep-seated earnestness, of tact with consummate ability, gave him his preëminence, and helps him maintain it. The type, of course, varies according to time and place, from the West Indies in the sixteenth century to New England in the nineteenth, and from the Mississippi bottoms to cities like New Orleans or New York.

The Music of Negro religion is that plaintive rhythmic melody, with its touching minor cadences, which, despite caricature and defilement, still remains the most original and beautiful expression of human life and longing yet born on American soil. Sprung from the African forests, where its counterpart can still be heard, it was adapted, changed, and intensified by the tragic soul-life of the slave, until, under the stress of law and whip, it became the one true expression of a people's sorrow, despair, and hope.

Finally the Frenzy of "Shouting," when the Spirit of the Lord passed by, and, seizing the devotee, made him mad with supernatural joy, was the last essential of Negro religion and the one more devoutly believed in than all the rest. It varied in expression from the silent rapt countenance or the low murmur and moan to the mad abandon of physical fervor,—the stamping, shrieking, and shouting, the rushing to and fro and wild waving of arms, the weeping and laughing, the vision and the trance. All this is nothing new in the world, but old as religion, as Delphi* and Endor. And so firm a hold did it have on the Negro, that many generations firmly believed that without this visible manifestation of the God there could be no true communion with the Invisible.

These were the characteristics of Negro religious life as developed up to the time of Emancipation. Since under the peculiar circumstances of the black man's environment they were the one expression of his higher life, they are of deep interest to the student of his development, both socially and psychologically. Numerous are the attractive lines of inquiry that here group themselves. What did slavery mean to the African savage? What was his attitude toward the World and Life? What seemed to him good and evil,—

God and Devil? Whither went his longings and strivings, and wherefore were his heart-burnings and disappointments? Answers to such questions can come only from a study of Negro religion as a development, through its gradual changes from the heathenism of the Gold Coast* to the institutional Negro church of Chicago.

Moreover, the religious growth of millions of men, even though they be slaves, cannot be without potent influence upon their contemporaries. The Methodists and Baptists of America owe much of their condition to the silent but potent influence of their millions of Negro converts. Especially is this noticeable in the South, where theology and religious philosophy are on this account a long way behind the North, and where the religion of the poor whites is a plain copy of Negro thought and methods. The mass of "gospel" hymns which has swept through American churches and well-nigh ruined our sense of song consists largely of debased imitations of Negro melodies made by ears that caught the jingle but not the music, the body but not the soul, of the Jubilee songs. It is thus clear that the study of Negro religion is not only a vital part of the history of the Negro in America, but an interesting part of American history.

The Negro church of to-day is the social centre of Negro life in the United States, and the most characteristic expression of African character. Take a typical church in a small Virginia town: it is the "First Baptist"—a roomy brick edifice seating five hundred or more persons, tastefully finished in Georgia pine, with a carpet, a small organ, and stained-glass windows. Underneath is a large assembly room with benches. This building is the central club-house of a community of a thousand or more Negroes. Various organizations meet here,—the church proper, the

Sunday-school, two or three insurance societies, women's societies, secret societies, and mass meetings of various kinds. Entertainments, suppers, and lectures are held beside the five or six regular weekly religious services. Considerable sums of money are collected and expended here, employment is found for the idle, strangers are introduced, news is disseminated and charity distributed. At the same time this social, intellectual, and economic centre is a religious centre of great power. Depravity, Sin, Redemption, Heaven, Hell, and Damnation are preached twice a Sunday after the crops are laid by; and few indeed of the community have the hardihood to withstand conversion. Back of this more formal religion, the Church often stands as a real conserver of morals, a strengthener of family life, and the final authority on what is Good and Right.

Thus one can see in the Negro church to-day, reproduced in microcosm, all the great world from which the Negro is cut off by color-prejudice and social condition. In the great city churches the same tendency is noticeable and in many respects emphasized. A great church like the Bethel of Philadelphia has over eleven hundred members, an edifice seating fifteen hundred persons and valued at one hundred thousand dollars, an annual budget of five thousand dollars, and a government consisting of a pastor with several assisting local preachers, an executive and legislative board, financial boards and tax collectors; general church meetings for making laws; sub-divided groups led by class leaders, a company of militia, and twenty-four auxiliary societies. The activity of a church like this is immense and far-reaching, and the bishops who preside over these organizations throughout the land are among the most powerful Negro rulers in the world.

Such churches are really governments of men, and consequently a little investigation reveals the curious fact that, in the South, at least, practically every American Negro is a church member. Some, to be sure, are not regularly enrolled, and a few do not habitually attend services; but, practically, a proscribed people must have a social centre, and that centre for this people is the Negro church. The census of 1890 showed nearly twenty-four thousand Negro churches in the country, with a total enrolled membership of over two and a half millions, or ten actual church members to every twenty-eight persons, and in some Southern States one in every two persons. Besides these there is the large number who, while not enrolled as members, attend and take part in many of the activities of the church. There is an organized Negro church for every sixty black families in the nation, and in some States for every forty families, owning, on an average, a thousand dollars' worth of property each, or nearly twenty-six million dollars in all.

Such, then, is the large development of the Negro church since Emancipation. The question now is, What have been the successive steps of this social history and what are the present tendencies? First, we must realize that no such institution as the Negro church could rear itself without definite historical foundations. These foundations we can find if we remember that the social history of the Negro did not start in America. He was brought from a definite social environment,—the polygamous clan life under the headship of the chief and the potent influence of the priest. His religion was nature-worship, with profound belief in invisible surrounding influences, good and bad, and his worship was through incantation and sacrifice. The first rude change in this life was the slave ship and the West Indian sugar-fields. The plantation organization replaced the clan and tribe, and the white master replaced the chief with far greater and more despotic powers. Forced and long-continued toil became the rule of life, the old ties of blood relationship and kinship disappeared, and instead of the family appeared a new polygamy and polyandry, which, in some cases, almost reached promiscuity. It was a terrific social revolution, and yet some traces were retained of the former group life, and the chief remaining institution was the Priest or Medicine-man. He early appeared on the plantation and found his function as the healer of the sick, the interpreter of the Unknown, the comforter of the sorrowing, the supernatural avenger of wrong, and the one who rudely but picturesquely expressed the longing, disappointment, and resentment of a stolen and oppressed people. Thus, as bard, physician, judge, and priest, within the narrow limits allowed by the slave system, rose the Negro preacher, and under him the first church was not at first by any means Christian nor definitely organized; rather it was an adaptation and mingling of heathen rites among the members of each plantation, and roughly designated as Voodooism. Association with the masters, missionary effort and motives of expediency gave these rites an early veneer of Christianity, and after the lapse of many generations the Negro church became Christian.

Two characteristic things must be noticed in regard to the church. First, it became almost entirely Baptist and Methodist in faith; secondly, as a social institution it antedated by many decades the monogamic Negro home. From the very circumstances of its beginning, the church was confined to the plantation, and consisted primarily of a series of disconnected units; although, later on, some freedom of movement was allowed, still this geographical limitation was always important and was one cause of the spread of the decentralized and democratic Baptist faith among the slaves. At the same time, the visible rite of baptism appealed strongly to their mystic temperament. To-day the Baptist Church is still largest in membership among Negroes, and has a million and a half communicants. Next in popularity came the churches organized in connection with the white neighboring churches, chiefly Baptist and Methodist, with a few Episcopalian and others. The Methodists still form the second greatest denomination, with nearly a million members. The faith of these two leading denominations was more suited to the slave church from the prominence they gave to religious feeling and fervor. The Negro membership in other denominations has always been small and relatively unimportant, although the Episcopalians and Presbyterians are gaining among the more intelligent classes to-day, and the Catholic Church is making headway in certain sections. After Emancipation, and still earlier in the North, the Negro churches largely severed such affiliations as they had had with the white churches, either by choice or by compulsion. The Baptist churches became independent, but the Methodists were compelled early to unite for purposes of episcopal government. This gave rise to the great African Methodist Church, the greatest Negro organization in the world, to the Zion Church and the Colored Methodist, and to the black conferences and churches in this and other denominations.

The second fact noted, namely, that the Negro church antedates the Negro home, leads to an explanation of much that is paradoxical in this communistic institution and in the morals of its members. But especially it leads us to regard this institution as peculiarly the expression of the inner ethical life of a people in a sense seldom true elsewhere. Let us turn, then, from the outer physical development of the church to the more important inner ethical life of the people who compose it. The Negro has already been pointed out many times as a religious animal,—a being of that deep emotional nature which turns instinctively toward the supernatural. Endowed with a rich tropical imagination and a keen, delicate appreciation of Nature, the transplanted African lived in a world animate with gods and devils, elves and witches; full of strange influences,—of Good to be implored, of Evil to be propitiated. Slavery, then, was to him the dark triumph of Evil over him. All the hateful powers of the Under-world were striving against him, and a spirit of revolt and revenge filled his heart. He called up all the resources of heathenism to aid,—exorcism and witch-craft, the mysterious Obi worship with its barbarious rites, spells, and blood-sacrifice even, now and then, of human victims. Weird midnight orgies and mystic conjurations were invoked, the witch-woman and the voodoo-priest became the centre of Negro group life, and that vein of vague superstition which characterizes the unlettered Negro even to-day was deepened and strengthened.

In spite, however, of such success as that of the fierce Maroons,* the Danish blacks, and others, the spirit of revolt gradually died away under the untiring energy and superior strength of the slave masters. By the middle of the eighteenth century the black slave had sunk, with hushed murmurs, to his place at the bottom of a new economic system, and was unconsciously ripe for a new philosophy of life. Nothing suited his condition then better than the doctrines of passive submission embodied in the newly learned Christianity. Slave masters early realized this, and cheerfully aided religious propaganda within certain bounds. The long system of repression and degradation of the Negro tended to emphasize the elements of his character which made him a valuable chattel: courtesy became humility, moral strength degenerated into submission, and the exquisite native appreciation of the beautiful became an infinite capacity for dumb suffering. The Negro, losing the joy of this world, eagerly seized upon the offered conceptions of the next; the avenging Spirit of the Lord enjoining patience in this world, under sorrow and tribulation until the Great Day when He should lead His dark children home,—this became his comforting dream. His preacher repeated the prophecy, and his bards sang,—

"Children, we all shall be free
When the Lord shall appear!"

This deep religious fatalism, painted so beautifully in "Uncle Tom,"* came soon to breed, as all fatalistic faiths will, the sensualist side by side with the martyr. Under the lax moral life of the plantation, where marriage was a farce, laziness a virtue, and property a theft, a religion of resignation and submission degenerated easily, in less strenuous minds, into a philosophy of indulgence and crime. Many of the worst characteristics of the Negro masses of to-day had their seed in this period of the slave's ethical growth. Here it was that the Home was ruined under the very shadow of the Church, white and black; here habits of shiftlessness took root, and sullen hopelessness replaced hopeful strife.

With the beginning of the abolition movement and

the gradual growth of a class of free Negroes came a change. We often neglect the influence of the freedman before the war, because of the paucity of his numbers and the small weight he had in the history of the nation. But we must not forget that his chief influence was internal,—was exerted on the black world; and that there he was the ethical and social leader. Huddled as he was in a few centres like Philadelphia, New York, and New Orleans, the masses of the freedmen sank into poverty and listlessness; but not all of them. The free Negro leader early arose and his chief characteristic was intense earnestness and deep feeling on the slavery question. Freedom became to him a real thing and not a dream. His religion became darker and more intense, and into his ethics crept a note of revenge, into his songs a day of reckoning close at hand. The "Coming of the Lord" swept this side of Death, and came to be a thing to be hoped for in this day. Through fugitive slaves and irrepressible discussion this desire for freedom seized the black millions still in bondage, and became their one ideal of life. The black bards caught new notes, and sometimes even dared to sing,—

"O Freedom, O Freedom, O Freedom over me!
Before I'll be a slave
I'll be buried in my grave,
And go home to my Lord
And be free."

For fifty years Negro religion thus transformed itself and identified itself with the dream of Abolition, until that which was a radical fad in the white North and an anarchistic plot in the white South had become a religion to the black world. Thus, when Emancipation finally came, it seemed to the freedman a literal

Coming of the Lord. His fervid imagination was stirred as never before, by the tramp of armies, the blood and dust of battle, and the wail and whirl of social upheaval. He stood dumb and motionless before the whirlwind: what had he to do with it? Was it not the Lord's doing, and marvellous in his eyes? Joyed and bewildered with what came, he stood awaiting new wonders till the inevitable Age of Reaction swept over the nation and brought the crisis of to-day.

It is difficult to explain clearly the present critical stage of Negro religion. First, we must remember that living as the blacks do in close contact with a great modern nation, and sharing, although imperfectly, the soul-life of that nation, they must necessarily be affected more or less directly by all the religious and ethical forces that are to-day moving the United States. These questions and movements are, however, overshadowed and dwarfed by the (to them) all-important question of their civil, political, and economic status. They must perpetually discuss the "Negro Problem,"—must live, move, and have their being in it, and interpret all else in its light or darkness. With this come, too, peculiar problems of their inner life,—of the status of women, the maintenance of Home, the training of children, the accumulation of wealth, and the prevention of crime. All this must mean a time of intense ethical ferment, of religious heart-searching and intellectual unrest. From the double life every American Negro must live, as a Negro and as an American, as swept on by the current of the nineteenth while yet struggling in the eddies of the fifteenth century,—from this must arise a painful self-consciousness, an almost morbid sense of personality and a moral hesitancy which is fatal to self-confidence. The worlds within and without the

Veil of Color are changing, and changing rapidly, but not at the same rate, not in the same way; and this must produce a peculiar wrenching of the soul, a peculiar sense of doubt and bewilderment. Such a double life, with double thoughts, double duties, and double social classes, must give rise to double words and double ideals, and tempt the mind to pretence or revolt, to hypocrisy or radicalism.

In some such doubtful words and phrases can one perhaps most clearly picture the peculiar ethical paradox that faces the Negro of to-day and is tingeing and changing his religious life. Feeling that his rights and his dearest ideals are being trampled upon, that the public conscience is ever more deaf to his righteous appeal, and that all the reactionary forces of prejudice, greed, and revenge are daily gaining new strength and fresh allies, the Negro faces no enviable dilemma. Conscious of his impotence, and pessimistic, he often becomes bitter and vindictive; and his religion, instead of a worship, is a complaint and a curse, a wail rather than a hope, a sneer rather than a faith. On the other hand, another type of mind, shrewder and keener and more tortuous too, sees in the very strength of the anti-Negro movement its patent weaknesses, and with Jesuitic casuistry is deterred by no ethical considerations in the endeavor to turn this weakness to the black man's strength. Thus we have two great and hardly reconcilable streams of thought and ethical strivings; the danger of the one lies in anarchy, that of the other in hypocrisy. The one type of Negro stands almost ready to curse God and die, and the other is too often found a traitor to right and a coward before force; the one is wedded to ideals remote, whimsical, perhaps impossible of realization; the other forgets that life is more than meat and the body more than raiment. But, after all, is not this simply the writhing of the age translated into black,—the triumph of the Lie which today, with its false culture, faces the hideousness of the anarchist assassin?

To-day the two groups of Negroes, the one in the North, the other in the South, represent these divergent ethical tendencies, the first tending toward radicalism, the other toward hypocritical compromise. It is no idle regret with which the white South mourns the loss of the old-time Negro,—the frank, honest, simple old servant who stood for the earlier religious age of submission and humility. With all his laziness and lack of many elements of true manhood, he was at least open-hearted, faithful, and sincere. To-day he is gone, but who is to blame for his going? Is it not those very persons who mourn for him? Is it not the tendency, born of Reconstruction and Reaction, to found a society on lawlessness and deception, to tamper with the moral fibre of a naturally honest and straightforward people until the whites threaten to become ungovernable tyrants and the blacks criminals and hypocrites? Deception is the natural defence of the weak against the strong, and the South used it for many years against its conquerors; to-day it must be prepared to see its black proletariat turn that same two-edged weapon against itself. And how natural this is! The death of Denmark Vesey* and Nat Turner proved long since to the Negro the present hopelessness of physical defence. Political defence is becoming less and less available, and economic defence is still only partially effective. But there is a patent defence at hand,—the defence of deception and flattery, of cajoling and lying. It is the same defence which peasants of the Middle Age used and which left its stamp on their character for centuries. To-day the young Negro of the South who would succeed cannot be frank and outspoken, honest and self-assertive, but rather he is daily tempted to be silent and wary, politic and sly; he must flatter and be pleasant, endure petty insults with a smile, shut his eyes to wrong; in too many cases he sees positive personal advantage in deception and lying. His real thoughts, his real aspirations, must be guarded in whispers; he must not criticise, he must not complain. Patience, humility, and adroitness must, in these growing black youth, replace impulse, manliness, and courage. With this sacrifice there is an economic opening, and perhaps peace and some prosperity. Without this there is riot, migration, or crime. Nor is this situation peculiar to the Southern United States, is it not rather the only method by which undeveloped races have gained the right to share modern culture? The price of culture is a Lie.

On the other hand, in the North the tendency is to emphasize the radicalism of the Negro. Driven from his birthright in the South by a situation at which every fibre of his more outspoken and assertive nature revolts, he finds himself in a land where he can scarcely earn a decent living amid the harsh competition and the color discrimination. At the same time, through schools and periodicals, discussions and lectures, he is intellectually quickened and awakened. The soul, long pent up and dwarfed, suddenly expands in new-found freedom. What wonder that every tendency is to excess,—radical complaint, radical remedies, bitter denunciation or angry silence. Some sink, some rise. The criminal and the sensualist leave the church for the gambling-hell and the brothel, and fill the slums of Chicago and Baltimore; the better classes segregate themselves from the group-life of both white and black, and form an aristocracy, cultured but pessimistic, whose bitter criticism stings while it points out no way of escape. They despise the submission and subserviency of the Southern Negroes, but offer no other means by which a poor and oppressed minority can exist side by side with its masters. Feeling deeply and keenly the tendencies and opportunities of the age in which they live, their souls are bitter at the fate which drops the Veil between; and the very fact that this bitterness is natural and justifiable only serves to intensify it and make it more maddening.

Between the two extreme types of ethical attitude which I have thus sought to make clear wavers the mass of the millions of Negroes, North and South; and their religious life and activity partake of this social conflict within their ranks. Their churches are differentiating,—now into groups of cold, fashionable devotees, in no way distinguishable from similar white groups save in color of skin; now into large social and business institutions catering to the desire for information and amusement of their members, warily avoiding unpleasant questions both within and without the black world, and preaching in effect if not in word: *Dum vivimus, vivamus.**

But back of this still broods silently the deep religious feeling of the real Negro heart, the stirring, unguided might of powerful human souls who have lost the guiding star of the past and seek in the great night a new religious ideal. Some day the Awakening will come, when the pent-up vigor of ten million souls shall sweep irresistibly toward the Goal, out of the Valley of the Shadow of Death, where all that makes life worth living—Liberty, Justice, and Right—is marked "For White People Only."

Chapter XI

Of the Passing of
the First-Born

O sister, sister, thy first-begotten,
The hands that cling and the feet that follow,
The voice of the child's blood crying yet,
Who hath remembered me? who hath forgotten?
Thou hast forgotten, O summer swallow,
But the world shall end when I forget.

SWINBURNE.

"Unto you a child is born," sang the bit of yellow paper that fluttered into my room one brown October morning. Then the fear of fatherhood mingled wildly with the joy of creation; I wondered how it looked and how it felt—what were its eyes, and how its hair curled and crumpled itself. And I thought in awe of her,—she who had slept with Death to tear a man-child from underneath her heart, while I was unconsciously wandering. I fled to my wife and child, repeating the while to myself half wonderingly, "Wife and child? Wife and child?"—fled fast and faster than boat and steam-car, and yet must ever impatiently await them; away from the hard-voiced city, away from the flickering sea into my own Berkshire Hills that sit all sadly guarding the gates of Massachusetts.

Up the stairs I ran to the wan mother and whimpering babe, to the sanctuary on whose altar a life at my bidding had offered itself to win a life, and won. What is this tiny formless thing, this newborn wail from an unknown world,—all head and voice? I handle it curiously, and watch perplexed its winking, breathing, and sneezing. I did not love it then; it seemed a ludicrous thing to love; but her I loved, my girl-mother, she whom now I saw unfolding like the glory of the morning—the transfigured woman. Through her I came to love the wee thing, as it grew strong; as its little soul unfolded itself in twitter and cry and half-formed word, and as its eyes caught the gleam and flash of life. How beautiful he was, with his olive-tinted flesh and dark gold ringlets, his eyes of mingled blue and brown, his perfect little limbs, and the soft voluptuous roll which the blood of Africa had moulded into his features! I held him in my arms, after we had sped far away from our Southern home,—held him, and glanced at the hot red soil of Georgia and the breathless city of a hundred hills, and felt a vague unrest. Why was his hair tinted with gold? An evil omen was golden hair in my life. Why had not the brown of his eyes crushed out and killed the blue?— for brown were his father's eyes, and his father's father's. And thus in the Land of the Color-line I saw, as it fell across my baby, the shadow of the Veil.

Within the Veil was he born, said I; and there within shall he live,—a Negro and a Negro's son. Holding in that little head—ah, bitterly!—the unbowed pride of a hunted race, clinging with that tiny dimpled hand—ah, wearily!—to a hope not hopeless but unhopeful, and seeing with those bright wondering eyes that peer into my soul a land whose freedom is to us a mockery and whose liberty a lie. I saw the shadow of the Veil as it passed over my baby, I saw the cold city towering above the blood-red land. I held my face beside his little cheek, showed him the star-children and the twinkling lights as they began to flash, and stilled with an even-song the unvoiced terror of my life.

So sturdy and masterful he grew, so filled with bubbling life, so tremulous with the unspoken wisdom of a life but eighteen months distant from the All-life,—we were not far from worshipping this revelation of the divine, my wife and I. Her own life builded and moulded itself upon the child; he tinged her every dream and idealized her every effort. No hands but hers must touch and garnish those little limbs; no dress or frill must touch them that had not wearied her fingers; no voice but hers could coax him off to Dreamland, and she and he together spoke some soft and unknown tongue and in it held communion. I too mused above his little white bed; saw the strength of my own arm stretched onward through the ages through the newer strength of his; saw the dream of my black fathers stagger a step onward in the wild phantasm of the world; heard in his baby voice the voice of the Prophet that was to rise within the Veil.

And so we dreamed and loved and planned by fall and winter, and the full flush of the long Southern spring, till the hot winds rolled from the fetid Gulf, till the roses shivered and the still stern sun quivered its awful light over the hills of Atlanta. And then one night the little feet pattered wearily to the wee white bed, and the tiny hands trembled; and a warm flushed face tossed on the pillow, and we knew baby was sick. Ten days he lay there,—a swift week and three endless days, wasting, wasting away. Cheerily the mother nursed him the first days, and laughed into the little eyes that smiled again. Tenderly then she hovered round him, till the smile fled away and Fear crouched beside the little bed.

Then the day ended not, and night was a dreamless terror, and joy and sleep slipped away. I hear now that Voice at midnight calling me from dull and dreamless trance,—crying, "The Shadow of Death! The Shadow of Death!" Out into the starlight I crept, to rouse the gray physician,—the Shadow of Death, the Shadow of Death. The hours trembled on; the night listened; the ghastly dawn glided like a tired thing across the lamplight. Then we two alone looked upon the child as he turned toward us with great eyes, and stretched his stringlike hands,—the Shadow of Death! And we spoke no word, and turned away.

He died at eventide, when the sun lay like a brooding sorrow above the western hills, veiling its face; when the winds spoke not, and the trees, the great green trees he loved, stood motionless. I saw his breath beat quicker and quicker, pause, and then his little soul leapt like a star that travels in the night and left a world of darkness in its train. The day changed not; the same tall trees peeped in at the windows, the same green grass glinted in the setting sun. Only in the chamber of death writhed the world's most piteous thing—a childless mother.

I shirk not. I long for work. I pant for a life full of striving. I am no coward, to shrink before the rugged rush of the storm, nor even quail before the awful shadow of the Veil. But hearken, O Death! Is not this my life hard enough,—is not that dull land that stretches its sneering web about me cold enough,—is not all the world beyond these four little walls pitiless enough, but that thou must needs enter here,—thou, O Death? About my head the thundering storm beat like a heartless voice, and the crazy forest pulsed with the curses of the weak; but what cared I, within my home beside my wife and baby boy? Wast thou so jealous of one little coign of happiness that thou must needs enter there,—thou, O Death?

A perfect life was his, all joy and love, with tears to make it brighter,—sweet as a summer's day beside the Housatonic. The world loved him; the women kissed his curls, the men looked gravely into his wonderful eyes, and the children hovered and fluttered about him. I can see him now, changing like the sky from sparkling laughter to darkening frowns, and then to wondering thoughtfulness as he watched the world. He knew no color-line, poor dear—and the Veil, though it shadowed him, had not yet darkened half his sun. He loved the white matron, he loved his black nurse; and in his little world walked souls alone, uncolored and unclothed. I—yea, all men—are larger and purer by the infinite breadth of that one little life. She who in simple clearness of vision sees beyond the stars said when he had flown, "He will be happy There; he ever loved beautiful things." And I, far more ignorant, and blind by the web of mine own weaving, sit alone winding words and muttering, "If still he be, and he be There, and there be a There, let him be happy, O Fate!"

Blithe was the morning of his burial, with bird and song and sweet-smelling flowers. The trees whispered to the grass, but the children sat with hushed faces. And yet it seemed a ghostly unreal day,—the wraith of Life. We seemed to rumble down an unknown street behind a little white bundle of posies, with the shadow of a song in our ears. The busy city dinned about us; they did not say much, those pale-faced hurrying men and women; they did not say much,—they only glanced and said, "Niggers!"

We could not lay him in the ground there in

Georgia, for the earth there is strangely red; so we bore him away to the northward, with his flowers and his little folded hands. In vain, in vain!—for where, O God! beneath thy broad blue sky shall my dark baby rest in peace,—where Reverence dwells, and Goodness, and a Freedom that is free?

All that day and all that night there sat an awful gladness in my heart,—nay, blame me not if I see the world thus darkly through the Veil,—and my soul whispers ever to me saying, "Not dead, not dead, but escaped; not bond, but free." No bitter meanness now shall sicken his baby heart till it die a living death, no taunt shall madden his happy boyhood. Fool that I was to think or wish that this little soul should grow choked and deformed within the Veil! I might have known that yonder deep unworldly look that ever and anon floated past his eyes was peering far beyond this narrow Now. In the poise of his little curl-crowned head did there not sit all that wild pride of being which his father had hardly crushed in his own heart? For what, forsooth, shall a Negro want with pride amid the studied humiliations of fifty million fellows? Well sped, my boy, before the world had dubbed your ambition insolence, had held your ideals unattainable, and taught you to cringe and bow. Better far this nameless void that stops my life than a sea of sorrow for you.

Idle words; he might have borne his burden more bravely than we,—aye, and found it lighter too, some day; for surely, surely this is not the end. Surely there shall yet dawn some mighty morning to lift the Veil and set the prisoned free. Not for me,—I shall die in my bonds,—but for fresh young souls who have not known the night and waken to the morning; a morning when men ask of the workman, not "Is he white?" but "Can he work?" When men ask artists, not "Are they black?" but "Do they know?" Some morning this may be, long, long years to come. But now there wails, on that dark shore within the Veil, the same deep voice, *Thou shalt forego!* And all have I foregone at that command, and with small complaint,—all save that fair young form that lies so coldly wed with death in the nest I had builded.

If one must have gone, why not I? Why may I not rest me from this restlessness and sleep from this wide waking? Was not the world's alembic, Time, in his young hands, and is not my time waning? Are there so many workers in the vineyard that the fair promise of this little body could lightly be tossed away? The wretched of my race that line the alleys of the nation sit fatherless and unmothered; but Love sat beside his cradle, and in his ear Wisdom waited to speak. Perhaps now he knows the All-love, and needs not to be wise. Sleep, then, child,—sleep till I sleep and waken to a baby voice and the ceaseless patter of little feet—above the Veil.

Of Alexander Crummell

Then from the Dawn it seemed there came, but faint
As from beyond the limit of the world,
Like the last echo born of a great cry,
Sounds, as if some fair city were one voice
Around a king returning from his wars.

TENNYSON.

This is the story of a human heart,—the tale of a black boy who many long years ago began to struggle with life that he might know the world and know himself. Three temptations he met on those dark dunes that lay gray and dismal before the wonder-eyes of the child: the temptation of Hate, that stood out against the red dawn; the temptation of Despair, that darkened noonday; and the temptation of Doubt, that ever steals along with twilight. Above all, you must hear of the vales he crossed,—the Valley of Humiliation and the Valley of the Shadow of Death.

I saw Alexander Crummell first at a Wilberforce* commencement season, amid its bustle and crush. Tall, frail, and black he stood, with simple dignity and an unmistakable air of good breeding. I talked with him apart, where the storming of the lusty young orators could not harm us. I spoke to him politely, then curiously, then eagerly, as I began to feel the fineness of his character,—his calm courtesy, the sweetness of his strength, and his fair blending of the hope and truth of life. Instinctively I bowed before this man, as one bows before the prophets of the world. Some seer he seemed, that came not from the crimson Past or the gray To-come, but from the pulsing Now,—that mocking world which seemed to me at once so light and dark, so splendid and sordid. Fourscore years had he wandered in this same world of mine, within the Veil.

He was born with the Missouri Compromise* and lay a-dying amid the echoes of Manila* and El Caney: stirring times for living, times dark to look back upon, darker to look forward to. The black-faced lad that paused over his mud and marbles seventy years ago saw puzzling vistas as he looked down the world. The slave-ship still groaned across the Atlantic, faint cries burdened the Southern breeze, and the great black father whispered mad tales of cruelty into those young ears. From the low doorway the mother silently watched her boy at play, and at nightfall sought him eagerly lest the shadows bear him away to the land of slaves.

So his young mind worked and winced and shaped curiously a vision of Life; and in the midst of that vision ever stood one dark figure alone,—ever with the hard, thick countenance of that bitter father, and a form that fell in vast and shapeless folds. Thus the temptation of Hate grew and shadowed the growing child,—gliding stealthily into his laughter, fading into his play, and seizing his dreams by day and night with rough, rude turbulence. So the black boy asked of sky and sun and flower the never-answered Why? and loved, as he grew, neither the world nor the world's rough ways.

Strange temptation for a child, you may think; and yet in this wide land to-day a thousand thousand dark children brood before this same temptation, and feel its cold and shuddering arms. For them, perhaps, some one will some day lift the Veil,—will come tenderly and cheerily into those sad little lives and brush the brooding hate away, just as Beriah Green strode in upon the life of Alexander Crummell. And before the bluff, kind-hearted man the shadow seemed less dark. Beriah Green had a school in Oneida County, New York, with a score of mischievous boys. "I'm going to bring a black boy here to educate," said Beriah Green, as only a crank and an abolitionist would have dared to say. "Oho!" laughed the boys. "Ye-es," said his wife; and Alexander came. Once before, the black boy had sought a school, had travelled, cold and hungry, four hundred miles up into free New Hampshire, to Canaan. But the godly farmers hitched ninety yoke of oxen to the abolition schoolhouse and dragged it into the middle of the swamp. The black boy trudged away.

The nineteenth was the first century of human sympathy,—the age when half wonderingly we began to descry in others that transfigured spark of divinity which we call Myself; when clodhoppers and peasants, and tramps and thieves, and millionaires and—sometimes—Negroes, became throbbing souls whose warm pulsing life touched us so nearly that we half gasped with surprise, crying, "Thou too! Hast Thou seen Sorrow and the dull waters of Hopelessness? Hast Thou known Life?" And then all helplessly we peered into those Other-worlds, and wailed, "O World of Worlds, how shall man make you one?"

So in that little Oneida school there came to those schoolboys a revelation of thought and longing beneath one black skin, of which they had not dreamed before. And to the lonely boy came a new dawn of sympathy and inspiration. The shadowy, formless thing—the temptation of Hate, that hovered between him and the world—grew fainter and less sinister. It did not wholly fade away, but diffused itself and lingered thick at the edges. Through it the child now first saw the blue and gold of life,—the sun-swept road that ran 'twixt heaven and earth until in one far-off wan wavering line they met and kissed. A vision of life came to the growing boy,—mystic, wonderful. He raised his head, stretched himself, breathed deep of the fresh new air. Yonder, behind the forests, he heard strange sounds; then glinting through the trees he saw, far, far away, the bronzed hosts of a nation calling,—calling faintly, calling loudly. He heard the hateful clank of their chains; he felt them cringe and grovel, and there rose within him a protest and a prophecy. And he girded himself to walk down the world.

A voice and vision called him to be a priest,—a seer to lead the uncalled out of the house of bondage. He saw the headless host turn toward him like the whirling of mad waters,—he stretched forth his hands eagerly, and then, even as he stretched them, suddenly there swept across the vision the temptation of Despair.

They were not wicked men,—the problem of life is not the problem of the wicked,—they were calm, good men, Bishops of the Apostolic Church of God, and strove toward righteousness. They said slowly, "It is all very natural—it is even commendable; but the

General Theological Seminary of the Episcopal Church cannot admit a Negro." And when that thin, half-grotesque figure still haunted their doors, they put their hands kindly, half sorrowfully, on his shoulders, and said, "Now,—of course, we—we know how *you* feel about it; but you see it is impossible,— that is—well—it is premature. Sometime, we trust— sincerely trust—all such distinctions will fade away; but now the world is as it is."

This was the temptation of Despair; and the young man fought it doggedly. Like some grave shadow he flitted by those halls, pleading, arguing, half angrily demanding admittance, until there came the final No: until men hustled the disturber away, marked him as foolish, unreasonable, and injudicious, a vain rebel against God's law. And then from that Vision Splendid all the glory faded slowly away, and left an earth gray and stern rolling on beneath a dark despair. Even the kind hands that stretched themselves toward him from out the depths of that dull morning seemed but parts of the purple shadows. He saw them coldly, and asked, "Why should I strive by special grace when the way of the world is closed to me?" All gently yet, the hands urged him on,—the hands of young John Jay,* that daring father's daring son; the hands of the good folk of Boston, that free city. And yet, with a way to the priesthood of the Church open at last before him, the cloud lingered there; and even when in old St. Paul's the venerable Bishop raised his white arms above the Negro deacon—even then the burden had not lifted from that heart, for there had passed a glory from the earth.

And yet the fire through which Alexander Crummell went did not burn in vain. Slowly and more soberly he took up again his plan of life. More critically he studied the situation. Deep down below the slavery and servitude of the Negro people he saw their fatal weaknesses, which long years of mistreatment had emphasized. The dearth of strong moral character, of unbending righteousness, he felt, was their great shortcoming, and here he would begin. He would gather the best of his people into some little Episcopal chapel and there lead, teach, and inspire them, till the leaven spread, till the children grew, till the world hearkened, till—till—and then across his dream gleamed some faint after-glow of that first fair vision of youth—only an after-glow, for there had passed a glory from the earth.

One day—it was in 1842, and the springtide was struggling merrily with the May winds of New England—he stood at last in his own chapel in Providence, a priest of the Church. The days sped by, and the dark young clergyman labored; he wrote his sermons carefully; he intoned his prayers with a soft, earnest voice; he haunted the streets and accosted the wayfarers; he visited the sick, and knelt beside the dying. He worked and toiled, week by week, day by day, month by month. And yet month by month the congregation dwindled, week by week the hollow walls echoed more sharply, day by day the calls came fewer and fewer, and day by day the third temptation sat clearer and still more clearly within the Veil; a temptation, as it were, bland and smiling, with just a shade of mockery in its smooth tones. First it came casually, in the cadence of a voice: "Oh, colored folks? Yes." Or perhaps more definitely: "What do you *expect?*" In voice and gesture lay the doubt—the temptation of Doubt. How he hated it, and stormed at it furiously! "Of course they are capable," he cried; "of course they can learn and strive and achieve—" and "Of course," added the temptation softly, "they do nothing of the sort." Of all the three temptations, this one struck the deepest. Hate? He had outgrown so childish a thing. Despair? He had steeled his right arm against it, and fought it with the vigor of determination. But to doubt the worth of his life-work,—to doubt the destiny and capability of the race his soul loved because it was his; to find listless squalor instead of eager endeavor; to hear his own lips whispering, "They do not care; they cannot know; they are dumb driven cattle,—why cast your pearls before swine?"—this, this seemed more than man could bear; and he closed the door, and sank upon the steps of the chancel, and cast his robe upon the floor and writhed.

The evening sunbeams had set the dust to dancing in the gloomy chapel when he arose. He folded his vestments, put away the hymn-books, and closed the great Bible. He stepped out into the twilight, looked back upon the narrow little pulpit with a weary smile, and locked the door. Then he walked briskly to the Bishop, and told the Bishop what the Bishop already knew. "I have failed," he said simply. And gaining courage by the confession, he added: "What I need is a larger constituency. There are comparatively few Negroes here, and perhaps they are not of the best. I must go where the field is wider, and try again." So the Bishop sent him to Philadelphia, with a letter to Bishop Onderdonk.

Bishop Onderdonk lived at the head of six white steps,—corpulent, red-faced, and the author of several thrilling tracts on Apostolic Succession. It was after dinner, and the Bishop had settled himself for a pleasant season of contemplation, when the bell must needs ring, and there must burst in upon the Bishop a letter and a thin, ungainly Negro. Bishop Onderdonk read the letter hastily and frowned. Fortunately, his mind was already clear on this point; and he cleared his brow and looked at Crummell. Then he said, slowly and impressively: "I will receive you into this diocese on one condition: no Negro priest can sit in my church convention, and no Negro church must ask for representation there."

I sometimes fancy I can see that tableau: the frail black figure, nervously twitching his hat before the massive abdomen of Bishop Onderdonk; his thread-bare coat thrown against the dark woodwork of the bookcases, where Fox's "Lives of the Martyrs" nestled happily beside "The Whole Duty of Man." I seem to see the wide eyes of the Negro wander past the Bishop's broadcloth to where the swinging glass doors of the cabinet glow in the sunlight. A little blue fly is trying to cross the yawning keyhole. He marches briskly up to it, peers into the chasm in a surprised sort of way, and rubs his feelers reflectively; then he essays its depths, and, finding it bottomless, draws back again. The dark-faced priest finds himself wondering if the fly too has faced its Valley of Humiliation, and if it will plunge into it,—when lo! it spreads its tiny wings and buzzes merrily across, leaving the watcher wingless and alone.

Then the full weight of his burden fell upon him. The rich walls wheeled away, and before him lay the cold rough moor winding on through life, cut in twain by one thick granite ridge,—here, the Valley of Humiliation; yonder, the Valley of the Shadow of Death. And I know not which be darker,—no, not I. But this I know: in yonder Vale of the Humble stand to-day a million swarthy men, who willingly would

"... bear the whips and scorns of time,*
The oppressor's wrong, the proud man's contumely,
The pangs of despised love, the law's delay,
The insolence of office, and the spurns
That patient merit of the unworthy takes,"—

all this and more would they bear did they but know that this were sacrifice and not a meaner thing. So surged the thought within that lone black breast. The Bishop cleared his throat suggestively; then, recollecting that there was really nothing to say, considerately said nothing, only sat tapping his foot impatiently. But Alexander Crummell said, slowly and heavily: "I will never enter your diocese on such terms." And saying this, he turned and passed into the Valley of the Shadow of Death. You might have noted only the physical dying, the shattered frame and hacking cough; but in that soul lay deeper death than that. He found a chapel in New York,—the church of his father; he labored for it in poverty and starvation, scorned by his fellow priests. Half in despair, he wandered across the sea, a beggar with outstretched hands. Englishmen clasped them,—Wilberforce and Stanley, Thirwell and Ingles, and even Froude and Macaulay; Sir Benjamin Brodie bade him rest awhile at Queen's College in Cambridge, and there he lingered, struggling for health of body and mind, until he took his degree in '53. Restless still, and unsatisfied, he turned toward Africa, and for long years, amid the spawn of the slave-smugglers, sought a new heaven and a new earth.

So the man groped for light; all this was not Life,—it was the world-wandering of a soul in search of itself, the striving of one who vainly sought his place in the world, ever haunted by the shadow of a death that is more than death,—the passing of a soul that has missed its duty. Twenty years he wandered,—twenty years and more; and yet the hard rasping question kept gnawing within him, "What, in God's name, am I on earth for?" In the narrow New York parish his soul seemed cramped and smothered. In the fine old air of the English University he heard the millions wailing over the sea. In the wild fever-cursed swamps of West Africa he stood helpless and alone.

You will not wonder at his weird pilgrimage,—you who in the swift whirl of living, amid its cold paradox and marvellous vision, have fronted life and asked its riddle face to face. And if you find that riddle hard to read, remember that yonder black boy finds it just a little harder; if it is difficult for you to find and face your duty, it is a shade more difficult for him; if your heart sickens in the blood and dust of battle, remember that to him the dust is thicker and the battle fiercer. No wonder the wanderers fall! No wonder we point to thief and murderer, and haunting prostitute, and the never-ending throng of unhearsed dead! The Valley of the Shadow of Death gives few of its pilgrims back to the world.

But Alexander Crummell it gave back. Out of the temptation of Hate, and burned by the fire of Despair, triumphant over Doubt, and steeled by Sacrifice against Humiliation, he turned at last home across the waters, humble and strong, gentle and determined. He bent to all the gibes and prejudices, to all hatred and discrimination, with that rare courtesy which is the armor of pure souls. He fought among his own, the low, the grasping, and the wicked, with that unbending righteousness which is the sword of the just. He never faltered, he seldom complained; he simply worked, inspiring the young, rebuking the old, helping the weak, guiding the strong.

So he grew, and brought within his wide influence all that was best of those who walk within the Veil. They who live without knew not nor dreamed of that full power within, that mighty inspiration which the dull gauze of caste decreed that most men should not know. And now that he is gone, I sweep the Veil away and cry, Lo! the soul to whose dear memory I bring this little tribute. I can see his face still, dark and heavy-lined beneath his snowy hair; lighting and shading, now with inspiration for the future, now in innocent pain at some human wickedness, now with sorrow at some hard memory from the past. The more I met Alexander Crummell, the more I felt how much that world was losing which knew so little of him. In another age he might have sat among the elders of the land in purple-bordered toga; in another country mothers might have sung him to the cradles.

He did his work,—he did it nobly and well; and yet I sorrow that here he worked alone, with so little human sympathy. His name to-day, in this broad land, means little, and comes to fifty million ears laden with no incense of memory or emulation. And herein lies the tragedy of the age: not that men are poor,—all men know something of poverty; not that men are wicked,—who is good? not that men are ignorant,— what is Truth? Nay, but that men know so little of men.

He sat one morning gazing toward the sea. He smiled and said, "The gate is rusty on the hinges." That night at star-rise a wind came moaning out of the west to blow the gate ajar, and then the soul I loved fled like a flame across the Seas, and in its seat sat Death.

I wonder where he is to-day? I wonder if in that dim world beyond, as he came gliding in, there rose on some wan throne a King,—a dark and pierced Jew, who knows the writhings of the earthly damned, saying, as he laid those heart-wrung talents down, "Well done!" while round about the morning stars sat singing.

Chapter

Of the Coming of John

What bring they 'neath the midnight,
    Beside the River-sea?
They bring the human heart wherein
    No nightly calm can be;
That droppeth never with the wind,
    Nor drieth with the dew;
O calm it, God; thy calm is broad
    To cover spirits too.
        The river floweth on.

MRS. BROWNING.

Carlisle Street runs westward from the centre of Johnstown, across a great black bridge, down a hill and up again, by little shops and meat-markets, past single-storied homes, until suddenly it stops against a wide green lawn. It is a broad, restful place, with two large buildings outlined against the west. When at evening the winds come swelling from the east, and the great pall of the city's smoke hangs wearily above the valley, then the red west glows like a dreamland down Carlisle Street, and, at the tolling of the supper-bell, throws the passing forms of students in dark silhouette against the sky. Tall and black, they move slowly by, and seem in the sinister light to flit before the city like dim warning ghosts. Perhaps they are; for this is Wells Institute, and these black students have few dealings with the white city below.

And if you will notice, night after night, there is one dark form that ever hurries last and late toward the twinkling lights of Swain Hall,—for Jones is never on time. A long, straggling fellow he is, brown and hard-haired, who seems to be growing straight out of his clothes, and walks with a half-apologetic roll. He used perpetually to set the quiet dining-room into waves of merriment, as he stole to his place after the bell had tapped for prayers; he seemed so perfectly awkward. And yet one glance at his face made one forgive him much,—that broad, good-natured smile in which lay no bit of art or artifice, but seemed just bubbling good-nature and genuine satisfaction with the world.

He came to us from Altamaha, away down there beneath the gnarled oaks of Southeastern Georgia, where the sea croons to the sands and the sands listen till they sink half drowned beneath the waters, rising only here and there in long, low islands. The white folk of Altamaha voted John a good boy,—fine plough-hand, good in the rice-fields, handy every-where, and always good-natured and respectful. But they shook their heads when his mother wanted to send him off to school. "It'll spoil him,—ruin him," they said; and they talked as though they knew. But full half the black folk followed him proudly to the station, and carried his queer little trunk and many bundles. And there they shook and shook hands, and the girls kissed him shyly and the boys clapped him on the back. So the train came, and he pinched his little sister lovingly, and put his great arms about his mother's neck, and then was away with a puff and a roar into the great yellow world that flamed and flared about the doubtful pilgrim. Up the coast they hurried, past the squares and palmettos of Savannah, through the cotton-fields and through the weary night, to Millville, and came with the morning to the noise and bustle of Johnstown.

And they that stood behind, that morning in Altamaha, and watched the train as it noisily bore playmate and brother and son away to the world, had thereafter one ever-recurring word,—"When John comes." Then what parties were to be, and what speakings in the churches; what new furniture in the front room,—perhaps even a new front room; and there would be a new schoolhouse, with John as teacher; and then perhaps a big wedding; all this and more—when John comes. But the white people shook their heads.

At first he was coming at Christmas-time,—but the vacation proved too short; and then, the next summer,—but times were hard and schooling costly, and so, instead, he worked in Johnstown. And so it drifted to the next summer, and the next,—till playmates scattered, and mother grew gray, and sister went up to the Judge's kitchen to work. And still the legend lingered,—"When John comes."

Up at the Judge's they rather liked this refrain; for they too had a John—a fair-haired, smooth-faced boy, who had played many a long summer's day to its close with his darker namesake. "Yes, sir! John is at Princeton, sir," said the broad-shouldered gray-haired Judge every morning as he marched down to the post-office. "Showing the Yankees what a Southern gentleman can do," he added; and strode home again with his letters and papers. Up at the great pillared house they lingered long over the Princeton letter,—the Judge and his frail wife, his sister and growing daughters. "It'll make a man of him," said the Judge, "college is the place." And then he asked the shy little waitress, "Well, Jennie, how's your John?" and added reflectively, "Too bad, too bad your mother sent him off,—it will spoil him." And the waitress wondered.

Thus in the far-away Southern village the world lay waiting, half consciously, the coming of two young men, and dreamed in an inarticulate way of new things that would be done and new thoughts that all would think. And yet it was singular that few thought of two Johns,—for the black folk thought of one John, and he was black; and the white folk thought of another John, and he was white. And neither world thought the other world's thought, save with a vague unrest.

Up in Johnstown, at the Institute, we were long puzzled at the case of John Jones. For a long time the clay seemed unfit for any sort of moulding. He was loud and boisterous, always laughing and singing, and never able to work consecutively at anything. He did not know how to study; he had no idea of thoroughness; and with his tardiness, carelessness, and appalling good-humor, we were sore perplexed. One night we sat in faculty-meeting, worried and serious; for Jones was in trouble again. This last escapade was too much, and so we solemnly voted "that Jones, on account of repeated disorder and inattention to work, be suspended for the rest of the term."

It seemed to us that the first time life ever struck Jones as a really serious thing was when the Dean told him he must leave school. He stared at the gray-haired man blankly, with great eyes. "Why,—why," he faltered, "but—I haven't graduated!" Then the Dean slowly and clearly explained, reminding him of the tardiness and the carelessness, of the poor lessons and neglected work, of the noise and disorder, until the fellow hung his head in confusion. Then he said quickly, "But you won't tell mammy and sister,—you won't write mammy, now will you? For if you won't I'll go out into the city and work, and come back next term and show you something." So the Dean promised faithfully, and John shouldered his little trunk, giving neither word nor look to the giggling boys, and walked down Carlisle Street to the great city, with sober eyes and a set and serious face.

Perhaps we imagined it, but someway it seemed to us that the serious look that crept over his boyish face that afternoon never left it again. When he came back to us he went to work with all his rugged strength. It was a hard struggle, for things did not come easily to him,—few crowding memories of early life and teaching came to help him on his new way; but all the world toward which he strove was of his own building, and he builded slow and hard. As the light dawned lingeringly on his new creations, he sat rapt and silent before the vision, or wandered alone over the green campus peering through and beyond the world of men into a world of thought. And the thoughts at times puzzled him sorely; he could not see just why the circle was not square, and carried it out fifty-six decimal places one midnight,—would have gone further, indeed, had not the matron rapped for lights out. He caught terrible colds lying on his back in the meadows of nights, trying to think out the solar system; he had grave doubts as to the ethics of the Fall of Rome, and strongly suspected the Germans of being thieves and rascals, despite his textbooks; he pondered long over every new Greek word, and wondered why this meant that and why it couldn't mean something else, and how it must have felt to think all things in Greek. So he thought and puzzled along for himself,—pausing perplexed where others skipped merrily, and walking steadily through the difficulties where the rest stopped and surrendered.

Thus he grew in body and soul, and with him his clothes seemed to grow and arrange themselves; coat sleeves got longer, cuffs appeared, and collars got less soiled. Now and then his boots shone, and a new dignity crept into his walk. And we who saw daily a new thoughtfulness growing in his eyes began to expect something of this plodding boy. Thus he passed out of the preparatory school into college, and we who watched him felt four more years of change, which almost transformed the tall, grave man who bowed to us commencement morning. He had left his queer thought-world and come back to a world of motion and of men. He looked now for the first time sharply about him, and wondered he had seen so little before. He grew slowly to feel almost for the first time the Veil that lay between him and the white world; he first noticed now the oppression that had not seemed oppression before, differences that erstwhile seemed natural, restraints and slights that in his boyhood days had gone unnoticed or been greeted with a laugh. He felt angry now when men did not call him "Mister," he clenched his hands at the "Jim Crow" cars, and chafed at the color-line that hemmed in him and his. A tinge of sarcasm crept into his speech, and a vague bitterness into his life; and he sat long hours wondering and planning a way around these crooked things. Daily he found himself shrinking from the choked and narrow life of his native town. And yet he always planned to go back to Altamaha,—always planned to work there. Still, more and more as the day approached he hesitated with a nameless dread; and even the day after graduation he seized with eagerness the offer of the Dean to send him North with the quartette during the summer vacation, to sing for the Institute. A breath of air before the plunge, he said to himself in half apology.

It was a bright September afternoon, and the streets of New York were brilliant with moving men. They reminded John of the sea, as he sat in the square and watched them, so changelessly changing, so bright and dark, so grave and gay. He scanned their rich and faultless clothes, the way they carried their hands, the shape of their hats; he peered into the hurrying carriages. Then, leaning back with a sigh, he said, "This is the World." The notion suddenly seized him to see where the world was going; since many of the richer and brighter seemed hurrying all one way. So when a tall, light-haired young man and a little talkative lady came by, he rose half hesitatingly and followed them. Up the street they went, past stores and gay shops, across a broad square, until with a hundred others they entered the high portal of a great building.

He was pushed toward the ticket-office with the others, and felt in his pocket for the new five-dollar bill he had hoarded. There seemed really no time for hesitation, so he drew it bravely out, passed it to the busy clerk, and received simply a ticket but no change. When at last he realized that he had paid five dollars to enter he knew not what, he stood stockstill amazed. "Be careful," said a low voice behind him; "you must not lynch the colored gentleman simply because he's in your way," and a girl looked up roguishly into the eyes of her fair-haired escort. A shade of annoyance passed over the escort's face. "You *will* not understand us at the South," he said half impatiently, as if continuing an argument. "With all your professions, one never sees in the North so cordial and intimate relations between white and black as are everyday occurrences with us. Why, I remember my closest playfellow in boyhood was a little Negro named after me, and surely no two,—*well!*" The man stopped short and flushed to the roots of his hair, for there directly beside his reserved orchestra chairs sat the Negro he had stumbled over in the hallway. He hesitated and grew pale with anger, called the usher and gave him his card, with a few peremptory words, and slowly sat down. The lady deftly changed the subject.

All this John did not see, for he sat in a half-daze minding the scene about him; the delicate beauty of the hall, the faint perfume, the moving myriad of men, the rich clothing and low hum of talking seemed all a part of a world so different from his, so strangely more beautiful than anything he had known, that he sat in dreamland, and started when, after a hush, rose high and clear the music of Lohengrin's swan.* The infinite beauty of the wail lingered and swept through every muscle of his frame, and put it all a-tune. He closed his eyes and grasped the elbows of the chair, touching unwittingly the lady's arm. And the lady drew away. A deep longing swelled in all his heart to rise with that clear music out of the dirt and dust of that low life that held him prisoned and befouled. If he could only live up in the free air where birds sang and setting suns had no touch of blood! Who had called him to be the slave and butt of all? And if he had called, what right had he to call when a world like this lay open before men?

Then the movement changed, and fuller, mightier harmony swelled away. He looked thoughtfully across the hall, and wondered why the beautiful gray-haired woman looked so listless, and what the little man could be whispering about. He would not like to be listless and idle, he thought, for he felt with the music the movement of power within him. If he but had some master-work, some life-service, hard,—aye, bitter hard, but without the cringing and sickening servility, without the cruel hurt that hardened his heart and soul. When at last a soft sorrow crept across the violins, there came to him the vision of a far-off home, the great eyes of his sister, and the dark drawn face of his mother. And his heart sank below the waters, even as the sea-sand sinks by the shores of Altamaha, only to be lifted aloft again with that last ethereal wail of the swan that quivered and faded away into the sky.

If left John sitting so silent and rapt that he did not for some time notice the usher tapping him lightly on the shoulder and saying politely, "Will you step this way, please, sir?" A little surprised, he arose quickly at the last tap, and, turning to leave his seat, looked full into the face of the fair-haired young man. For the first time the young man recognized his dark boyhood playmate, and John knew that it was the Judge's son. The White John started, lifted his hand, and then froze into his chair; the black John smiled lightly, then grimly, and followed the usher down the aisle. The manager was sorry, very, very sorry,—but he explained that some mistake had been made in selling the gentleman a seat already disposed of; he would refund the money, of course,—and indeed felt the matter keenly, and so forth, and—before he had finished John was gone, walking hurriedly across the square and down the broad streets, and as he passed the park he buttoned his coat and said, "John Jones, you're a natural-born fool." Then he went to his lodgings and wrote a letter, and tore it up; he wrote another, and threw it in the fire. Then he seized a scrap of paper and wrote: "Dear Mother and Sister—I am coming—John."

"Perhaps," said John, as he settled himself on the train, "perhaps I am to blame myself in struggling against my manifest destiny simply because it looks hard and unpleasant. Here is my duty to Altamaha plain before me; perhaps they'll let me help settle the Negro problems there,—perhaps they won't. 'I will go in to the King, which is not according to the law; and if I perish, I perish.'" And then he mused and dreamed, and planned a life-work; and the train flew south.

Down in Altamaha, after seven long years, all the world knew John was coming. The homes were scrubbed and scoured,—above all, one; the gardens and yards had an unwonted trimness, and Jennie bought a new gingham. With some finesse and negotiation, all the dark Methodist and Presbyterians were induced to join in a monster welcome at the Baptist Church; and as the day drew near, warm discussions arose on every corner as to the exact extent and nature of John's accomplishments. It was noontide on a gray and cloudy day when he came. The black town flocked to the depot, with a little of the white at the edges,—a happy throng, with "Good-mawnings" and "Howdys" and laughing and joking and jostling. Mother sat yonder in the window watching; but sister Jennie stood on the platform, nervously fingering her dress, tall and lithe, with soft brown skin and loving eyes peering from out a tangled wilderness of hair. John rose gloomily as the train stopped, for he was thinking of the "Jim Crow" car; he stepped to the platform, and paused: a little dingy station, a black crowd gaudy and dirty, a half-mile of dilapidated shanties along a straggling ditch of mud. An overwhelming sense of the sordidness and narrowness of it all seized him; he looked in vain for his mother, kissed coldly the tall, strange girl who called him brother, spoke a short, dry word here and there; then, lingering neither for hand-shaking nor gossip, started silently up the street, raising his hat merely to the last eager old aunty, to her open-mouthed astonishment. The people were distinctly bewildered. This silent, cold man,—was this John? Where was his smile and hearty hand-grasp? "'Peared kind o' down in the mouf," said the Methodist preacher thoughtfully. "Seemed monstus stuck up," complained a Baptist sister. But the white postmaster from the edge of the crowd expressed the opinion of his folks plainly. "That damn Nigger," said he, as he shouldered the mail and arranged his tobacco, "has gone North and got plum full o' fool notions; but they won't work in Altamaha." And the crowd melted away.

The meeting of welcome at the Baptist Church was a failure. Rain spoiled the barbecue, and thunder turned the milk in the ice-cream. When the speaking came at night, the house was crowded to overflowing. The three preachers had especially prepared themselves, but somehow John's manner seemed to throw a blanket over everything,—he seemed so cold and preoccupied, and had so strange an air of restraint that the Methodist brother could not warm up to his theme and elicited not a single "Amen"; the Presbyterian prayer was but feebly responded to, and even the Baptist preacher, though he wakened faint enthusiasm, got so mixed up in his favorite sentence that he had to close it by stopping fully fifteen minutes sooner than he meant. The people moved uneasily in their seats as John rose to reply. He spoke slowly and methodically. The age, he said, demanded new ideas; we were far different from those men of the seventeenth and eighteenth centuries,—with broader ideas of human brotherhood and destiny. Then he spoke of the rise of charity and popular education, and particularly of the spread of wealth and work. The question was, then, he added reflectively, looking at the low discolored ceiling, what part the Negroes of this land would take in the striving of the new century. He sketched in vague outline the new Industrial School that might rise among these pines, he spoke in detail of the charitable and philanthropic work that might be organized, of money that might be saved for banks and business. Finally he urged unity, and deprecated especially religious and denominational bickering. "To-day," he said, with a smile, "the world cares little whether a man be Baptist or Methodist, or indeed a churchman at all, so long as he is good and true. What difference does it make whether a man be baptized in river or washbowl, or not at all? Let's leave all that littleness, and look higher." Then, thinking of nothing else, he slowly sat down. A painful hush seized that crowded mass. Little had they understood of what he said, for he spoke an unknown tongue, save the last word about baptism; that they knew, and they sat very still while the clock ticked. Then at last a low suppressed snarl came from the Amen corner, and an old bent man arose, walked over the seats, and climbed straight up into the pulpit. He was wrinkled and black, with scant gray and tufted hair; his voice and hands shook as with palsy; but on his face lay the intense rapt look of the religious fanatic. He seized the Bible with his rough, huge hands; twice he raised it inarticulate, and then fairly burst into words, with rude and awful eloquence. He quivered, swayed, and bent; then rose aloft in perfect majesty, till the people moaned and wept, wailed and shouted, and a wild shrieking arose from the corners where all the pent-up feeling of the hour gathered itself and rushed into the air. John never knew clearly what the old man said; he only felt himself held up to scorn and scathing denunciation for trampling on the true Religion, and he realized with amazement that all unknowingly he had put rough, rude hands on something this little world held sacred. He arose silently, and passed out into the night. Down toward the sea he went, in the fitful starlight, half conscious of the girl who followed timidly after him. When at last he stood upon the bluff, he turned to his little sister and looked upon her sorrowfully, remembering with sudden pain how little thought he had given her. He put his arm about her and let her passion of tears spend itself on his shoulder.

Long they stood together, peering over the gray unresting water.

"John," she said, "does it make every one—unhappy when they study and learn lots of things?"

He paused and smiled. "I am afraid it does," he said.

"And, John, are you glad you studied?"

"Yes," came the answer, slowly but positively.

She watched the flickering lights upon the sea, and said thoughtfully, "I wish I was unhappy,—and—and," putting both arms about his neck, "I think I am, a little, John."

It was several days later that John walked up to the Judge's house to ask for the privilege of teaching the Negro school. The Judge himself met him at the front door, stared a little hard at him, and said brusquely, "Go 'round to the kitchen door, John, and wait." Sitting on the kitchen steps, John stared at the corn, thoroughly perplexed. What on earth had come over him? Every step he made offended some one. He had come to save his people, and before he left the depot he had hurt them. He sought to teach them at the church, and had outraged their deepest feelings. He had schooled himself to be respectful to the Judge, and then blundered into his front door. And all the time he had meant right,—and yet, and yet, somehow he found it so hard and strange to fit his old surroundings again, to find his place in the world about him. He could not remember that he used to have any difficulty in the past, when life was glad and gay. The world seemed smooth and easy then. Perhaps,—but his sister came to the kitchen door just then and said the Judge awaited him.

The Judge sat in the dining-room amid his morning's mail, and he did not ask John to sit down. He plunged squarely into the business. "You've come for the school, I suppose. Well, John, I want to speak to you plainly. You know I'm a friend to your people. I've helped you and your family, and would have done more if you hadn't got the notion of going off. Now I like the colored people, and sympathize with all their reasonable aspirations; but you and I both know, John, that in this country the Negro must remain subordinate, and can never expect to be the equal of white men. In their place, your people can be honest and respectful; and God knows, I'll do what I can to help them. But when they want to reverse nature, and rule white men, and marry white women, and sit in my parlor, then, by God! we'll hold them under if we have to lynch every Nigger in the land. Now, John, the question is, are you, with your education and Northern notions, going to accept the situation and teach the darkies to be faithful servants and laborers as your fathers were,—I knew your father, John, he belonged to my brother, and he was a good Nigger. Well—well, are you going to be like him, or are you going to try to put fool ideas of rising and equality into these folks' heads, and make them discontented and unhappy?"

"I am going to accept the situation, Judge Henderson," answered John, with a brevity that did not escape the keen old man. He hesitated a moment, and then said shortly, "Very well,—we'll try you awhile. Good-morning."

It was a full month after the opening of the Negro school that the other John came home, tall, gay, and headstrong. The mother wept, the sisters sang. The whole white town was glad. A proud man was the Judge, and it was a goodly sight to see the two swinging down Main Street together. And yet all did not go smoothly between them, for the younger man could not and did not veil his contempt for the little town, and plainly had his heart set on New York. Now the one cherished ambition of the Judge was to see his son mayor of Altamaha, representative to the legislature, and—who could say?—governor of Georgia. So the argument often waxed hot between them. "Good heavens, father," the younger man would say after dinner, as he lighted a cigar and stood by the fireplace, "you surely don't expect a young fellow like me to settle down permanently in this— this God-forgotten town with nothing but mud and Negroes?" "I did," the Judge would answer laconically; and on this particular day it seemed from the gathering scowl that he was about to add something more emphatic, but neighbors had already begun to drop in to admire his son, and the conversation drifted.

"Heah that John is livenin' things up at the darky school," volunteered the postmaster, after a pause.

"What now?" asked the Judge, sharply.

"Oh, nothin' in particulah,—just his almighty air and uppish ways. B'lieve I did heah somethin' about his givin' talks on the French Revolution, equality, and such like. He's what I call a dangerous Nigger."

"Have you heard him say anything out of the way?"

"Why, no,—but Sally, our girl, told my wife a lot of rot. Then, too, I don't need to heah: a Nigger what won't say 'sir' to a white man, or—"

"Who is this John?" interrupted the son.

"Why, it's little black John, Peggy's son,—your old playfellow."

The young man's face flushed angrily, and then he laughed.

"Oh," said he, "it's the darky that tried to force himself into a seat beside the lady I was escorting—"

But Judge Henderson waited to hear no more. He had been nettled all day, and now at this he rose with a half-smothered oath, took his hat and cane, and walked straight to the schoolhouse.

For John, it had been a long, hard pull to get things started in the rickety old shanty that sheltered his school. The Negroes were rent into factions for and against him, the parents were careless, the children irregular and dirty, and books, pencils, and slates largely missing. Nevertheless, he struggled hopefully on, and seemed to see at last some glimmering of dawn. The attendance was larger and the children were a shade cleaner this week. Even the booby class in reading showed a little comforting progress. So John settled himself with renewed patience this afternoon.

"Now, Mandy," he said cheerfully, "that's better; but you mustn't chop your words up so: 'If—the—man—goes.' Why, your little brother even wouldn't tell a story that way, now would he?"

"Naw, suh, he cain't talk."

"All right; now let's try again: 'If the man—'"

"John!"

The whole school started in surprise, and the teacher half arose, as the red, angry face of the Judge appeared in the open doorway.

"John, this school is closed. You children can go home and get to work. The white people of Altamaha are not spending their money on black folks to have their heads crammed with impudence and lies. Clear out! I'll lock the door myself."

Up at the great pillared house the tall young son wandered aimlessly about after his father's abrupt departure. In the house there was little to interest him; the books were old and stale, the local newspaper flat, and the women had retired with headaches and sewing. He tried a nap, but it was too warm. So he sauntered out into the fields, complaining disconsolately, "Good Lord! how long will this imprisonment last!" He was not a bad fellow,—just a little spoiled and self-indulgent, and as headstrong as his proud father. He seemed a young man pleasant to look upon, as he sat on the great black stump at the edge of the pines idly swinging his legs and smoking. "Why, there isn't even a girl worth getting up a respectable flirtation with," he growled. Just then his eye caught a tall, willowy figure hurrying toward him on the narrow path. He looked with interest at first, and then burst into a laugh as he said, "Well, I declare, if it isn't Jennie, the little brown kitchen-maid! Why, I never noticed before what a trim little body she is. Hello, Jennie! Why, you haven't kissed me since I came home," he said gaily. The young girl stared at him in surprise and confusion,—faltered something inarticulate, and attempted to pass. But a wilful mood had seized the young idler, and he caught at her arm. Frightened, she slipped by; and half mischievously he turned and ran after her through the tall pines.

Yonder, toward the sea, at the end of the path, came John slowly, with his head down. He had turned wearily homeward from the schoolhouse; then, thinking to shield his mother from the blow, started to meet his sister as she came from work and break the news of his dismissal to her. "I'll go away," he said slowly; "I'll go away and find work, and send for them. I cannot live here longer." And then the fierce, buried anger surged up into his throat. He waved his arms and hurried wildly up the path.

The great brown sea lay silent. The air scarce breathed. The dying day bathed the twisted oaks and mighty pines in black and gold. There came from the wind no warning, not a whisper from the cloudless sky. There was only a black man hurrying on with an ache in his heart, seeing neither sun nor sea, but starting as from a dream at the frightened cry that woke the pines, to see his dark sister struggling in the arms of a tall and fair-haired man.

He said not a word, but, seizing a fallen limb, struck him with all the pent-up hatred of his great black arm; and the body lay white and still beneath the pines, all bathed in sunshine and in blood. John looked at it dreamily, then walked back to the house briskly, and said in a soft voice, "Mammy, I'm going away—I'm going to be free."

She gazed at him dimly and faltered, "No'th, honey, is yo' gwine No'th agin?"

He looked out where the North Star glistened pale above the waters, and said. "Yes, mammy, I'm going—North."

Then, without another word, he went out into the narrow lane, up by the straight pines, to the same winding path, and seated himself on the great black stump, looking at the blood where the body had lain. Yonder in the gray past he had played with that dead boy, romping together under the solemn trees. The night deepened; he thought of the boys at Johnstown. He wondered how Brown had turned out, and Carey? And Jones,—Jones? Why, *he* was Jones, and he wondered what they would all say when they knew, when they knew, in that great long dining-room with its hundreds of merry eyes. Then as the sheen of the starlight stole over him, he thought of the gilded ceiling of that vast concert hall, heard stealing toward him the faint sweet music of the swan. Hark! was it music, or the hurry and shouting of men? Yes, surely! Clear and high the faint sweet melody rose and fluttered like a living thing, so that the very earth trembled as with the tramp of horses and murmur of angry men.

He leaned back and smiled toward the sea, whence rose the strange melody, away from the dark shadows where lay the noise of horses galloping, galloping on. With an effort he roused himself, bent forward, and looked steadily down the pathway, softly humming the "Song of the Bride,"*—

"Freudig geführt, ziehet dahin."

Amid the trees in the dim morning twilight he watched their shadows dancing and heard their horses thundering toward him, until at last they came sweeping like a storm, and he saw in front that haggard white-haired man, whose eyes flashed red with fury. Oh, how he pitied him,—pitied him,—and wondered if he had the coiling twisted rope. Then, as the storm burst round him, he rose slowly to his feet and turned his closed eyes toward the Sea.

And the world whistled in his ears.

Chapter XIV

Of the Sorrow Songs

> I walk through the churchyard
>   To lay this body down;
> I know moon-rise, I know star-rise;
> I walk in the moonlight, I walk in the starlight;
> I'll lie in the grave and stretch out my arms,
> I'll go to judgment in the evening of the day,
> And my soul and thy soul shall meet that day,
>   When I lay this body down.
>
> NEGRO SONG.

They that walked in darkness sang songs in the olden days—Sorrow Songs—for they were weary at heart. And so before each thought that I have written in this book I have set a phrase, a haunting echo of these weird old songs in which the soul of the black slave spoke to men. Ever since I was a child these songs have stirred me strangely. They came out of the South unknown to me, one by one, and yet at once I knew them as of me and of mine. Then in after years when I came to Nashville I saw the great temple* builded of these songs towering over the pale city. To me Jubilee Hall seemed ever made of the songs themselves, and its bricks were red with the blood and dust of toil. Out of them rose for me morning, noon, and night, bursts of wonderful melody, full of the voices of my brothers and sisters, full of the voices of the past.

Little of beauty has America given the world save the rude grandeur God himself stamped on her bosom; the human spirit in this new world has expressed itself in vigor and ingenuity rather than in beauty. And so by fateful chance the Negro folk-song—the rhythmic cry of the slave—stands to-day not simply as the sole American music, but as the most beautiful expression of human experience born this side the seas. It has been neglected, it has been, and is, half despised, and above all it has been persistently mistaken and misunderstood; but notwithstanding, it still remains as the singular spiritual heritage of the nation and the greatest gift of the Negro people.

Away back in the thirties the melody of these slave songs stirred the nation, but the songs were soon half forgotten. Some, like "Near the lake where drooped the willow," passed into current airs and their source was forgotten; others were caricatured on the "minstrel" stage and their memory died away. Then in war-time came the singular Port Royal experiment* after the capture of Hilton Head, and perhaps for the first time the North met the Southern slave face to face and heart to heart with no third witness. The Sea Islands of the Carolinas, where they met, were filled with a black folk of primitive type, touched and moulded less by the world about them than any others outside the Black Belt. Their appearance was uncouth, their language funny, but their hearts were human and their singing stirred men with a mighty power. Thomas Wentworth Higginson* hastened to tell of these songs, and Miss McKim* and others urged upon the world their rare beauty. But the world listened only half credulously until the Fisk Jubilee Singers sang the slave songs so deeply into the world's heart that it can never wholly forget them again.

There was once a blacksmith's son born at Cadiz, New York, who in the changes of time taught school in Ohio and helped defend Cincinnati from Kirby Smith. Then he fought at Chancellorsville and Gettysburg and finally served in the Freedman's Bureau at Nashville. Here he formed a Sunday-school class of black children in 1866, and sang with them and taught them to sing. And then they taught him to sing, and when once the glory of the Jubilee songs passed into the soul of George L. White, he knew his life-work was to let those Negroes sing to the world as they had sung to him. So in 1871 the pilgrimage of the Fisk Jubilee Singers began. North to Cincinnati they rode,—four half-clothed black boys and five girl-women,—led by a man with a cause and a purpose. They stopped at Wilberforce, the oldest of Negro schools, where a black bishop blessed them. Then they went, fighting cold and starvation, shut out of hotels, and cheerfully sneered at, ever northward; and ever the magic of their song kept thrilling hearts, until a burst of applause in the Congregational Council at Oberlin revealed them to the world. They came to New York and Henry Ward Beecher* dared to welcome them, even though the metropolitan dailies sneered at his "Nigger Minstrels." So their songs conquered till they sang across the land and across the sea, before Queen and Kaiser, in Scotland and Ireland, Holland and Switzerland. Seven years they sang, and brought back a hundred and fifty thousand dollars to found Fisk University.

Since their day they have been imitated—sometimes well, by the singers of Hampton and Atlanta, sometimes ill, by straggling quartettes. Caricature has sought again to spoil the quaint beauty of the music, and has filled the air with many debased melodies which vulgar ears scarce know from the real. But the true Negro folk-song still lives in the hearts of those who have heard them truly sung and in the hearts of the Negro people.

What are these songs, and what do they mean? I know little of music and can say nothing in technical phrase, but I know something of men, and knowing them, I know that these songs are the articulate message of the slave to the world. They tell us in these eager days that life was joyous to the black slave, careless and happy. I can easily believe this of some, of many. But not all the past South, though it rose from the dead, can gainsay the heart-touching witness of these songs. They are the music of an unhappy people, of the children of disappointment; they tell of death and suffering and unvoiced longing toward a truer world, of misty wanderings and hidden ways.

The songs are indeed the siftings of centuries; the music is far more ancient than the words, and in it we can trace here and there signs of development. My grandfather's grandmother was seized by an evil Dutch trader two centuries ago; and coming to the valleys of the Hudson and Housatonic, black, little, and lithe, she shivered and shrank in the harsh north winds, looked longingly at the hills, and often crooned a heathen melody to the child between her knees, thus:

The child sang it to his children and they to their children's children, and so two hundred years it has travelled down to us and we sing it to our children, knowing as little as our fathers what its words may mean, but knowing well the meaning of its music.

This was primitive African music; it may be seen in larger form in the strange chant which heralds "The Coming of John":

> "You may bury me in the East,
> You may bury me in the West,
> But I'll hear the trumpet sound in that morning,"

—the voice of exile.

Ten master songs, more or less, one may pluck from this forest of melody—songs of undoubted Negro origin and wide popular currency, and songs peculiarly characteristic of the slave. One of these I have just mentioned. Another whose strains begin this book is "Nobody knows the trouble I've seen." When, struck with a sudden poverty, the United States refused to fulfill its promises of land to the freedmen, a brigadier-general went down to the Sea Islands to carry the news. An old woman on the outskirts of the throng began singing this song; all the mass joined with her, swaying. And the soldier wept.

The third song is the cradle-song of death which all men know,—"Swing low, sweet chariot,"—whose bars begin the life story of "Alexander Crummell." Then there is the song of many waters, "Roll, Jordan, roll," a mighty chorus with minor cadences. There were many songs of the fugitive like that which opens "The Wings of Atalanta," and the more familiar "Been a-listening." The seventh is the song of the End and the Beginning—"My Lord, what a mourning! when the stars begin to fall"; a strain of this is placed before "The Dawn of Freedom." The song of groping—"My way's cloudy"—begins "The Meaning of Progress"; the ninth is the song of this chapter—"Wrestlin' Jacob, the day is a-breaking,"—a pæan of hopeful strife. The last master song is the song of songs—"Steal away,"—sprung from "The Faith of the Fathers."

There are many others of the Negro folk-songs as striking and characteristic as these, as, for instance, the three strains in the third, eighth, and ninth chapters; and others I am sure could easily make a selection on more scientific principles. There are, too, songs that seem to be a step removed from the more primitive types: there is the maze-like medley, "Bright sparkles," one phrase of which heads "The Black Belt"; the Easter carol, "Dust, dust and ashes"; the dirge, "My mother's took her flight and gone home"; and that burst of melody hovering over "The Passing of the First-Born"—"I hope my mother will be there in that beautiful world on high."

These represent a third step in the development of the slave song, of which "You may bury me in the East" is the first, and songs like "March on" (chapter six) and "Steal away" are the second. The first is African music, the second Afro-American, while the third is a blending of Negro music with the music heard in the foster land. The result is still distinctively Negro and the method of blending original, but the elements are both Negro and Caucasian. One might go further and find a fourth step in this development, where the songs of white America have been distinctively influenced by the slave songs or have incorporated whole phrases of Negro melody, as "Swanee River" and "Old Black Joe." Side by side, too, with the growth has gone the debasements and imitations—the Negro "minstrel" songs, many of the "gospel" hymns, and some of the contemporary "coon" songs,—a mass of music in which the novice may easily lose himself and never find the real Negro melodies.

In these songs, I have said, the slave spoke to the world. Such a message is naturally veiled and half articulate. Words and music have lost each other and new and cant phrases of a dimly understood theology have displaced the older sentiment. Once in a while we catch a strange word of an unknown tongue, as the "Mighty Myo," which figures as a river of death; more often slight words or mere doggerel are joined to music of singular sweetness. Purely secular songs are few in number, partly because many of them were turned into hymns by a change of words, partly because the frolics were seldom heard by the stranger, and the music less often caught. Of nearly all the songs, however, the music is distinctly sorrowful. The ten master songs I have mentioned tell in word and music of trouble and exile, of strife and hiding; they grope toward some unseen power and sigh for rest in the End.

The words that are left to us are not without interest, and, cleared of evident dross, they conceal much of real poetry and meaning beneath conventional theology and unmeaning rhapsody. Like all primitive folk, the slave stood near to Nature's heart. Life was a "rough and rolling sea" like the brown Atlantic of the Sea Islands; the "Wilderness" was the home of God, and the "lonesome valley" led to the way of life. "Winter'll soon be over," was the picture of life and death to a tropical imagination. The sudden wild thunder-storms of the South awed and impressed the Negroes,—at times the rumbling seemed to them "mournful," at times imperious:

"My Lord calls me,
He calls me by the thunder,
The trumpet sounds it in my soul."

The monotonous toil and exposure is painted in many words. One sees the ploughmen in the hot, moist furrow, singing:

"Dere's no rain to wet you,
Dere's no sun to burn you,
Oh, push along, believer,
I want to go home."

The bowed and bent old man cries, with thrice-repeated wail:

"O Lord, keep me from sinking down,"

and he rebukes the devil of doubt who can whisper:

"Jesus is dead and God's gone away."

Yet the soul-hunger is there, the restlessness of the savage, the wail of the wanderer, and the plaint is put in one little phrase:

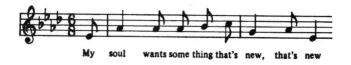

My soul wants some thing that's new, that's new

Over the inner thoughts of the slaves and their relations one with another the shadow of fear ever hung, so that we get but glimpses here and there, and also with them, eloquent omissions and silences. Mother and child are sung, but seldom father; fugitive and weary wanderer call for pity and affection, but there is little of wooing and wedding; the rocks and the mountains are well known, but home is unknown. Strange blending of love and helplessness sighs through the refrain:

"Yonder's my ole mudder,
Been waggin' at de hill so long;
'Bout time she cross over,
Git home bime-by."

Elsewhere comes the cry of the "motherless" and the "Farewell, farewell, my only child."

Love-songs are scarce and fall into two categories—the frivolous and light, and the sad. Of deep successful love there is ominous silence, and in one of the oldest of these songs there is a depth of history and meaning:

Poor Ro - sy, poor gal; Poor Ro - sy,
poor gal; Ro - sy break my poor heart.
Heav'n shall - a - be my home.

A black woman said of the song, "It can't be sung without a full heart and a troubled sperrit." The same voice sings here that sings in the German folk-song:

"Jetz Geh i' an's brunele, trink' aber net."

Of death the Negro showed little fear, but talked of it familiarly and even fondly as simply a crossing of the waters, perhaps—who knows?—back to his ancient forests again. Later days transfigured his fatalism, and amid the dust and dirt the toiler sang:

> "Dust, dust and ashes, fly over my grave,
> But the Lord shall bear my spirit home."

The things evidently borrowed from the surrounding world undergo characteristic change when they enter the mouth of the slave. Especially is this true of Bible phrases. "Weep, O captive daughter of Zion," is quaintly turned into "Zion, weep-a-low," and the wheels of Ezekiel are turned every way in the mystic dreaming of the slave, till he says:

> "There's a little wheel a-turnin' in-a-my heart."

As in olden time, the words of these hymns were improvised by some leading minstrel of the religious band. The circumstances of the gathering, however, the rhythm of the songs, and the limitations of allowable thought, confined the poetry for the most part to single or double lines, and they seldom were expanded to quatrains or longer tales, although there are some few examples of sustained efforts, chiefly paraphrases of the Bible. Three short series of verses have always attracted me,—the one that heads this chapter, of one line of which Thomas Wentworth Higginson has fittingly said, "Never, it seems to me, since man first lived and suffered was his infinite longing for peace uttered more plaintively." The second and third are descriptions of the Last Judgment,—the one a late improvisation, with some traces of outside influence:

> "Oh, the stars in the elements are falling,
> And the moon drips away into blood,

And the ransomed of the Lord are returning
  unto God,
Blessed be the name of the Lord."

And the other earlier and homelier picture from the low coast lands:

"Michael, haul the boat ashore,
Then you'll hear the horn they blow,
Then you'll hear the trumpet sound,
Trumpet sound the world around,
Trumpet sound for rich and poor,
Trumpet sound the Jubilee,
Trumpet sound for you and me."

Through all the sorrow of the Sorrow Songs there breathes a hope—a faith in the ultimate justice of things. The minor cadences of despair change often to triumph and calm confidence. Sometimes it is faith in life, sometimes a faith in death, sometimes assurance of boundless justice in some fair world beyond. But whichever it is, the meaning is always clear: that sometime, somewhere, men will judge men by their souls and not by their skins. Is such a hope justified? Do the Sorrow Songs sing true?

The silently growing assumption of this age is that the probation of races is past, and that the backward races of to-day are of proven inefficiency and not worth the saving. Such an assumption is the arrogance of peoples irreverent toward Time and ignorant of the deeds of men. A thousand years ago such an assumption, easily possible, would have made it difficult for the Teuton* to prove his right to life. Two thousand years ago such dogmatism, readily welcome, would have scouted the idea of blond races ever leading civilization. So wofully unorganized is sociological knowledge that the meaning of progress, the meaning of "swift" and "slow" in human doing, and the limits of human perfectability, are veiled, unanswered sphinxes on the shores of science. Why should Æschylus* have sung two thousand years before Shakespeare was born? Why has civilization flourished in Europe, and flickered, flamed, and died in Africa? So long as the world stands meekly dumb before such questions, shall this nation proclaim its ignorance and unhallowed prejudices by denying freedom of opportunity to those who brought the Sorrow Songs to the Seats of the Mighty?

Your country? How came it yours? Before the Pilgrims landed we were here. Here we have brought our three gifts and mingled them with yours: a gift of story and song—soft, stirring melody in an ill-harmonized and unmelodious land; the gift of sweat and brawn to beat back the wilderness, conquer the soil, and lay the foundations of this vast economic empire two hundred years earlier than your weak hands could have done it; the third, a gift of the Spirit. Around us the history of the land has centred for thrice a hundred years; out of the nation's heart we have called all that was best to throttle and subdue all that was worst; fire and blood, prayer and sacrifice, have billowed over this people, and they have found peace only in the altars of the God of Right. Nor has our gift of the Spirit been merely passive. Actively we have woven ourselves with the very warp and woof of this nation,—we fought their battles, shared their sorrow, mingled our blood with theirs, and generation after generation have pleaded with a headstrong, careless people to despise not Justice, Mercy, and Truth, lest the nation be smitten with a curse. Our song, our toil, our cheer, and warning have been given to this nation in blood-brotherhood. Are not these

gifts worth the giving? Is not this work and striving?
Would America have been America without her Negro
people?

Even so is the hope that sang in the songs of my
fathers well sung. If somewhere in this whirl and
chaos of things there dwells Eternal Good, pitiful yet
masterful, then anon in His good time America shall
rend the Veil and the prisoned shall go free. Free, free
as the sunshine trickling down the morning into these
high windows of mine, free as yonder fresh young
voices welling up to me from the caverns of brick and
mortar below—swelling with song, instinct with life,
tremulous treble and darkening bass. My children, my
little children, are singing to the sunshine, and thus
they sing:

- long   the   heav - en - ly   way,

And the traveller girds himself, and sets his face toward the Morning, and goes his way.

The Afterthought

Hear my cry, O God the Reader; vouchsafe that this my book fall not still-born into the world wilderness. Let there spring, Gentle One, from out its leaves vigor of thought and thoughtful deed to reap the harvest wonderful. Let the ears of a guilty people tingle with truth, and seventy millions sigh for the righteousness which exalteth nations, in this drear day when human brotherhood is mockery and a snare. Thus in Thy good time may infinite reason turn the tangle straight, and these crooked marks on a fragile leaf be not indeed

THE END

Glossary

of Names, Historical Terms, and Foreign Words

Chapter I

12 **carpet-bagger:** the unflattering nickname for Northerners who came South after the Civil War. Allegedly, they had so little that they could carry all their belongings in a carpetbag and were looking for personal gain.

12 **Fifteenth Amendment:** This amendment to the U.S. Constitution states that "The right of citizens to vote shall not be denied or abridged . . . on account of race, color, or previous condition of servitude." It was ratified by the states in 1870. **Note:** It would be another 50 years before women would be allowed to vote, so in effect, black men were voting before white women.

13 **revolution of 1876:** In the hotly contested presidential election of that year, Rutherford B. Hayes won because he promised to remove troops from the South. In so doing, he jeopardized the progress African Americans had made during Reconstruction.

13 **Canaan:** the Promised Land of the Old Testament.

15 *Sturm und Drang:* a German term meaning "storm and stress," or turmoil.

Chapter II

19 **Emancipation Proclamation:** the proclamation issued by President Lincoln in January, 1863, that freed those African Americans held in bondage in the rebellious southern states.

19 **Butler:** General Benjamin Butler commanded Fort Monroe in Virginia during the Civil War.

19 **Fremont:** General John C. Fremont led a force in the Civil War.

20 **Chase:** Salmon P. Chase was the Secretary of War during the Civil War.

21 **Sherman:** William Tecumseh Sherman was the Union general who led the famous "March to the Sea" during the Civil War.

21 **American Missionary Association . . . *Amistad:*** The American Missionary Association (AMA) was established in 1846 to raise funds to charter a ship to return kidnapped Africans from the slave ship *Amistad* to their homeland. In 1839, the *Amistad* had sailed from Cuba with 53 captives from Sierra Leone. One of the captives, Cinque, led a successful mutiny, but the Cuban sailors tricked him and steered the ship to the slaveholding United States instead of back to Africa. Once in the United States, the Africans were jailed and charged with murder and piracy. Former U.S. President John Quincy Adams argued the Africans' case before the Supreme Court, and they were set free.

24 **Sumner:** Charles Sumner was a U.S. senator from Massachusetts who was against slavery.

28 **Ninth Crusade:** Du Bois compares the Northern teachers' educational mission to the eight Crusades, or religious wars, that Christians launched against Muslims to regain the Holy Land in the Middle Ages.

31 **Lee:** General Robert E. Lee, commander of the Confederate Army during the Civil War.

31 **Thirteenth Amendment:** This amendment to the U.S. Constitution, ratified in 1865, made the keeping of slaves illegal.

Fourteenth Amendment: This amendment, ratified in 1868, gave full citizenship rights to all persons born in the United States. It also nullified the provision in Article I of the Constitution that stated that for purposes of representation in the Congress, blacks would be counted as 3/5 of a person.

Fifteenth Amendment: the amendment giving black men the right to vote (see notes for Chapter I).

33 ***toto cœlo:*** Latin for "the whole extent of the heavens," or in every possible way.

35 **Edmund Ware, Samuel Armstrong, and Erasmus Cravath:** northern white educators who came to the South to help educate newly freed blacks after the Civil War.

Fisk, Howard, Atlanta, Hampton: black colleges established shortly after the Civil War.

Chapter III

44 **Price:** Joseph C. Price (1854–1893) was an African-American minister and orator who raised money for black schools.

44 **Jefferson Davis:** president of the Confederacy from 1861 to 1865.

45 **Socrates** (470–399 B.C.): a Greek philosopher and the celebrated teacher of Plato.

45 **St. Francis of Assisi** (1182–1226): founder of the Franciscan order of monks.

45 **Spanish-American War:** the victorious 1898 war against Spain that gave the United States control of the Philippines, Guam, Puerto Rico, and Cuba.

46 **Roosevelt:** Theodore Roosevelt was President of the United States from 1901 to 1909.

46 **Abolitionists:** the people who worked to abolish (end) slavery in the United States.

48 **Maroons:** a group of Africans in Jamaica who escaped slavery and formed their own self-

contained community high up in the hills. The Maroons fiercely and successfully defended themselves against those who tried to re-enslave them and encouraged others who were enslaved to run away and join them.

48 **Danish blacks:** a reference to the 1733 uprising by Africans enslaved on the Virgin Islands then held by Denmark. In a well-executed plan the Africans spent several days killing every white they could find before the militia was able to regain control.

48 **Cato of Stono:** In 1739, more than 100 enslaved Africans led by Cato rebelled in Stono, near Charleston, South Carolina. They took arms from a warehouse and killed 30 whites.

48 **Phyllis:** Phillis Wheatley (1753–1784) was born in Africa, captured as a child, and brought to Boston, where she became a celebrated poet.

48 **Attucks:** Crispus Attucks (1723–1770), the son of an African man and a Native American woman, was the first person killed in the historic Boston Massacre. A monument on Boston Common preserves his memory.

48 **Salem and Poor:** Peter Salem and Salem Poor were African Americans who were distinguished soldiers in the American Revolutionary War.

48 **Banneker:** Benjamin Banneker (1731–1806) was a black mathematician and astronomer born in Maryland. He assisted in the survey to lay out Washington, D.C. in 1790 and published an annual almanac for farmers from 1792 to 1802.

48 **Derham:** Dr. James Derham was an 18th-century black physician described as "very learned."

48 **Cuffes:** Paul Cuffe (1759–1817) was a successful shipbuilder and shipowner in New Bedford, Massachusetts. He and his brother John withheld their taxes on the grounds that they were not allowed to vote, and a court granted them voting rights.

48 **Haytian revolt:** Under the leadership of Toussaint

L'Ouverture, blacks in Haiti overthrew the slavery regime in 1793.

48 **Gabriel . . . Vesey . . . Nat Turner:** Gabriel (also known as Gabriel Prosser) led an uprising of more than 1000 armed slaves, but a violent rainstorm led to the rebellion's failure. Denmark Vesey, a carpenter who had purchased his freedom, planned a slave revolt that involved so many people (around 9000) that word leaked out before it could be completed. Nat Turner led a rebellion in which 57 whites were killed within 24 hours. Gabriel, Vesey, and Turner all were captured and hanged.

49 **Walker's wild appeal:** In 1829, David Walker published an *Appeal to the Coloured Citizens of the World, but in particular, and very expressly, to those of The United States of America* urging enslaved Africans to rise up against their "masters." Walker was found dead shortly after he published a third edition in 1830.

49 **Forten:** James Forten (1766–1842) developed a sail-handling device and owned a sail loft that made him the wealthiest black man in Philadelphia. He used much of his money to promote the abolition of slavery.

49 **Purvis:** Robert Purvis (1810–1898) was one of the black leaders who helped organize the American Anti-Slavery Society in Philadelphia and was an active participant in the Underground Railroad.

49 **Shad:** Abraham Shadd, a free black abolitionist who opposed the movement to transport free-born and emancipated blacks to Africa.

49 **Du Bois:** Alexander Du Bois, the grandfather of W. E. B. Du Bois.

49 **Barbadoes:** James G. Barbadoes (1796–1841) was a black businessman and abolitionist in Boston in the 1830s. He was also the secretary of the Massachusetts General Colored Association.

49 **Remond:** Charles Lenox Remond (1810–1874) was another black leader from Salem,

Massachusetts who traveled around lecturing and soliciting support for the antislavery movement.

49 **Nell:** William C. Nell (1816–1874) was a historian who wrote *Services of Colored Americans in the Wars of 1776 and 1812,* published in 1852.

49 **Wells-Brown:** William Wells Brown (1814–1884) was an antislavery lecturer and the author of *Narrative of William Wells Brown, A Fugitive Slave, Written By Himself,* published in 1847. He also wrote the 1853 novel *Clotel; or the President's Daughter.*

50 **John Brown's raid:** Brown, a white man, led an attack to capture the arsenal at Harpers Ferry, Virginia in 1859. His plan was to use the weapons to arm enslaved blacks for rebellion. He was captured and hanged.

50 **Elliot:** Robert B. Elliott (1842–1884) was the speaker of the house in the South Carolina legislature in 1874.

50 **Bruce:** Blanche Kelso Bruce (1841–1898) was the first African American to serve a full term in the U.S. Senate. He organized the first school for blacks in Missouri.

50 **Langston:** John Mercer Langston (1829–1897), a lawyer and educator, was the official representative of the U.S. government to Haiti in 1877. He was an ancestor of Langston Hughes, the famous poet and author.

50 **Alexander Crummell** (1819–1898): an African-American clergyman to whom Du Bois pays tribute in Chapter XII. (Chap. III)

50 **Bishop Daniel Payne:** a distinguished bishop in the African Methodist Episcopal Church and a founder of Wilberforce University.

50 **Revolution of 1876:** In the hotly contested presidential election of that year, Rutherford B. Hayes won because he promised to remove troops from the South. In so doing, he

jeopardized the progress African Americans had made during Reconstruction.

53   **recent course . . . Philippines:** At that time, the United States was dominating the people of Cuba, Puerto Rico, and the Philippines—lands it had won from Spain—and it had illegally taken over Hawaii, forcing the queen from her throne at gunpoint.

53   **Grimkes:** Archibald Grimke was a distinguished Boston attorney; his brother the Rev. Francis Grimke was a graduate of Princeton.

53   **Kelly Miller:** a Howard University professor who founded the American Negro Academy (along with Du Bois and several others). This national organization encouraged "scholarly" blacks to take the lead in shaping the image of African Americans in the fight against those who despised them.

53   **J. W. E. Bowen:** John Wesley Edward Bowen (1855–1933) earned degrees from the University of New Orleans and Gammon Theological Seminary and received a Ph.D. from Boston University in 1887. He was pastor of several churches, a college professor, and the editor of *The Voice of the Negro.*

57   **Governor Aycock:** Charles Brantley Aycock (1859–1912) was the governor of North Carolina from 1901 to 1905. He funded public education for both blacks and whites in the state.

57   **Senator Morgan:** John Tyler Morgan (1824–1907) was a white supremacist U. S. senator from Alabama.

57   **Thomas Nelson Page:** Page (1853–1922) wrote novels that romanticized the Old South and plantation life.

57   **Senator Ben Tillman:** Tillman (1847–1918), a racist U.S. senator from South Carolina, opposed giving African Americans the right to vote and defended lynching.

Chapter IV

64 **Cicero "pro Archia Poeta":** Marcus Tullius Cicero (106–43 b.c.) was a Roman orator and philosopher. His speech *pro Archia Poeta* (in Latin) supports the Greek poet Archias' claim to Roman citizenship and contains a famous passage defending the study of literature.

72 **Jim Crow car:** a railroad car reserved for blacks. Racist Jim Crow laws, enacted in the South beginning in 1875, banned blacks from all public accommodations used by whites—hotels, restaurants, theaters, schools, trains, buses, etc.

Chapter V

74 *réclame:* a French term meaning "publicity" or "exaggerated acclaim."

74 **Lachesis:** one of the Fates from Greek mythology. She is the one who spins life's thread and determines its length.

74 **Mercury:** the Roman god of commerce, who also served as a messenger to the other gods.

74 **Boeotia . . . Atalanta . . . Hippomenes:** References to a famous Greek myth. Atalanta, a maiden huntress from Boeotia, a region of ancient Greece, agreed to marry any man who could beat her in a footrace. Hippomenes outran her by dropping three golden apples along the path, which she stopped to pick up.

75 **the Bourse:** the marketplace or stock exchange.

75 **Third Estate:** a term for a social group who has newly gained political power. Historically it has referred to the common people, as opposed to the nobility or the clergy. The news media is often referred to as the fourth estate.

75 **Pluto:** the Roman god of the underworld, whose name is associated with wealth.

75 **Ceres:** the Roman goddess of agriculture.

76 **Apollo:** the Greek and Roman god of sunlight, prophecy and music.

76 *parvenu:* a French term for a person who has suddenly risen to a higher social class and is not yet accepted by members of that class.

78 **Mammonism:** devotion to money and wealth. In the New Testament, *Mammon* is the false god of wealth.

79 **Dido . . . Troy:** In Virgil's epic poem *The Aeneid,* Dido, the queen of Carthage, kills herself when Aeneas, the defender of Troy, leaves her.

79 **Pharaohs:** the rulers of ancient Egypt.

79 **Plato** (427–347 B.C.): a renowned Greek philosopher and teacher.

79 *trivium* **and** *quadrivium:* In medieval universities, the seven liberal arts were grouped in two divisions. The lower division, the *trivium,* consisted of grammar, rhetoric, and logic. The upper division, the *quadrivium,* consisted of arithmetic, music, geometry and astronomy.

79 **Oxford . . . Leipsic . . . Yale . . . Columbia:** major institutions of higher learning.

80 **Parnassus:** a mountain in Greece that was sacred to the god Apollo and the creative Muses.

80 **"Entbehren sollst du, sollst entbehren":** a line from *Faust* by the German poet Goethe. The translation is "Deny yourself. You must deny yourself."

80 **Academus . . . Cambridge:** Academus is the school for advanced learning founded by Plato. Cambridge is a prestigious university in England.

81 **sixth, seventh, and eighth commandments:** the commandments against killing, committing adultery, and stealing.

Chapter VI

85 **Jamestown:** the site in Virginia where the first 20 Africans were brought in 1619.

86 ***tertium quid:*** a Latin term meaning "a third party of uncertain status."

86 ***dilettante:*** a French term meaning "amateur."

87 **Zeitgeist:** a German term for the general intellectual, moral and cultural climate of an era.

88 **Dr. Johnson:** Dr. Samuel Johnson (1709–1784) published a dictionary in 1755 and also wrote poetry, essays, criticism and biography.

94 ***a priori:*** a Latin term for something that requires no proof because it is self-evident.

98 ***gaucherie:*** a French term for awkwardness or clumsiness.

102 **Rhinegold:** a legendary hoard of gold at the bottom of the Rhine river in Germany. From it was made a ring with a magic curse. Richard Wagner's opera *Das Rheingold* was based on this legend.

103 **Shakespeare . . . Balzac . . . Dumas:** famous world writers. William Shakespeare (1564–1616) is considered the greatest English playwright. Honore Balzac (1799–1850) was a French novelist. Alexandre Dumas the elder (1802–1870) was a popular African-French novelist and playwright who wrote *The Three Musketeers*. His son Alexandre Dumas the younger (1824–1895) was also a successful writer.

103 **Aristotle** (384–322 B.C.): a Greek philosopher who studied under Plato and taught Alexander the Great.

103 **Aurelius:** the 4th-century Roman author of a history of the Roman emperors.

103 **Pisgah:** a mountain ridge in ancient Moab (now the country of Jordan) from whose summit Moses viewed the Promised Land.

103 **Philistine and Amalekite:** Philistines and Amalekites were the oldest enemies of the Israelites during Biblical times. Here the words are metaphors for the forces standing against the education of black folk.

Chapter VII

104 **Hernando de Soto . . . Great Sea:** Hernando de Soto (1500?–1542) was a Spaniard who landed in Florida and explored what was to become the United States, getting all the way to the Mississippi River. He was looking for the Great Sea, or Pacific Ocean, but never reached it.

105 **Sam Hose:** an African-American farmer near Atlanta who killed a white man in an argument. A lynch mob of over 2000 white men, women, and children killed Hose, burned his body, then fought for pieces of his flesh for souvenirs.

105 **Oglethorpe:** James Edward Oglethorpe (1696–1785) was an English philanthropist and the founder of the state of Georgia.

105 **Whitefield:** George Whitefield (1714–1770) was an English evangelist who came to Georgia to do missionary work. He defended slavery and supported the landholders who wanted the removal of restrictions on importing slaves.

105 **Darien . . . took place:** In 1899, hundreds of black residents of McIntosh County, Georgia, gathered to prevent a lynching. They were later tried for insurrection.

105 **Moravians of Ebenezer:** members of a religious movement founded in Bohemia and Moravia in the 15th century. Moravians had established two settlements in Georgia—Ebenezer and New Ebenezer.

105 **Haytian Terror of Toussaint:** Under the leadership of Toussaint L'Ouverture, blacks in Haiti overthrew the slavery regime in 1793.

106 **statute of 1808:** In 1807 the U.S. Congress passed a law banning "the importation of slaves into the U.S. or the territories." It became effective January 1, 1808.

107 **panic of 1837 . . . Jackson . . . Van Buren:** The Panic of 1837 was a financial crisis in which state banks failed and many people lost their savings and businesses. The policies of President Andrew Jackson had led to the crisis but his successor, President Martin Van Buren, was blamed for it.

108 **Rhine-pfalz . . . Naples . . . Cracow:** the Rhine-pfalz is a state in Germany, west of the Rhine River. Naples is a city and port in Italy. Cracow (Krakow) is a major city in Poland.

115 *nouveau riche:* French for "the newly rich."

118 **Land of Canaan:** an ancient land in Palestine that is often used as a metaphor for a place of hope and promise.

Chapter VIII

127 **Chrysomallus . . . Fleece . . . Jason . . . Argonauts:** references to the Greek myth in which Jason and his sailors on the ship *Argo* (Argonauts) go in search of the Golden Fleece shorn from the ram Chrysomallus.

127 *parvenu:* a French term for a person who has suddenly risen to a higher social class and is not yet accepted by members of that class.

131 **ante-bellum:** existing before the Civil War.

Chapter IX

153 *tertium quid:* a Latin term meaning "a third party of uncertain status."

156 **Carlyle:** Thomas Carlyle (1795–1881) was a Scottish essayist and historian who attacked the

sham and corruption of modern society. One of his many publications was *Heroes and Hero Worship*, published in 1840.

164 **ipso facto:** a Latin term meaning "by the very nature of a thing."

173 **Phillis Wheatley . . . Sam Hose:** Wheatley was a famous African-American poet of the 18th century (see notes for Chapter III). Sam Hose was an African-American farmer lynched by a mob for killing a white man (see notes for Chapter VII).

Chapter X

176 **Delphi . . . Endor:** At Delphi, a city in ancient Greece, there was an oracle, or priestess, through whom the god Apollo was thought to communicate. The Witch of Endor, mentioned in the Old Testament, was a sorceress who could communicate with spirits.

177 **Gold Coast:** the ancient name of the area that is now Ghana, so called because the people there were gold traders.

182 **Maroons . . . Danish blacks:** The Maroons were Africans in Jamaica who escaped slavery and formed their own community. The Danish blacks mentioned staged a slave rebellion in 1733, in the Virgin Islands belonging to Denmark. (See notes for Chapter III.)

183 **"Uncle Tom":** the main character in the novel *Uncle Tom's Cabin* by Harriet Beecher Stowe. This book, published in 1852, was credited with influencing people to want to end slavery.

187 **Denmark Vesey and Nat Turner:** leaders of slave rebellions (see notes for Chapter III).

189 **Dum vivimus vivamus:** Latin for "while we live, let us live."

Chapter XII

197 **Wilberforce:** a university in Ohio named for William Wilberforce (1759-1833), a British philanthropist, antislavery activist, and member of the House of Commons.

198 **Missouri Compromise:** the law enacted in March 1820, prohibiting the holding of slaves north of the southern boundary of Missouri. This law was intended to maintain a balance of slave and non-slave states. Crummell was born in 1819.

198 **Manila and El Caney:** Manila, capital of the Philippines, and El Caney, a village in Cuba, were sites of victorious U.S. battles at the end of the Spanish-American war of 1898. Crummell died in 1898.

201 **John Jay** (1817–1894): a lawyer, diplomat and prominent white abolitionist. His father, William (1789–1858) also favored emancipating enslaved Africans.

204 **". . . bear the whips and scorns of time, . . .":** Du Bois quotes the famous soliloquy from Shakespeare's play *Hamlet,* in which Hamlet considers suicide.

Chapter XIII

215 **Lohengrin's swan:** a reference to the 1850 opera *Lohengrin,* by the German composer Richard Wagner, about a knight who appears in a boat drawn by a swan.

226 **"Song of the Bride":** The opera *Lohengrin* contains a famous wedding march, still played at weddings today. Du Bois quotes the first two lines.

Chapter XIV

227 **great temple . . . songs:** Jubilee Hall at Fisk University, built with funds raised by a student group who travelled worldwide singing spirituals.

228 **Port Royal experiment:** a program begun in Port Royal, South Carolina in 1863, in which newly freed people were educated by Northern white teachers and worked cotton plantations with the hope of owning the land.

228 **Thomas Wentworth Higginson** (1823–1911): a white clergyman and abolitionist who was colonel of the first black regiment to serve in the Civil War. The story of that regiment was dramatized in the movie *Glory*. Higginson discusses slave songs in his memoir, *Army Life in a Black Regiment*.

228 **Miss McKim:** Lucy McKim was a Northerner who went South as part of the Port Royal experiment (see note above). She collected slave songs in the Sea Islands of South Carolina.

229 **Henry Ward Beecher** (1813–1887): Beecher, a white abolitionist and the brother of Harriet Beecher Stowe, was pastor of a church in Brooklyn, New York.

237 **Teuton:** a Germanic person.

238 **Æschylus . . . Shakespeare:** Aeschylus (525–456 B.C.) was an ancient Greek playwright who specialized in tragedy. Shakespeare (1564–1616) is considered the greatest English playwright.

Related Readings

CONTENTS

Atlanta Exposition Address

by Booker T. Washington

In "Of Mr Booker T. Washington and Others," Du Bois criticizes the views of Washington, who was the founder of Tuskegee Institute and the most influential African-American leader at that time. The "Atlanta Compromise" refers to the position Washington took in the following speech, made at the Cotton States and International Exposition in Atlanta on September 18, 1895.

One third of the population of the South is of the Negro race. No enterprise seeking the material, civil, or moral welfare of this section can disregard this element of our population and reach the highest success. I but convey to you, Mr. President and Directors, the sentiment of the masses of my race when I say that in no way have the value and manhood of the American Negro been more fittingly and generously recognized than by the managers of this magnificent exposition at every stage of its progress. It is a recognition that will do more to cement the friendship of the two races than any occurrence since the dawn of our freedom.

Not only this, but the opportunity here afforded will awaken among us a new era of industrial progress. Ignorant and inexperienced, it is not strange that in the first years of our new life we began at the top instead of at the bottom; that a seat in Congress or the State Legislature was more sought than real estate or industrial skill; that the political convention or stump-speaking had more attraction than starting a dairy farm or truck garden.

A ship lost at sea for many days suddenly sighted a friendly vessel. From the mast of the unfortunate vessel was seen a signal: "Water, water; we die of thirst!" The answer from the friendly vessel at once came back: "Cast down your bucket where you are." A second time the signal, "Water, water; send us water!" ran up from the distressed vessel, and was answered: "Cast down your bucket where you are." And a third and fourth signal for water was answered, "Cast down your bucket where you are." The captain of the distressed vessel, at last heeding the injunction, cast down his bucket, and it came up full of fresh, sparkling water from the mouth of the Amazon River. To those of my race who depend upon bettering their condition in a foreign land, or who underestimate the importance of cultivating friendly relations with the Southern white man who is their next-door neighbor, I would say: "Cast down your bucket where you are"—cast it down in making friends, in every manly way, of the people of all races by whom we are surrounded.

Cast it down in agriculture, mechanics, in commerce, in domestic service, and in the professions. And in this connection it is well to bear in mind that whatever other sins the South may be called to bear, when it comes to business, pure and simple, it is in the South that the Negro is given a man's chance in the commercial world, and in nothing is this Exposition more eloquent than in emphasizing this chance. Our greatest danger is that in the great leap from slavery to freedom we may overlook the fact that the masses of us are to live by the productions of our hands, and fail to keep in mind that we shall prosper in proportion as we learn to dignify and glorify common labor, and put brains and skill into the common occupations of life; shall prosper in proportion as we learn to draw the line between the superficial and the substantial, the ornamental gew-gaws of life and the useful. No race can prosper till it learns that there is as much dignity in tilling a field as in writing a poem. It is at the bottom of life we must begin, and not at the top. Nor should we permit our grievances to overshadow our opportunities.

To those of the white race who look to the incoming of those of foreign birth and strange tongue and habits for the prosperity of the South, were I permitted, I would repeat what I say to my own race, "Cast down your bucket where you are." Cast it down among the eight million Negroes whose habits you know, whose fidelity and love you have tested in days when to have proved treacherous meant the ruin of your firesides. Cast down your bucket among these people who have without strikes and labor wars tilled your fields, cleared your forests, builded your railroads and cities, brought forth treasures from the bowels of the earth, and helped make possible this magnificent representation of the progress of the South. Casting down your bucket among my people, helping and encouraging them as you are doing on these grounds, and, with education of head, hand, and heart, you will find that they will buy your surplus land, make blossom the waste places in your fields, and run your factories. While doing this, you can be sure in the future, as in the past, that you and your families will be surrounded by the most patient, faithful, law-abiding, and unresentful people that the world has seen. As we have proved our loyalty to you in the past, in nursing your children, watching by the sick bed of your mothers and fathers, and often following them with tear-dimmed eyes to their graves, so in the future, in our humble way, we shall stand by you with a devotion that no foreigner can approach, ready to lay down our lives, if need be, in defense of yours, interlacing our industrial, commercial, civil, and religious life with yours in a way that shall make the interests of both races one. In all things that are purely social we can be as separate as the fingers, yet one as the hand in all things essential to mutual progress.

There is no defense or security for any of us except in the highest intelligence and development of all. If anywhere there are efforts tending to curtail the fullest growth of the Negro, let these efforts be turned into stimulating, encouraging, and making him the most useful and intelligent citizen. Effort or means so invested will pay a thousand per cent interest. These efforts will be twice blessed—"Blessing him that gives and him that takes."

There is no escape through law of man or God from the inevitable:

> The laws of changeless justice bind
> Oppressor with oppressed;
> And close as sin and suffering joined
> We march to fare abreast.

Nearly sixteen millions of hands will aid you in pulling the load upward, or they will pull, against you, the load downward. We shall constitute one third and more of the ignorance and crime of the South, or one third its intelligence and progress; we shall contribute one third to the business and industrial prosperity of the South, or we shall prove a veritable body of death, stagnating, depressing, retarding every effort to advance the body politic.

Gentlemen of the Exposition, as we present to you our humble effort at an exhibition of our progress, you must not expect overmuch. Starting thirty years ago with ownership here and there in a few quilts and pumpkins and chickens (gathered from miscellaneous sources), remember, the path that has led from these to the inventions and production of agricultural implements, buggies, steam engines, newspapers, books, statuary carving, paintings, the management of drugstores and banks, has not been trodden without contact with thorns and thistles. While we take pride in what we exhibit as a result of our independent efforts, we do not for a moment forget that our part in this exhibition would fall far short of your expectations but for the constant help that has come to our educational life, not only from the Southern states, but especially from Northern philanthropists, who have made their gifts a constant stream of blessing and encouragement.

The wisest among my race understand that the agitation of questions of social equality is the extremest folly, and that progress in the enjoyment of all the privileges that will come to us must be the result of severe and constant struggle rather than of artificial forcing. No race that has anything to contribute to the markets of the world is long, in any degree, ostracized. It is important and right that all privileges of the law be ours, but it is vastly more important that we be prepared for the exercise of those privileges. The opportunity to earn a dollar in a factory just now is worth infinitely more than the opportunity to spend a dollar in an opera house.

In conclusion, may I repeat that nothing in thirty years has given us more hope and encouragement, and drawn us so near to you of the white race, as this opportunity offered by the Exposition; and here bending, as it were, over the altar that represents the results of the struggles of your race and mine, both starting practically empty-handed three decades ago, I pledge that, in your effort to work out the great and intricate problem which God has laid at the doors of the South, you shall have at all times the patient, sympathetic help of my race; only let this be constantly in mind, that while, from representations in these buildings of the product of field, of forest, of mine, of factory, letters, and art, much good will come, yet far above and beyond material benefits will be that higher good, that, let us pray God, will come in a blotting out of sectional differences and racial animosities and suspicions, in a determination to administer absolute justice, in a willing obedience among all classes to the mandates of law. This, coupled with our material prosperity, will bring into our beloved South a new heaven and a new earth.

Booker T. and W. E. B.

by Dudley Randall

Dudley Randall, a Detroit poet who founded Broadside Press, imagines a rhyming debate between Booker T. Washington and W. E. B. Du Bois.

"It seems to me," said Booker T.,
"It shows a mighty lot of cheek
To study chemistry and Greek
When Mister Charlie needs a hand
5   To hoe the cotton on his land,
And when Miss Ann looks for a cook,
Why stick your nose inside a book?"

"I don't agree," said W.E.B.,
"If I should have the drive to seek
10   Knowledge of chemistry or Greek,
I'll do it. Charles and Miss can look
Another place for hand or cook.
Some men rejoice in skill of hand,
And some in cultivating land,
15   But there are others who maintain
The right to cultivate the brain."

"It seems to me," said Booker T.,
"That all you folks have missed the boat
Who shout about the right to vote,

20 And spend vain days and sleepless nights
In uproar over civil rights.
Just keep your mouths shut, do not grouse,
But work, and save, and buy a house."

"I don't agree," said W.E.B.,
25 "For what can property avail
If dignity and justice fail.
Unless you help to make the laws,
They'll steal your house with trumped-up
     clause.
A rope's as tight, a fire as hot,
30 No matter how much cash you've got.
Speak soft, and try your little plan,
But as for me, I'll be a man."

"It seems to me," said Booker T.—

"I don't agree,"
30 Said W.E.B.

Address to the Fourth International Convention of the Negro Peoples of the World

by Marcus Garvey

In "Of Mr. Booker T. Washington and Others," Du Bois speaks of that class of African Americans who "distrust the white race generally, and . . . think that the Negro's only hope lies in emigration beyond the borders of the United States." An independent black nation in Africa was one of the goals of Marcus Garvey's Universal Negro Improvement Association, which claimed 2 million members from the United States, the Caribbean and Africa. Garvey called for "a country of our own" in this speech at New York's Carnegie Hall on August 1, 1924.

Delegates to the Fourth International Convention of the Negro Peoples of the World, Ladies and Gentlemen:

The pleasure of addressing you at this hour is great.

You have re-assembled yourselves in New York, coming from all parts of the world to this Annual Convention, because you believe that by unity you can alleviate the unfortunate condition in which racially we find ourselves.

We are glad to meet as Negroes, notwithstanding the stigma that is placed upon us by a soulless and conscienceless world because of our backwardness.

As usual, I am not here to flatter you, I am not here to tell you how happy and prosperous we are as a people, because that is all false. The Negro is not happy, but, to the contrary, is extremely miserable. He is miserable because the world is closing fast around him, and if he does not strike out now for his own preservation, it is only a question of a few more decades when he will be completely out-done in a world of strenuous competition for a place among the fittest of God's creation.

Negro Dying Out

The Negro is dying out, and he is going to die faster and more rapidly in the next fifty years than he has in the past three hundred years. There is only one thing to save the Negro, and that is an immediate realization of his own responsibilities. Unfortunately we are the most careless and indifferent people in the world! We are shiftless and irresponsible, and that is why we find ourselves the wards of an inherited materialism that has lost its soul and its conscience. It is strange to hear a Negro leader speak in this strain, as the usual course is flattery, but I would not flatter you to save my own life and that of my own family. There is no value in flattery. Flattery of the Negro for another quarter of a century will mean hell and damnation to the race. How can any Negro leader flatter us about progress and the rest of it, when the world is preparing more than ever to bury the entire race? Must I flatter you when England, France, Italy, Belgium and Spain are all concentrating on robbing every square inch of African territory—the land of our fathers? Must I flatter you when the cry is being loudly raised for a white America, Canada, Australia and Europe, and a yellow and brown Asia? Must I flatter you when I find all other peoples preparing themselves for the struggle to survive, and you still smiling, eating, dancing, drinking and sleeping away your time, as if yesterday were the beginning of the age of pleasure? I would rather be dead than be a member of your race without thought of the morrow, for it portends evil to him that thinketh not. Because I cannot flatter you I am here to tell, emphatically, that if we do not seriously reorganize ourselves as a people and face the world with a program of African nationalism our days in civilization are numbered, and it will be only a question of time when the Negro will be as completely and complacently dead as the North American Indian, or the Australian Bushman.

Progress on Sand

You talk about the progress we have made in America and elsewhere, among the people of our acquaintance, but what progress is it? A progress that can be snatched away from you in forty-eight hours, because it has been built upon sand.

You must thank God for the last two generations of whites in our western civilization; thank God that they were not made of sterner stuff, and character and a disposition to see all races their rivals and competitors in the struggle to hold and possess the world, otherwise, like the Indian, we would have been nearly all dead.

The progress of the Negro in our civilization was tolerated because of indifference, but that indifference exists no longer. Our whole civilization is becoming intolerant, and because of that the whole world of races has started to think.

Can you blame the white man for thinking, when red and yellow men are knocking at his door? Can you blame the tiger for being on the defensive when the lion approaches? And thus we find that generations ago, when the Negro was not given a thought as a world competitor he is now regarded as an encumbrance in a civilization to which he has materially contributed little. Men do not build for others, they build for themselves. The age and our religion demand it. What are you going to expect, that white men are going to build up America and elsewhere and hand it over to us? If we are expecting that we are crazy, we have lost our reason.

If you were white, you would see the rest in hell before you would deprive your children of bread to give it to others. You would give that which you did not want, but not that which is to be the sustenance of your family, and so the world thinks; yet a Du Bois and the National Association for the Advancement of Colored People will tell us by flattery that the day is coming when a white President of the United States of America will get out of the White House and give the position to a Negro, that the day is coming when a Mr. Hughes will desert the Secretaryship of State and give it to the Negro, James Weldon Johnson; that the time is just around the corner of constitutional rights when the next Ambassador to the Court of Saint James will be a black man from Mississippi or from North Carolina. Do you think that white men who have suffered, bled and died to make America and the world what it is, are going to hand over to a parcel of lazy Negroes the things that they prize most?

Stop flattering yourselves, fellowmen, and let us go to work. Do you hear me? Go to work! Go to work in the morn of a new creation and strike, not because of the noonday sun, but plod on and on, until you have succeeded in climbing the hills of opposition and reached the height of self-progress, and from that pinnacle bestow upon the world a civilization of your own, and hand down to your children and posterity of your own a worthy contribution to the age of human materialism.

We of the Universal Negro Improvement Association are fair and just. We do not expect the white man to rob himself, and to deprive himself, for our racial benefit. How could you reasonably expect that, in an age like this, when men have divided themselves into racial and national groups, when the one group has its own interest to protect as against that of the other?

The laws of self-preservation force every human group to look after itself and protect its own interest; hence so long as the American white man or any other white man, for that matter, realizes his responsibility, he is bound to struggle to protect that which is his and his own, and I feel that the Negro today who has been led by the unscrupulous of our race has been grossly misguided, in the direction of expecting too much from the civilization of others.

The Carpet-Bagger

Immediately after emancipation, we were improperly led in the South by this same group and ultimately lost our vote and voice. The carpet-bagger and the thoughtless, selfish Negro politician and leader sold the race back into slavery. And the same attempt is now being made in the North by that original group, prompted by the dishonest white political boss and the unscrupulous Negro politician. The time has come for both races to seriously adjust their differences and settle the future of our respective peoples. The selfish of both races will not stop to think and act, but the responsibility becomes more so ours, who have the vision of the future.

Criminals Out of Jail

Because of my attempt to lead my race into the only solution that I see would benefit both groups, I have been maliciously and wickedly maligned, and by members of our own race. I have been plotted against, framed up, indicated and convicted, the story which you so well know. That was responsible for our not having a Convention last year. I thank you, however, for the tribute you paid me during that period in postponing the Convention through respect to my enforced absence. Last August I spent three months in the Tombs in New York, but I was as happy then as I am now. I was sent there by the evil forces that have always fought and opposed reform movements, but I am as ready now to go back to the Tombs or elsewhere as I was when I was forced to leave you. The jail does not make a criminal, the criminal makes himself. There are more criminals out of jail than in jail, the only difference is that the majority of those who are out, are such skillful criminals that they know how to keep themselves out. They have tried to besmirch my name so as to prevent me doing the good that I desire to do in the interest of the race. It amuses me sometimes to hear the biggest crooks in the Negro Race referring to me as a criminal. As I have said before, Negro race leaders are the biggest crooks in the world. It is because of their crookedness that we have not made more progress. If you think I am not telling the truth in this direction you may quiz any of the white political bosses, and those who will tell the truth will reveal a tale most shocking as far as our Negro leaders are concerned. This is true of the group of fellows of our race that lead universally as well as nationally. They will sell the souls of their mothers and their country into perdition. That is why the Universal Negro Improvement Association has to make such a fight, and that is why the opposition is as hard and marked. You can pay the Negro leader to hang his race and block every effort of self-help. This is not commonly so among other races. We must give credit to the great white race, to the extent that they will fight among themselves, that they will cheat each other in business, but when it approaches the future and destiny of the race, a halt is immediately called. Not so with the Negro, he does not know when and where to stop in hurting himself.

Reorganizing the Race

I repeat that we must reorganize ourselves as a people, if we are to go forward, and I take this opportunity, as you assemble yourselves here from all parts of the world, to sound the warning note.

To review the work of our Association for the past two years is to recount the exploits of a continuous struggle to reach the top. Our organization has been tested during the past two years beyond that of any other period in the history of Negro movements. I am glad to say, however, that we have survived all the intrigues, barriers, and handicaps placed in the way. Some of our enemies thought that they would have been able to crush our movement when I was convicted and sentenced to prison. They had depended upon that, as the trump card in their effort to crush the new spirit of freedom among Negroes, but like all such efforts, it was doomed to failure. I will bring to your recollection a similar effort made a little over nineteen hundred years ago when on Calvary's Mount, the Jews after inspiring the Romans, attempted to crucify the man, Christ, the leader of the Christian religion. They thought that after the crucifixion, after he was buried, that they would have silenced the principles of Christianity forever, but how successful they were, is made manifest today when we find hundreds of millions of souls the world over professing the principles for which the man died on Calvary's cross. As in the rise of Christianity, so do we have the spiritual rise of the Universal Negro Improvement Association throughout the world. They tried to crucify it in America, and it has arisen in Africa a thousand fold. They tried to crucify it on the American continent, and it is now sweeping the whole world. You cannot crucify a principle; you cannot nail the souls of men to a cross; you cannot imprison it; you cannot bury it. It will rise like the spirit of the Great Redeemer and take its flight down the ages, until men far and near have taken up the cry for which the principle was crucified.

We of the Universal Negro Improvement Association are stronger today than we ever were before. We are strong in spirit, strong in determination; we are unbroken in every direction; we stand firm facing the world, determined to carve out and find a place for the four hundred millions of our suffering people. We call upon humanity everywhere to listen to the cry of the new Negro. We ask the human heart for a response, because Africa's sun cannot be downed. Africa's sun is rising, gradually rising, and soon shall take its place among the brilliant constellations of nations. The Negro wants a nation, nothing less, nothing more; and why shouldn't we be nationally free, nationally independent, nationally unfettered? We want a nationality similar to that of the English, the French, the Italian, the German, to that of the white American, to that of the yellow Japanese; we want nationality and government because we realize that the American nation in a short while will not be large enough to accommodate two competitive rivals, one black and the other white.

Black Man's Aspirations

There is no doubt about it that the black man of America today aspires to the White House, to the Cabinet, and to the Senate, and the House. He aspires to be head of State and municipal governments. What are you going to do with him? He cannot be satisfied in the midst of a majority group that seeks to protect its interest at all hazards; then the only alternative is to give the Negro a place of his own. That is why we appeal to the sober white minds of America, and not the selfish ones. The selfish ones will see nothing more than the immediate present, but the deep thinking white man will see the result of another fifty or one hundred years, when these two peoples will be brought together in closer contact of rivalry. As races we practically represent a similar intelligence today. We have graduated from the same schools, colleges and universities. What can you do with men who are equally and competently fitted in mind, but give them an equal chance, and if there is no chance of equality, there must be dissatisfaction on the one hand. That dissatisfaction we have in our midst now. We have it manifested by W. E. B. Du Bois, by James Weldon Johnson; we have it manifested by the organization known as the National Association for the Advancement of Colored People, that seeks to bring about social equality, political equality, and industrial equality, things that are guaranteed us under the Constitution, but which, in the face of a majority race, we cannot demand, because of the terrible odds against us. In the midst of this, then, what can we do but seek an outlet of our own unless, we intend to fight a losing game. Reason will dictate that there is no benefit to be derived from fighting always a losing game. We will lose until we have completely lost our stand in America.

The Period of Self-Protection

To repeat myself, we talk about progress. What progress have we made when everything we do is done through the good will and grace of the liberal white man of the present day? But can he always afford to be liberal? Do you not realize that in another few decades he will have on his hands a problem of his own—a problem to feed his own children, to take care of his own flesh and blood? In the midst of that crisis, when he finds not even enough to feed himself, what will become of the Negro? The Negro naturally must die to give way, and make room for others who are better prepared to live. That is the danger, men; and that is why we have the Universal Negro Improvement Association. The condition that I have referred to will not only be true of America and of continental Europe; it will be true wherever the great white race lives. There will not be room enough for them, and others who seek to compete with them. That is why we hear the cry of Egypt for the Egyptians, India for the Indians, Asia for the Asiatics, and we raise the cry of Africa for the Africans; those at home and those abroad. That is why we ask England to be fair, to be just and considerate; that is why we ask France, Italy, Spain and Belgium to be fair, just and considerate; that is why we ask them to let the black man restore himself to his own country; and that is why we are determined to see it done. No camouflage, and no promise of good-will, will solve the problem. What guarantee have we, what lease have we on the future that the man who treats us kindly today will perpetuate it through his son or his grandson tomorrow?

Races and peoples are only safeguarded when they are strong enough to protect themselves, and that is why we appeal to the four hundred million Negroes of the world to come together for self-protection and self-preservation. We do not want what belongs to the great white race, or the yellow race. We want only those things that belong to the black race. Africa is ours. To win Africa we will give up America, we will give up our claim in all other parts of the world; but we must have Africa. We will give up the vain desire of having a seat in the White House in America, of having a seat in the House of Lords in England, of being President of France, for the chance and opportunity of filling these positions in a country of our own.

That is how the Universal Negro Improvement Association differs from other organizations. Other organizations, especially in America, are fighting for a political equality which they will never get, and never win, in the face of a majority opposition. We win so much today and lose so much tomorrow. We will lose our political strength in the North in another few years, as we lost it in the South during Reconstruction. We fill one position today, but lose two tomorrow, and so we will drift on and on, until we have been completely obliterated from western civilization.

Changes Among Negroes

You may ask me what good has the Universal Negro Improvement Association done, what has it accomplished within the last six years? We will point to you the great changes that have taken place in Africa, the West Indies and America. In the West Indies, black men have been elevated to high positions by the British Government, so as to off-set and counteract the sweeping influence of the Universal Negro Improvement Association. Several of the Colonies have been given larger constitutional rights. In Africa, the entire West Coast has been benefited. Self-government has been given to several of the African Colonies, and native Africans have been elevated to higher positions, so as to offset the sweeping spirit of the Universal Negro Improvement Association throughout the Continent of Africa. In America, several of our men have been given prominent positions; Negro commissions have been appointed to attend to affairs of state; Negro Consuls have also been appointed. Things that happened in America within the last six years to advance the political status, the social and industrial status of the Negro were never experienced before. All that is traceable to the Universal Negro Improvement Association within the last six years. In the great game of politics you do not see the immediate results at your door, but those who are observant will be able to trace the good that is being done from the many directions whence it comes. If you were to take a survey of the whole world of Negroes you will find that we are more highly thought of in 1922 than we were in 1914. England, France and the European and Colonial powers regard the Universal Negro Improvement Association with a certain amount of suspicion because they believe that we are antagonistic. But we are not. We are not antagonistic to France, to England or Italy, nor any of the white Powers in Europe. We are only demanding a square deal for our race. Did we not fight to help them? Did we not sacrifice our blood, give up our all, to save England, to save France, Italy and America during the last war? Then why shouldn't we expect some consideration for the service rendered? That is all we ask; and we are now pressing that claim to the throne of white justice. We are told that God's throne is white, although we believe it to be black. But if it is white, we are placing our plea before that throne of God, asking Him to so touch the hearts of our fellow-men as to let them yield to us the things that are ours, as it was right to yield to Caesar the things that were Caesar's.

As we deliberate on the many problems confronting us during the month of August, let us not lose control of ourselves; let us not forget that we are the guardians of four hundred millions; let us not forget that it is our duty to so act and legislate as to help humanity everywhere, whether it be black or white. We shall be called upon during this month to take up certain matters that are grave, but dispassionately we shall discuss them; and whenever the interest of the different race groups clash, let it be our duty to take the other fellow's feelings into our consideration. If we must be justly treated, then we ourselves must treat all men similarly. So, let no prejudice cause us to say or do anything against the interest of the white man, or the yellow man; let us realize that the white man has the right to live, the yellow man has the right to live, and all that we desire to do is to impress them with the fact that we also have the right to live.

from Coming of Age in Mississippi

by Anne Moody

If Du Bois was one of the fathers of the civil rights movement, Anne Moody was one of its daughters. She became involved in the movement as a college student, participating in sit-ins and working for voting rights and literacy projects. Following is an excerpt from her autobiography. Anne (called Essie by her family) recalls how she was affected by the 1955 lynching of Emmett Till, a Chicago boy who was her own age— fourteen.

Not only did I enter high school with a new name, but also with a completely new insight into the life of Negroes in Mississippi. I was now working for one of the meanest white women in town, and a week before school started Emmett Till was killed.

Up until his death, I had heard of Negroes found floating in a river or dead somewhere with their bodies riddled with bullets. But I didn't know the mystery behind these killings then. I remember once when I was only seven I heard Mama and one of my aunts talking about some Negro who had been beaten to death. "Just like them low-down skunks killed him they will do the same to us," Mama had said. When I asked her who killed the man and why, she said, "An Evil Spirit killed him. You gotta be a good girl or it will kill you too." So since I was seven, I had lived in fear of that "Evil Spirit." It took me eight years to learn what that spirit was.

I was coming from school the evening I heard about Emmett Till's death. There was a whole group of us, girls and boys, walking down the road headed home. A group of about six high school boys were walking a few paces ahead of me and several other girls. We were laughing and talking about something that had happened in school that day. However, the six boys in front of us weren't talking very loud. Usually they kept up so much noise. But today they were just walking and talking among themselves. All of a sudden they began to shout at each other. . . .

"That boy wasn't but fourteen years old and they killed him. Now what kin a fourteen-year-old boy do with a white woman? What if he did whistle at her, he might have thought [she] was pretty." . . .

What they were saying shocked me. . . . We walked on behind them for a while listening. Questions about who was killed, where, and why started running through my mind. I walked up to one of the boys.

"Eddie, what boy was killed?"

"Moody, where've you been?" he asked me. "Everybody talking about that fourteen-year-old boy who was killed in Greenwood by some white men. You don't know nothing that's going on besides what's in them books of yours, huh?"

Standing there before the rest of the girls, I felt so stupid. It was then that I realized I really didn't know what was going on all around me. It wasn't that I was dumb. It was just that ever since I was nine, I'd had to work after school and do my lessons on lunch hour. I never had time to learn anything, to hang around with people my own age. And you never were told anything by adults.

That evening when I stopped off at the house on my way to Mrs. Burke's, Mama was singing. Any other day she would have been yelling at Adline and Junior them to take off their school clothes. I wondered if she knew about Emmet Till. The way she was singing she had something on her mind and it wasn't pleasant either.

I got a shoe, you got a shoe,
All of God's chillun got shoes;
When I get to hebben, I'm gonna put on my shoes,
And gonna tromp all over God's hebben.
When I get to hebben I'm gonna put on my shoes,
And gonna walk all over God's hebben.

Mama was dishing up beans like she didn't know anyone was home. Adline, Junior, and James had just thrown their books down and sat themselves at the table. I didn't usually eat before I went to work. But I wanted to ask Mama about Emmett Till. So I ate and thought of some way of asking her.

"These beans are some good, Mama," I said, trying to sense her mood.

"Why is you eating anyway? You gonna be late for work. You know how Miss Burke is," she said to me.

"I don't have much to do this evening. I kin get it done before I leave work," I said.

The conversation stopped after that. Then Mama started humming that song again.

When I get to hebben, I'm gonna put on my shoes,
And gonna tromp all over God's hebben.

She put a plate on the floor for Jennie Ann and Jerry.

"Jennie Ann! you and Jerry sit down here and eat and don't put beans all over this floor."

Ralph, the baby, started crying, and she went in the bedroom to give him his bottle. I got up and followed her.

"Mama, did you hear about that fourteen-year-old Negro boy who was killed a little over a week ago by some white men?" I asked her.

"Where did you hear that?" she said angrily.

"Boy, everybody really thinks I am dumb or deaf or something. I heard Eddie them talking about it this evening coming from school."

"Eddie them better watch how they go around here talking. These white folks git a hold of it they gonna be in trouble," she said.

"What are they gonna be in trouble about, Mama? People got a right to talk, ain't they?"

"You go on to work before you is late. And don't you let on like you know nothing about that boy being killed before Miss Burke them. Just do your work like you don't know nothing," she said. "That boy's a lot better off in heaven than he is here," she continued and then started singing again.

On my way to Mrs. Burke's that evening, Mama's words kept running through my mind. "Just do your work like you don't know nothing." "Why is Mama acting so scared?" I thought. "And what if Mrs. Burke knew we knew? Why must I pretend I don't know? Why are these people killing Negroes? What did Emmett Till do besides whistle at that woman?"

By the time I got to work, I had worked my nerves up some. I was shaking as I walked up on the porch. "Do your work like you don't know nothing." But once I got inside, I couldn't have acted normal if Mrs. Burke were paying me to be myself.

I was so nervous, I spent most of the evening avoiding them going about the house dusting and sweeping. Everything went along fairly well until dinner was served.

"Don, Wayne, and Mama, y'all come on to dinner. Essie, you can wash up the pots and dishes in the sink now. Then after dinner you won't have as many," Mrs. Burke called to me.

If I had the power to mysteriously disappear at that moment, I would have. They used the breakfast table in the kitchen for most of their meals. The dining room was only used for Sunday dinner or when they had company. I wished they had company tonight so they could eat in the dining room while I was at the kitchen sink.

"I forgot the bread," Mrs. Burke said when they were all seated. "Essie, will you cut it and put it on the table for me?"

I took the cornbread, cut it in squares, and put it on a small round dish. Just as I was about to set it on the table, Wayne yelled at the cat. I dropped the plate and the bread went all over the floor.

"Never mind, Essie," Mrs. Burke said angrily as she got up and got some white bread from the breadbox.

I didn't say anything. I picked up the cornbread from around the table and went back to the dishes. As soon as I got to the sink, I dropped a saucer on the floor and broke it. Didn't anyone say a word until I had picked up the pieces.

"Essie, I bought some new cleanser today. It's setting on the bathroom shelf. See if it will remove the stains in the tub," Mrs. Burke said.

I went to the bathroom to clean the tub. By the time I got through with it, it was snow white. I spent a whole hour scrubbing it. I had removed the stains in no time but I kept scrubbing until they finished dinner.

from *Coming of Age in Mississippi*   289

When they had finished and gone into the living room as usual to watch TV, Mrs. Burke called me to eat. I took a clean plate out of the cabinet and sat down. Just as I was putting the first forkful of food in my mouth, Mrs. Burke entered the kitchen.

"Essie, did you hear about that fourteen-year-old boy who was killed in Greenwood?" she asked me, sitting down in one of the chairs opposite me.

"No, I didn't hear that," I answered, almost choking on the food.

"Do you know why he was killed?" she asked, and I didn't answer.

"He was killed because he got out of his place with a white woman. A boy from Mississippi would have known better than that. This boy was from Chicago. Negroes up North have no respect for people. They think they can get away with anything. He just came to Mississippi and put a whole lot of notions in the boys' heads here and stirred up a lot of trouble," she said passionately.

"How old are you, Essie?" she asked me after a pause.

"Fourteen. I will soon be fifteen though," I said.

"See, that boy was just fourteen too. It's a shame he had to die so soon." She was so red in the face, she looked as if she was on fire.

When she left the kitchen I sat there with my mouth open and my food untouched. I couldn't have eaten now if I were starving. "Just do your work like you don't know nothing" ran through my mind again and I began washing the dishes.

I went home shaking like a leaf on a tree. For the first time out of all her trying, Mrs. Burke had made me feel like rotten garbage. Many times she had tried to instill fear within me and subdue me and had given up. But when she talked about Emmett Till there was something in her voice that sent chills and fear all over me.

Before Emmett Till's murder, I had known the fear of hunger, hell, and the Devil. But now there was a new fear known to me—the fear of being killed just because I was black. This was the worst of my fears. I knew once I got food, the fear of starving to death would leave. I also was told that if I were a good girl, I wouldn't have to fear the Devil or hell. But I didn't know what one had to do or not do as a Negro not to be killed. Probably just being a Negro period was enough, I thought.

A few days later, I went to work and Mrs. Burke had about eight women over for tea. They were all sitting around in the living room when I got there. She told me she was having a "guild meeting," and asked me to help her serve the cookies and tea.

After helping her, I started cleaning the house. I always swept the hallway and porch first. As I was sweeping the hall, I could hear them talking. When I heard the word "nigger," I stopped sweeping and listened. Mrs. Burke must have sensed this, because she suddenly came to the door.

"Essie, finish the hall and clean the bathroom," she said hesitantly. "Then you can go for today. I am not making dinner tonight." Then she went back in the living room with the rest of the ladies.

Before she interrupted my listening, I had picked up the words "NAACP" and "that organization." Because they were talking about niggers, I knew NAACP had something to do with Negroes. All that night I kept wondering what could that NAACP mean?

Later when I was sitting in the kitchen at home doing my lessons, I decided to ask Mama. It was about twelve-thirty. Everyone was in bed but me. When Mama came in to put some milk in Ralph's bottle, I said, "Mama, what do NAACP mean?"

"Where did you git that from?" she asked me, spilling milk all over the floor.

"Mrs. Burke had a meeting tonight—"

"What kind of meeting?" she asked, cutting me off.

"I don't know. She had some women over—she said it was a guild meeting," I said.

"A guild meeting," she repeated.

"Yes, they were talking about Negroes and I heard some woman say 'that NAACP' and another 'that organization,' meaning the same thing."

"What else did they say?" she asked me.

"That's all I heard. Mrs. Burke must have thought I was listening, so she told me to clean the bathroom and leave."

"Don't you ever mention that word around Mrs. Burke or no other white person, you heah! Finish your lesson and cut that light out and go to bed," Mama said angrily and left the kitchen.

"With a Mama like that you'll never learn anything," I thought as I got into bed. All night long I thought about Emmett Till and the NAACP. I even got up to look up NAACP in my little concise dictionary. But I didn't find it.

The next day at school, I decided to ask my homeroom teacher Mrs. Rice the meaning of NAACP. When the bell sounded for lunch, I remained in my seat as the other students left the room.

"Are you going to spend your lunch hour studying again today, Moody?" Mrs. Rice asked me.

"Can I ask you a question, Mrs. Rice?" I asked her.

"You *may* ask me a question, yes, but I don't know if you *can* or not," she said.

"What does the word NAACP mean?" I asked.

"Why do you want to know?"

"The lady I worked for had a meeting and I overheard the word mentioned."

"What else did you hear?"

"Nothing. I didn't know what NAACP meant, that's all." I felt like I was on the witness stand or something.

"Well, next time your boss has another meeting you listen more carefully. NAACP is a Negro organization that was established a long time ago to help Negroes gain a few basic rights," she said.

"What's it gotta do with the Emmett Till murder?" I asked.

"They are trying to get a conviction in Emmett Till's case. You see the NAACP is trying to do a lot for the Negroes and get the right to vote for Negroes in the South. I shouldn't be telling you all this. And don't you dare breathe a word of what I said. It could cost me my job if word got out I was teaching my students such. I gotta go to lunch and you should go outside too because it's nice and sunny out today," she said leaving the room. "We'll talk more when I have time."

About a week later, Mrs. Rice had me over for Sunday dinner, and I spent about five hours with her. Within that time, I digested a good meal and accumulated a whole new pool of knowledge about Negroes being butchered and slaughtered by whites in the South. After Mrs. Rice had told me all this, I felt like the lowest animal on earth. At least when other animals (hogs, cows, etc.) were killed by man, they were used as food. But when man was butchered or killed by man, in the case of Negroes by whites, they were left lying on a road or found floating in a river or something.

Mrs. Rice got to be something like a mother to me. She told me anything I wanted to know. And made me promise that I would keep all this information she was passing on to me to myself. She said she couldn't, rather didn't, want to talk about these things to the other teachers, that they would tell Mr. Willis and she would be fired. At the end of that year she was fired. I never found out why. I haven't seen her since then.

from Warriors Don't Cry

by Melba Patillo Beals

When Melba Patillo was 16, she was one of the "Little Rock Nine" chosen to integrate Central High School in Little Rock, Arkansas in 1957. Claiming that he wanted to "prevent violence," Governor Orval Faubus called out the Arkansas National Guard, who blocked the students from entering the school. At the students' backs was an angry white mob, so the students had to flee. Three weeks later, there was a court hearing to determine whether the federal government could order the state governor to stop interfering with integration. Eventually, President Eisenhower brought in 1200 U.S. Army paratroopers to escort the students to school.

FAUBUS, U.S. GOVERNMENT HEAD INTO CRUCIAL
COLLISION IN FEDERAL COURT TODAY
—*Arkansas Gazette,* Friday, September 20, 1957

The first clash between the federal government and a state over school integration will reach a crucial stage at 10 a.m. today in Federal District Court at Little Rock. The immediate issue will be whether Governor Faubus and the Arkansas National Guard should be enjoined from further interference with integration at Little Rock Central High School.

The overriding historic issue will be whether the federal government has the constitutional authority to check a state governor when he uses the powers of his office to defy the federal court.

Sitting alone in my room, I couldn't stop thinking how Governor Faubus would for certain have to be in that courtroom. I couldn't imagine that he wouldn't be there. In my diary I wrote:

> *This is the day I hope to meet Governor Faubus face to face. I can't decide what to say to him. If only he will listen to me one minute, I know I can make him understand there is nothing so bad about me that he shouldn't allow white children to go to school with me.*
>
> *The weatherman says it's going to be 85 and up this afternoon. I'll regret wearing my cotton blouse and quilted skirt, but they're new and pretty. I want to look just right so the governor will know who I really am.*

The nine of us walked up the sidewalk toward the Federal Building at a brisk pace. Our group included Mrs. Bates, attorneys Thurgood Marshall and Wiley Branton, and a number of people I did not know. I was told they were community ministers and lawyers, coming along to protect us. Between awkward scraps of conversation, I could hear our footsteps on the sidewalk as we moved toward the official-looking building. I had never paid much attention to it before.

It was a muggy day, rather like the inside of a steam room. As we grew closer to our destination, there were more people and more chatter, but my mind was flooded with important things I wanted to say to the governor. One voice inside me said he didn't care what I thought, but the other said I should be prepared just in case.

I was a bit on edge. A small part of me was becoming accustomed to the fact that since the integration had begun, both my people and whites stared at me. Some of the faces lining the streets on that morning had welcome smiles, others were indifferent, while still others were undeniably angry. I wore dark glasses, which allowed me to peer out wherever I wanted without anybody being able to see how fearful I was.

I had never been in court before. I'd only seen pictures of judges. I felt frightened—frightened of the Federal Court, but mostly frightened of all those powerful government men, the governor's lawyers, who could make things happen just as they wanted.

I had read in the newspaper that attorneys for the federal government would be arguing that there was no evidence of the kind of violence that made it necessary to call out troops. Since the governor claimed our going to Central was what caused the trouble, we nine students were subpoenaed to tell what we had seen and experienced on that first day at Central High School. I was afraid of what would happen if we lost. Would that mean we could be sued or arrested? Would the news reporters make fun of us? What would my friends say?

"We're going to have to take the kids in through the side door," a man's voice said. My pace quickened as we were ushered past all the people milling about, through a very narrow, dimly lit marble hall, where our voices and footsteps echoed. We were led to the elevator, walking fast as if we were being chased. The door slid shut, and I stared straight ahead. My knees were trembling, and every inch of my body was perspiring. That elevator was so full that I could hear its guts grinding as it struggled to deliver us to the fourth-floor courtroom.

I hoped the opening elevator doors would admit fresh air. Instead, they revealed a crush of people, jammed body-to-body, shoving each other, desperately trying to get through that narrow hallway to go somewhere or do something. I was blinded by the glaring lights held high over the heads of the sea of people by news photographers trying to get pictures. We could hardly get out of the elevator and into the throng. Like sardines we wiggled and pushed, trying to forge a pathway. I stopped thinking about fresh, cool air, I just wanted to breathe and not be crushed. As we emerged, several reporters started shouting questions at us. I felt as though I were attending one of those Hollywood openings I'd seen on TV.

"What do you think of Governor Faubus?"

"How do you think the white students will treat you if you go back to Central?"

"Why do you want to go to the white school?"

"Are your parents buying knives and guns?"

"No," I shouted. "Nobody's buying weapons."

Mrs. Bates touched my shoulder. "Shhhhhhhhh!" she said. We had been cautioned not to talk back to reporters on this day. We were to say nothing until after the NAACP attorneys had made our case.

Flashing cameras and blinding lights followed as we inched our way through the corridor. The questions continued—rapid-fire, close in our faces. Perspiration trickled down the back of my neck. I could see beads of water on the noses and foreheads of many people crowded around me.

"Smile, kids," Mrs. Bates whispered. "Straighten your shoulders. Stand tall."

It felt as though there were about a hundred people in that hallway, where only half that many should have been squeezed in. Cameramen were perched on chairs and even on each other to get pictures. They must have been real anxious to be there because they were undoubtedly suffering in the sweltering heat and risking bodily injury as well.

"Melba, we're inside now. Take off those dark glasses. Please." I was embarrassed to be singled out that way by Mrs. Bates. The glare of the light hurt my eyes, and I didn't really want to look into the faces of all those people who seemed to be staring at me.

"Some of you'all think we're stars, but really, all these reporters are here to see if we're gonna get killed or not," teased one of the comics from our group.

Step by step, with enormous effort, we managed to get through the crush of human bodies. The courtroom was smaller than I'd imagined, about the size of an average living room, with wooden benches lining either side of a narrow aisle. I had heard someone say the courtroom only held 150 people. It was filled to overflowing. I was glad to see that a good number of the spectators were our people. Sections of the room were roped off. We were squeezed through the crowd and ushered to one of the areas in front, near the bailiff.

Reporters holding their notebooks sat in the jury box and in a small section at the rear of the room. As we took our seats, I noticed the United States and Arkansas flags displayed in the front of the room.

"Niggers stink. The room smells now," a voice called out from somewhere behind us. I turned around to see three white ladies directly behind me.

"I'll bet you don't even know your ABC's, monkeys," one of them said. "You monkeys. What are you looking at?" I glowered at her, trying not to say what I was really thinking. Where I came from adults didn't behave that way.

Suddenly uniformed soldiers were arriving. I turned my attention away from the woman heckling me as the soldiers paraded down the aisle with military precision. So these were the armed men who were keeping us away from school. These were the leaders of the Arkansas National Guard. Up close, they seemed much less intimidating. Some of them were no taller than I was.

Several men and one woman, all wearing business suits and carrying briefcases, were talking to the uniformed men. I figured they were the governor's attorneys. I asked where the governor was, expecting him any moment. That's when one of the attorneys told us that an elected official does not have to appear to answer a summons. Maybe I would not have the privilege of seeing the governor after all. I had hoped that seeing him in person would help me get over my dislike for him.

Suddenly, a whisper of concern made its way through our group. We were all aware that Thelma Mothershed had a heart condition, and now, right before our eyes, her lips and fingertips were turning blue. She struggled to catch her breath. All of us focused our attention on her, and instantly I knew it was a mistake. Not only might it alarm her, but our behavior could also alert school officials to her failing health. I assumed they had never bothered to check her school records; otherwise they might have stopped her going to the integration.

"Shhhh. Thelma will be just fine. Sit up straight. Think about what you'll say if you're called to testify." Mrs. Bates relieved our tension as she moved to sit beside Thelma.

"All rise. The Honorable Judge Ronald Davies presiding." The deep voice sounded like a circus ringmaster announcing the next act. I held my breath. I had read so much about him. What would he be like? A very small man wearing a black robe entered and moved swiftly toward the massive desk. His smooth dark hair was parted in the middle, framing his pleasant round face.

As he climbed up to the imposing leather chair and settled in, what stood out most of all were his huge eyes peering through thick horn-rimmed glasses. From where I sat, I could see only the top part of his black robe, his round face, and those all-seeing, all-knowing eyes.

Shortly after the hearing began, one of the governor's attorneys, Tom Harper, stood and made a motion that Judge Davies disqualify himself because he was biased due to his appointment by the federal government specifically for our case. Judge Davies pounded his gavel and ruled the motion for disqualification was not legally sufficient and not timely.

Next Wiley Branton asked the court's permission to file a supplementary complaint joining us in the government's petition against Faubus and two Arkansas National Guard commanders. Davies ruled it could be filed.

The governor's attorney Tom Harper then asked to have subpoenas withdrawn that had been served on Arkansas National Guard Commander Adjutant General Clinger and his assistant, saying men on military duty are exempt from subpoenas. Again the judge ruled against them.

Meanwhile, there was a commotion at the rear of

the room as reporters hustled back and forth, scribbling on note pads and whispering to each other. They behaved as though they had some divine right to do whatever was necessary to get the information they needed. They were an electrifying show unto themselves, separate and apart from the judge and lawyers.

The more I watched them, the more I thought I'd like to become one when I grew up. As a reporter, I would get to observe interesting events and write about them. I'd also get to behave with a know-it-all urgency, as though what I was doing were more important than anything else.

The seats were so hard that I was pleased Judge Davies moved things along swiftly, pounding his gavel, denying motions presented by the governor's attorneys, all the while speaking sternly. Finally, just before noon, Harper, once again speaking for Governor Faubus, asked if preliminary matters were taken care of.

"Well," the judge growled, "I haven't gotten the late mail, but I think so."

Continuing in a matter-of-fact tone, Harper then asked Judge Davies to dismiss the case because it involved constitutional issues that required a three-judge panel. Judge Davies ruled that the case would continue. In response to that ruling, Harper said, "May we be excused?"

Judge Davies spoke emphatically: "You are excused, gentlemen, but you understand that this is a moot question. The hearing will proceed."

Continuing to speak for all the governor's attorneys, Harper began reading a statement. "The position of Governor Faubus and the military officials of the state is that the governor and the state will not concede that the U.S. Court or anyone else can question the authority of the governor to exercise his judgment in administering the affairs of state, and since he does not concede this responsibility, we will not proceed further in this action."

To my amazement, Harper led the way as several men and one woman gathered their papers and followed him out the door. "Is this a protest?" someone asked. Reporters ran for the door like corralled horses through an open gate. I thought they'd hurt themselves. The judge pounded the gavel.

The attorneys for the Department of Justice called themselves "amicus curiae," saying they were prepared to offer more than one hundred witnesses to support the order for integration. Word was whispered down our line that "amicus curiae" meant friend of the court. But surely no real friend would keep us sitting on those hard seats long enough for a hundred people to testify. My heart sank as we nine eyeballed each other with grim expressions.

"We'll be too old for high school if we have to listen to all those people," I whispered aloud. To my delight, the judge announced the hundred witnesses would not begin until after recess.

In order to get to our lunch, we walked through a gauntlet of hot flashing lights and squeezed past people shouting questions. Once outside, we encountered the problem that had always plagued our people in Little Rock. There were no restaurants that would serve us, at least no decent ones.

The mighty Thurgood Marshall was forced to join us in a greasy joint that served wilted lettuce on overcooked hamburgers in the shabby section of our neighborhood known as Ninth Street. As he ate, he answered our questions. More than anything he seemed to be astonished that the governor's attorneys had walked out of the room so suddenly. "It must have been their plan all along," he said.

That afternoon the parade of witnesses presented by the Justice Department made one major point. They said the threat of violence due to integration was not sufficient for the governor to have called out troops. The mayor of Little Rock, the chairman of the school board, the superintendent of schools, the principal of Central High, and the Little Rock chief of police all testified that they found no threat of violence in Little Rock and had not requested that the governor send troops.

School Superintendent Virgil Blossom testified for a long time about the details of the school board's plan for integration, which had taken two years and two hundred meetings to devise. U.S. District Attorney Orso Cobb asked how many complaints he had gotten. Blossom said the school board had received only a few complaints and suggestions for improving the plan. "As a matter of fact, the plan has been very well received. I'm not saying I believe any majority of the people of Little Rock want integration," he said. "They don't. But they favor this plan as the best answer to a difficult problem." The judge asked the superintendent a question many people had asked me and one I had wondered about myself.

"How were these nine students chosen?"

"The Negroes were selected on the basis of scholarship, personal conduct, and health. We picked those who had the mental ability to do the job and had used it," Blossom answered.

For just a moment, I fretted they would discover Thelma's secret heart problem. But the fact was they had never had us examined by a doctor and there was no talk of doing so.

Then it was time to present our case. The nagging voice inside my head said how could I put my hand on the Bible and not tell the whole truth. Another voice argued that yes, Mother and I were chased, but in fact we weren't hurt—they didn't really touch us. So the truth was—we weren't injured on that day. Over and over again it had been explained to me that to say we were physically injured or attacked that first day on the school grounds or in the immediate area would be to support the governor's case. We knew he would use the slightest justification to delay integration for all eternity.

First to testify from our group was Ernest Green. He wanted to go to Central, he said, because it was closer to his home and would save time and money. He was asked whether he offered any assault against the troops. "No, sir, I didn't," he said with a broad smile.

Next, Elizabeth Eckford testified. She did not complain about the life-threatening mob that had traumatized her. She sat erect, speaking calmly, saying that a few white people lived not far from her house, yet there had been no racial disputes. I was relieved when the attorney said that there would be no need for the rest of us to testify. Had I been asked to place my hand on the Bible, I don't know what I might have been forced to say, perhaps truths that would have hurt us. I figured it was that divine force again moving us on to integration.

The attorneys for the United States made repeated references to the May 1954 decision. I had to stop listening. The very mention of that decision always made me sad. It brought back the face of the angry white man who had chased me down that day. Panic-filled recollections flooded my mind, blotting out the courtroom proceedings.

"Melba! Melba!" Minnijean was tugging at my arm. The others were excited.

The judge was announcing his decision, saying that the governor had "thwarted" the court-approved plan of integration by means of National Guard troops. The judge's voice was deep, his tone emphatic, as he said, "There is no real evidence here that we shouldn't proceed with the court-ordered integration of Central High School. The order is so entered." He pounded the gavel, stood, and walked out of the room.

"Oh, damn nigger-loving judge!" someone shouted, using all those words that Grandma said would lead a body to hell.

Mrs. Bates told us to remain seated until everyone else left the room. I sat very still for a long moment as everybody around me began moving. So, God, you really do want me to go back to that school. For a time it seemed as if I were all alone in a silent tunnel, and everyone else was way at the other end. I would always remember that judge and his huge, piercing dark eyes. There must be something wonderful in his heart, I thought. I would remember him in my prayers.

As a throng of reporters surged toward us, my heart was pounding, my breath coming in short spurts. I flashed my confident smile, but my knees wobbled. Those reporters went crazy, all shoving and shouting their questions at once. I thought they might injure us and themselves as they climbed over each other and tried to get their cameras into position. It was like nothing I had ever experienced before.

"Come Monday morning you'll be a genuine Central High student. How do you feel about that?" one reporter shouted his question above all others.

"Monday morning," I whispered, "I'm gonna be a Central High student—Monday morning!"

At 6:20 p.m. Friday evening, Governor Faubus made a big deal of removing the Arkansas National Guard from Central High. He appeared on television saying that he would appeal Judge Davies's ruling. He gave a long and impassioned speech, predicting once again that if integration took place, blood would run in the streets of Little Rock.

"You know he's smart like a fox," Grandma said. "He's got something in mind, suddenly moving those troops that way."

"Naw, I think he's just following the judge's orders. Anyhow, he's a defeated man. Let's celebrate." Mother raised her glass of lemonade. Grandma frowned. She disliked any one of us to do with milk or a cola what sinners did with liquor.

"To integration with peace and joy and harmony," Mother said, smiling, and took a sip of her lemonade.

"All right," Grandma said, lifting an imaginary glass into the air. "To life without all this ugliness. Maybe now things will quiet down and get back to normal."

That night I wrote in my diary:

Okay, God, so Grandma is right it's my turn to carry the banner. Please help me do thy will.

Over the weekend, Little Rock became an eerie city. Only those with urgent business walked the streets, with quick nervous strides. People from my community did not gather and visit as they usually would. Like me, they must have been frightened by the news reports that continued to describe roving gangs of segregationists crisscrossing the city, looking to do harm to any of our people they could find. Rumors persisted that various people we knew had been beaten or chased.

It felt awful not to have authorities to turn to in the midst of all the violence. I could see fear in the faces of the adults around me. I could hear it in their whispered conversations. All my life I had felt unprotected by city officials. If some major crisis took place, like a fire in our community, white firemen had always taken their time coming to help. They didn't fight to save our lives and property, as if neither had any value to them, so we had set up our own systems of summoning each other for help.

The integration dispute made me feel as though we were much more vulnerable. Whites had control of the police, the firemen, and the ambulances. They could decide who got help and who didn't. Even if the Ku Klux Klan ravaged one of our homes, we wouldn't call the police for help. None of us was certain which of our city officials wore civic uniforms by day and white sheets at night.

News reports described Governor Faubus as unruffled by all the turmoil. He was living his life and doing business as usual in the face of this crisis. One article said that through the two previous hectic weeks the governor had been sleeping soundly, eating regularly, chatting with his son in college, enjoying his fan mail, and relaxing as he read about his favorite president, Abraham Lincoln. He didn't sound to me like a man who was remorseful or planning to mend his ways, or a man who was suffering the inconvenience of having his normal way of life shattered, as were we.

On Sunday, I thought the news of more violence in the streets might cause Grandma and Mama to forget about church. I should have known better. It was cloudy, with thunderstorms expected, as we cautiously drove our regular route to church. It upset us to see that sidewalks usually filled with families on their way to Sunday service were empty. We heard the church bells toll, their echoing clang a protest to the silence that blanketed our community.

However, a hopeful mood was evident in the church service. The judge's positive decision for integration was God's will, Reverend Young said. And God would give us the strength to go forth. He said we needed to pray and work to heal our divided community.

He spoke of the many God-fearing, reasonable white people who supported our activities and of the white ministers joining forces to help stop the violence. He expressed gratitude and prayed for Mayor Woodrow Mann, who continued to defy Governor Faubus, accusing him of being wrong in opposing integration and the federal government. Our minister urged support for the nine of us who were integrating Central, mentioning the three of us who sat in church, Gloria, Ernie, and me.

Mumbles of "Yes, Lord" and "Amen" made me hope some people had changed their minds and that now most of my church family thought that I was doing the right thing. But nevertheless there were those who disagreed and were willing to show their feelings at every turn. One woman snagged me in the ladies' bathroom, saying, "The nice white lady I work for treated me like family up till now. These days she treats me like I'm just the colored help."

"Look," Mother said, "there's a price to be paid for freedom; we pay it now or we're in 'ball and chain' forever."

"Easy for you to talk, Mrs. Pattillo. You're an educated woman. I ain't got no sheepskin on my wall."

The church service seemed to last longer than usual. Afterward there was so much talk of integration that I felt wrung out. The only bright spot in my Sunday was Vince's offer to drive me home from church. Mother frowned at the suggestion. When I pleaded, she demanded that she trail us in her car. So we formed a two-car caravan, Vince in his brand-new square-back, red-and-white Chevy, and Grandma, Mama, and Conrad following close behind in our car.

"I guess I'd better not speed," he said, grinning that handsome smile. I was craning my neck to look back every now and then. "Yep, they're there," he said. I was embarrassed that Mother was following us so closely. To make things worse, Vince had one thing on his mind—integration, finding out about what we nine were doing, when we got together, how we studied, and what the NAACP said to us in meetings. I began feeling as though I were giving a news report.

"How does it feel to see your name in the paper, to be a celebrity that everybody's talking about?" I glanced at him in his Eisenhower jacket and slick shoes. He was sharp and wonderful. Why couldn't it be another place and time?

"Uncomfortable," I grumbled.

"Hey, there's got to be some good things in all the fuss they're making over you."

"It's all so new that I can't figure it out yet. Right now I'd give anything for just one day of normal school with old friends."

"Too late for that, you're a Central High student."

I had counted on our date as one last opportunity to feel normal joy before Monday came. Our conversation and his cute charms were supposed to stoke my daydreams so I'd have something to smile about when things went wrong at Central. No such luck. In less than twenty-four hours, I would face my first day inside Central High without this protective veil.

After Dreaming of President Johnson

by Howard Gordon

Du Bois speaks of the African American's "double-consciousness, this sense of always looking at one's self through the eyes of others." The following story shows how a young boy learns to see himself, and other African Americans, through the eyes of white society.

So many people can easily recall that precise moment when they learned of President Kennedy's assassination. And, they can remember exactly how they reacted to the news. They have never forgotten who they were with, or what they had eaten, or even which clothes they happened to be wearing.

Until recently, I remembered none of such carefully recorded details. I was always a boy of disturbingly vague dreams, and perhaps on November 22, 1963, I restlessly fell asleep in order to forget everything I had learned.

What I did remember was that my life was much like the world of other children. School was important to us only because it presented an opportunity to mold sacred friendships. All adults were to be viewed as disciplinarians who occupied one stratum in a three-tiered system. Parents, teachers, and the police, of course, were the gatekeepers of each of these despised tiers. And fun—the sort of fun children had passion for—could not be discovered with an attitude of looking forward to becoming an adult; it had to be found in comic books, in block parties, and in imaginary adventures.

I was an only child in a lower-income family. The year of my tenth birthday, my father packed our meager belongings into his pickup and moved us to the city. The city was Rochester. We had moved there from Benoit, a sleepy farming enclave of three hundred residents. Benoit was the kind of town where a father could send his child to the local store for a newspaper and know he'd return safely, know there was never a need to worry over city ruffians or the dangers of constant traffic. So quiet was Benoit that my father claimed he could hear moths pupating as he sat rocking on the front porch. Every summer evening, he sat there with my mother on their wicker sofa, and he would point out the endless stars among a web of constellations, all the while pretending to know their names, though never at all fooling my mother. But she went along with his dubious expertise, because both of us liked to hear him talk. His soft voice assured us he was in control, and he seemed to hum many of his words as if composing tunes we could cherish in another lifetime.

"MMM mmm you can hide out here," my father would tell us. Then he'd sigh wishfully.

And it made sense. Out there under the stars everything was so small and dark. Even our tiny farmhouse seemed hidden by the darkness. The three of us were like children playing in the tall grasses, listening and watching for something invisible or magic, yet hoping that, like us, whatever we found could just be left alone.

My father's aversion to the noise and crime of the big city created a perseverance for the harsh, western New York winters, which dropped savage snows into our valley and made the dirt roads as impenetrable as the meadows blanketed under knee-high drifts. During such storms, we risked the fifteen-mile trip into Rochester only once a month.

My mother and I bought groceries at the A&P while my father, hands on hips, patrolled the aisles for the hooligans who, he had often predicted, would swipe the food of hardworking folks right out of their grocery carts. I quickly learned to recognize these thugs, since my father had made a habit of pointing them out.

"Don't talk to him," he would warn me, as he ignored the friendly nod of a flat-nosed man. Or he might admonish me with, "Uh-um, stay away from them," directed at a horde of children in rumpled clothing who tugged at their mother's dress. They were curious but amiable children, asking me, "Who you be?" But I was aware of my father looming over us, his eyes red and cold, as though he were intoxicated by his own rage. As I became older, it was clear to me that my father hated these people because we were just like them. They, too, had very little money to spend, and only humble possessions. The only difference between us was the distance separating our homes.

What's more, my father hated these people in a way that made me fear him. I can't remember ever being afraid of anyone but my father. I now understand that he needed to keep us secure within our own isolation, yet horrified of stepping outside of it. If he could have had his way, we would have remained forever removed from their kind; but lack of income had made the need to relocate inevitable.

Once we had moved to Rochester, my father labored as an auto junkyard mechanic when he could find steady work; when he couldn't, he accepted seasonal employment on the custodial staff in one of the then still segregated cemeteries. My mother found a job as an occasional fruit-canner in an aged factory ten miles outside the city. It was she who had convinced my father we had to leave. He had held out for the quiet and simple life, but my mother was always more practical.

"Simple is what we'll be if we stay out here," she had argued.

He had thought about it for a moment, then answered her with one of his patented hums, a grumble of recognition that our lives were changing.

Much of that first year in Rochester somehow evaporated. Perhaps I simply became older and forgot, the way children tend to forget, the way they lose much of what happened early in their lives. But even now, I am always trying to remember. There are fragments. I do recollect that it was July when Sonny Liston knocked out Floyd Patterson and when the Mets, my father's favorite baseball team, finally ended their twenty-two game losing streak by beating the Los Angeles Dodgers. I remember the march, hundreds of thousands of people at the Lincoln Memorial.

We knew that we lived in hard times. Still, like every boy and girl my age, I was quickly schooled with the notion that each of us had an equal chance to live the American Dream. Ours was indeed a young country. The times were steeped in an ambience of limitless possibilities. The space race had yet to be won, and the new president was both a leader who promised us all a "Great Society" and a man whom every child could emulate.

Our family life became quite predictable; on Sundays we worshiped at the Church of God, and every Thursday evening I participated in the Brothers in Youth Fellowship, learning about equality under God and reinforcing that new direction in which the country seemed headed. Life at home was conducted under a simple philosophy: If you have a home, praise the Lord. If you lose your home, praise the Lord, and the next time you build one, make it His so that you will be blessed.

So we were blessed, my parents informed me. I learned to be thankful for the food on our dinner table, no matter how small the portions. Our survival in the face of poverty was an example of the divine intervention my parents often spoke about. Faithfully, we blessed each of our meals, and we chanted solemn prayers before slipping into bed. But, whenever I slept, I had a recurring dream, one that startled me awake.

Most dreams are so real that you begin to believe you are actually experiencing whatever you do in them. But this one dream was so far from real that I always knew I was asleep, or going mad, and that I had to hurry and awaken.

He was right there in front of me, telling me to come closer, and his face, rugged and lined, seemed to float so easily in a clearing of placards and effervescent smiles that I was unaware it was attached to a body. This was not just a man in front of me; it was the president of the United States—President Johnson. And he beckoned me, "Come here, little boy." I did. I let go of my father's hand and walked through the maze of bodies clad in flower-print dresses and dark three-piece suits. But this could not be real. I felt as if I were pressing my face against a television screen. I was finally standing right next to the man. He had been kissing babies. He seemed to shake everyone's hand. Such a big man. Huge hands. Balloons drifted over the crowd. Then he saw me again. My small hand was open. He looked right at me and smiled, but I hesitated. His stare seemed to say, "Well?" I felt ashamed and looked down at his rust-colored boots. Cowboy boots. Before I knew what was happening, the leader of the free world had turned around, shaken more hands, and was gone.

My father often reprimanded me for looking down and away from his gaze. I am awake now, and November 22, 1963, is clear again. A year that was gone is back. I didn't call it back. It just came on its own, as though it were a stain hidden somewhere but never really washed away. After dreaming of President Johnson, I no longer wanted to be like him—his ears were much too big, anyway.

In 1963, I am eleven, a shy and quiet child whose face can barely reach the middle of my father's chest, let alone his fierce eyes.

"A boy who can't return a stare will never be a man," he says.

I want very much to be a man. In the world in which I find myself growing up, nothing is greater or more significant. But I had hoped the metamorphosis into manhood would occur naturally and be as uneventful as losing one's baby teeth or gaining height. Instead, it has become clear to me that the process of becoming a man is a loudly announced rite of passage to be witnessed by the entire world.

"Wilson," my father shouts, "mmm look at me when I'm talking to you, boy."

Even my name draws unwanted attention. I hate it, and long for something common, like Peter or John.

My newest friend's name is John. He and I met in gym class on the second day of the school year. We played on the same sixth-grade kickball team, and we wrestled for five minutes without either of us being able to pin the other. I told Johnny that Peter was really my first name, but that everyone dishonors me by calling me Wilson. Johnny has agreed to call me Pete.

I have a reason for admiring a name that is not my own. My best friend is Oliver Trinidad. He and I have been neighbors since my family moved into the city. Oliver shares everything with me, including his new comic books. But one particular comic he had shown me during the summer is called *The Amazing Spider-Man,* whose superhero is secretly Peter Parker, an unlikely teenage crime fighter who is as shy and unassuming as am I.

Oliver and I walk home together from school as we always do. We stand in front of my apartment building. With his foot, Oliver prods a bird that sits on the sidewalk. The bird just seems to ball itself up tightly in its feathers, as if doing so will protect it from Oliver's toe. A lover of animals and anything small, I protest.

"Leave it alone, man."

"Aw, I ain't gonna hurt it doin' this."

"I can't come over later and play," I tell Oliver. He wants me to go with him to the woods, to a place we call the Backhills. But I tell him that Johnny has invited me to his home, where he promises to show me his collection of Marvel comics. I am excited because he has every back issue of *Spider-Man* along with my own favorites: *Fantastic Four, Sub-Mariner, Dr. Doom, Thor, Captain America, Incredible Hulk, Iron-Man, Avengers*—all of the hottest and most sought-after comic adventurers. But Spider-Man has become my recent obsession. Until I met Johnny, I hadn't really paid any attention to the superhero, hadn't read a single issue about him even though the series had been out at least a year. I thought, How can a little insect be a superhero? But Johnny told me that spiders are not insects, and that Spider-Man is the best. Unlike other superheroes, his mask completely hides his face. No one can know who he really is.

"So you hangin' out with that white boy now, huh?" Oliver says.

"But you're my friend, too," I say.

"Naw I ain't," Oliver says. And he gives the bird such a hard kick that his shoe makes a *twaaack!* sound. "So there," he says, and he runs next door to his own house. He stares at me from his porch. I look away.

The bird has landed six feet away in the middle of the road. It lies on one side, unmoving. Its beak is open, and one of its wings has partially unfolded. I decide not to see whether it is dead. A strange feeling strikes me, like I've eaten too much junk food and need to throw up but can't. The vomit reaches my throat, then reverses itself, and my entire body shakes as if it's cold. My legs are no good to me. They refuse to walk even thought I need to get away.

Johnny lives on Bertham Avenue, about three miles from my neighborhood. He gave me easy directions, though I feel disoriented long before I leave the Third Ward boundary. You learn to know the people and the neighborhood, because their personalities are unmistakably stamped into it. The artists used abandoned buildings and alley walls as canvasses for life-sized self-portraits and colorful graffiti. The romantics await rescue from their ghettoized existence by enduring nonstop ballads cranked from scratched 45s by the Marvelettes or the Impressions or Jackie Wilson; you know who the best dancers are because they automatically kick into the jerk or the popeye as soon as you pass by their porches, or every time a car turns the corner. There is no stargazing or storytelling within the city confines. And all of the singers here—

the confident ones, at least—congregate on street corners, harmonizing for all the world to hear, while those who lack the same bravado practice in bathrooms and alleys, hoping that the echo-chamber effect will disguise their group's off-key notes. On other corners stand members of the Fruit of Islam, soft-spoken young men with Caesar haircuts—men who dress in pin-striped gray and blue suits and plain but spotlessly polished shoes, and who are as recognizable by their radiant bow ties as they are for the sincere smiles that remain on their faces even if you do not purchase their bean pies or their *Muhammad Speaks* newspapers.

I know the hopes and talents and even the limitations of the people who occupy the neighborhood. I know their dreams and fears—know the gossip they pass among themselves.

And I know something else about these people, something they would never guess. I secretly hate them. They are loud. They shout their conversations at each other. They use imperfect English and have other conspicuous faults. Their coarse and knotty hair does not fall from their heads in wondrous dark bangs or curl into blond locks like the hair of Hollywood movie stars. Their noses have no length and are rarely pointed or hooked, they are crude and flat and nearly touch their jutted mouths, which do not have the perfectly thin lips that seem painted onto faces I admire. Nor are their clothes anything like those owned by people who appear on television or in my magazines. And these people do not own the stores my family shops in downtown or the banks from which my parents borrow money. They aren't the teachers in my school or the policemen who drive through our neighborhood, and they have as little chance of becoming bus drivers as they do of becoming secret service agents for President Kennedy.

Many of them are criminals. I read, and I am told this. They are the dark, sweating men who appear in WANTED posters, the evil men who must be apprehended for rape and murder and robbery of decent folks. I am beginning to understand my father's loathing. These are people who must be handcuffed and taken away—locked up with their own kind behind prison bars. I am told this in school, and I read about much of their crime in the newspapers.

These people make me hate myself, make me wish I had nothing in common with them. Maybe they are *bad guys,* the hooligans my father warns me about. They may represent the reasons a world holds out hope for real superheroes.

People stare at me as I make my way to Johnny's. It jump-starts my imagination. Many of them stop as I approach, then watch me until I pass. But I don't return their stares. Maybe they know I am somehow different. Perhaps they suspect I harbor some great secret, or even amazing powers that can never be understood. They stare at me as if I am really wearing blue tights and red boots.

Johnny had told me that he wanted to be Spider-Man. I hadn't argued. He looks a bit like Peter Parker. Nearly a year older than me, he is taller, lean, though not skinny, and he does wear glasses. Let him be Spider-Man. I know we will soon become the best of friends. I don't need Oliver Trinidad, or anyone like him. But Johnny and I will be like brothers. Together we will fight crime and protect the innocent. We'll swing over the rooftops, soar above obstacles, and somersault out of danger.

Johnny's gate is unlocked, but I climb over it anyway. Nimbly, I leap over the five steps onto the porch without losing my balance. The front door is open. I peek through the screen at a man couched in front of a television. His feet are propped up on a small table. The man has not heard my soft footfalls. I start to knock, but something tells me that I would disturb this man, that it would not be right to indicate my presence. The man has no shoulders, only a tremendously long neck that starts at his oversized ears and takes on the shape of a tree trunk stripped of its bark. His arms appear to grow right out of that neck. He turns to me slowly, and his eyes frown. This time, my own stare does not falter. His does. He turns back to the TV as he yells, "Betty."

A woman appears. She wipes her hands on an apron she is carrying and stoops to see me more clearly. She has a poisoned sort of look, a frosty half-smile of someone who has swallowed a bitter pill. And she, too, stares at me for a moment. But she never touches the screen door.

"Well, what do you want?" the woman says.

"Is Johnny home?" I say.

She looks at me again and her half-smile disappears. She turns toward the direction from which she entered the room.

"Johnny," she shouts, "there's a nigger out here to see you."

The woman walks away, but I can't move. My legs feel stuck to the porch, and a rushing sound fills my ears, as if there's a train inside my head. I'm getting that queasy feeling again, the rising sickness that tickles my throat. Something is happening on the television that I can't quite make out. A black car in a procession. A woman on top of the car. And something about the president being shot. Somehow I manage to step away from the screen door. I hear Johnny, or someone, coming, but I jump off the porch and land on one knee. I don't know if I'm hurt; I just run.

And I run as if everything in front or behind me is an enemy, as if the big houses along the street have eyes instead of windows, and the lawns are traps beneath my sneakers. I run away from people and fire hydrants and from cars honking at me. I run until I reach my own street and see Oliver poking listlessly at the dead bird with a stick.

"Told you to leave that bird alone," I yell at him. I stare him down until he drops the stick.

We don't say anything for quite a while. But I'm glad to see him.

"Man, why you cryin'?" Oliver finally says.

"For nothin'," I say.

I wipe my eyes.

"You see the comics?"

"I don't need any stupid old comics," I tell him. He doesn't ask me about them again.

We stand on the corner watching cars flash by. Oliver offers me a candy cigarette. I forgot about the dead bird. It is no longer important. After a while, everything is back to normal again, and we're looking for something to do.

"Hey, wanna go to the Backhills?" Oliver says.

"Let's go," I say.

And we start running.

Communication and Reality

by Malcolm X

*Like Du Bois, black nationalist leader
Malcolm X was concerned with improving
African Americans' self-image and helping
them to identify with others of African
descent around the world. In this speech,
which he made to the Domestic Peace
Corps on December 12, 1964, he warns
people to think for themselves and not to
accept images created by the white press.*

First, I want to let you know I am very thankful for
the invitation to speak here this afternoon. Number
one, before a group such as this, and number two, I
always feel more at home in Harlem than anywhere
else I've ever been. The topic we are going to discuss
in a very informal way is Africa and the African
Revolution and its effect on the Afro-American.

I take time to mention that because I am one who
believes that what's happening on the African
continent has a direct bearing on what happens to you
and me in this country: The degree to which they get
independence, strength, and recognition on that
continent is inseparable from the degree to which we
get independence, strength, and recognition on this
continent, and I hope before the day is over to be able
to clarify that.

First, I would like to point out that since it is my
understanding that most of you are training to be

leaders in the community, the country, and the world, some advice that I would give is that whenever you occupy a position of responsibility never accept images that have been created for you by someone else. It is always better to form the habit of learning how to see things for yourself, listen to things for yourself, and think for yourself; then you are in a better position to judge for yourself.

We are living in a time when image-making has become a science. Someone can create a certain image and then use that image to twist your mind and lead you right up a blind path. An example: A few weeks ago, I was on a plane traveling from Algiers to Geneva. There were two white Americans sitting beside me, one a male, the other a female. I had met the male in the airport and we had struck up a conversation. He was an interpreter for the United Nations and was based in Geneva. The lady was with the American Embassy in Algeria. So we conversed for about forty minutes between Algiers and Geneva, a nice human conversation. I don't think they were trying to be white and they weren't trying to prove they weren't white. They weren't particularly trying to prove anything. It was just a conversation between three human beings. I certainly wasn't trying to make them think I wasn't black; race just didn't come into the conversation.

So, after we had this quiet, objective, friendly, and very informative conversation for about forty minutes, the lady looked at my briefcase and said, "I want to ask you a personal question. What kind of last name could you have that begins with an 'X'?" This was bugging her. I said, "That's it, 'X,'" like that. So she said, "Well, what's your first name?" I said, "Malcolm." She waited about ten minutes and said, "You're not Malcolm X?" and I said, "Yes." She said,

"But you're not what I was looking for." I told her right then and there about the danger of believing what she hears someone else say or believing what she reads that someone else has written and not keeping herself in a position to weigh things for herself.

So I just take time to mention that because it is very dangerous for you and me to form the habit of believing completely everything about anyone or any situation when we only have the press as our source of information. It is always better, if you don't want to be completely in the dark, to read about it. But don't come to a conclusion until you have an opportunity to do some personal, firsthand investigation for yourself.

The American press, in fact the FBI, can use the American press to create almost any kind of image they want of anyone on the local scene. And then you have other police agencies of an international stature that are able to use the world press in the same manner. If the press is able to project someone in the image of an extremist, no matter what that person says or does from then on, it is considered by the public as an act of extremism. No matter how good, constructive, or positive it is, because it's done by this person who has been projected as an extremist, the people who have been misled by the press have a mental block and the press knows that. The person can run and save someone from drowning in the middle of the Hudson, but still the act is looked upon with suspicion because the press has been used to create suspicion toward that person.

I point these things out—especially for you and me, those of us who are trying to come from behind. If we aren't aware, we'll find that all these modern methods of trickery will be used and we will be maneuvered into thinking that we are getting freedom or thinking that we are making progress when actually we will be going backward.

And one of the things that you and I as an oppressed people should be on guard against, as I said, is to be very careful about letting anyone paint our images for us. The world press as well as the American press can make the victim of the crime look like the criminal and can make the criminal look like the victim. You don't think that is possible for someone to do this to your mind, but all you have to do is take a look at what happened in the Congo. The world press projected the scene in the Congo as one wherein the people who were the victims of the crime were made to appear as if they were the actual criminals and the ones who were the actual criminals were made to appear as if they were the actual victims. The press did this, and by the press doing this, it made it almost impossible for the public to analyze the Congo situation with clarity and keep it in its proper perspective.

An example: Here we had African villages in the Congo that had no kind of air force whatsoever, they were completely without defense against air attacks; planes were dropping bombs on these African villages. The bombs were destroying women and children. But there was no great outcry here in America against such an inhuman act because the press very skillfully made it look like a humanitarian project by referring to the pilots as "American trained." And as soon as they put the word American in there, that was supposed to lend it some kind of respectability or legality.

They called them American-trained, anti-Castro Cuban pilots and since Castro is a word that is almost like a curse, the fact that they were anti-Castro pilots made whatever they were doing an act of humanitarianism. But still you can't overlook the fact that they were dropping bombs on villages in Africa that had no defense whatsoever against bombs. But they called this an act of humanitarianism and the public was made to accept it as an act of humanitarianism.

I have to point this out because it is an example of how the press can maneuver and manipulate your mind to make you think that mass murder is some kind of humanitarian project simply by making the image of the criminal appear to be that of a humanitarian and the image of the victim that of the criminal.

So it is good to keep this in mind because you can take it a step further. One of the principal images in that scene over there was Tshombe, who is a murderer. He murdered the rightful prime minister of the Congo; this cannot be denied. The rightful minister of the Congo was Patrice Lumumba. Now, the one who is responsible for having murdered him in cold blood—and the world knows it—was put over the Congo as its premier by the United States Government and this gave him some kind of image of respectability because America sanctioned him. Not only did America sanction him, she supplied him with sufficient funds wherein he could then go to South Africa and import hired killers, mercenaries they call them, but a mercenary is a hired killer.

So this man, Tshombe, who was a murderer hired by the United States and placed in a position of authority over the Congo, showed his nature by what he did with American money—he hired some more killers. But because he was appointed by America Tshombe wasn't looked upon as a murderer or a killer, and the American press gave the mercenaries an image of respectability. An image of respectability. Now these mercenaries, under Tshombe's sanction and support, were indiscriminately shooting African women and children as well as African men.

No one got upset over the loss of thousands of Congolese lives; they only got upset when the lives of a few whites were at stake. Because when the lives of the whites were at stake, the press immediately played on your sentiment by referring to these whites as innocent hostages, as nuns and priests and missionaries, and it gave them an image that you would sympathize with.

I must point this out because it shows you how tricky the press can be. The press can make you not have any sympathy whatsoever for the death of thousands of people who look just like yourself, but at the same time, they make tears roll down your face over the loss of a few lives that don't look anything like yourself. They manipulate your feelings.

So my advice to any of you who at any time think that you'll ever be placed in a position of responsibility—you owe it to others as well as to yourself to be very careful about letting others make up your mind for you. You have to learn how to see for yourself, hear for yourself, think for yourself, and then judge for yourself.

Secondly, I would like to say this: It concerns my own personal self, whose image they have projected in their own light. I am against any form of racism. We are all against racism. The only difference between you and me is that you want to fight racism and racists non-violently and lovingly and I'll fight them the way they fight me. Whatever weapon they use, that's the one I'll use. I go for talking the kind of language he talks. You can't communicate with a person unless you use the language he uses. If a man is speaking French, you can talk German all night long, he won't know what you're talking about. You have to find out what kind of language he understands and then you put it to him in the language that he understands.

I'm a Muslim, which means my religion is Islam. I believe in Allah. I believe in all of the prophets, whoever represented God on this earth. I believe what Muslims believe: prayer, fasting, charity, and the pilgrimage to the Holy Land, Mecca, which I've been fortunate to have made four or five times. I believe in the brotherhood of man, all men, but I don't believe in brotherhood with anybody who doesn't want brotherhood with me. I believe in treating people right, but I'm not going to waste my time trying to treat somebody right who doesn't know how to return that treatment. This is the only difference between you and me.

You believe in treating everybody right whether they put a rope around your neck or whether they put you in the grave. Well, my belief isn't that strong. I believe in the brotherhood of man, but I think that anybody who wants to lynch a Negro is not qualified for that brotherhood and I don't put forth any effort to get them into that brotherhood. You want to save him and I don't.

Despite the fact that I believe in the brotherhood of man as a Muslim, and in the religion of Islam, there is one fact also that I can't overlook: I'm an Afro-American and Afro-Americans have problems that go well beyond religion. We have problems that our religious organization in itself cannot solve and we have problems that no one organization can solve or no one leader can solve. We have a problem that is going to take the combined efforts of every leader and every organization if we are going to get a solution.

For that reason, I don't believe that as a Muslim it is possible for me to bring my religion into any discussion with non-Muslims without causing more division, animosity, and hostility; then we will only be involved in a self-defeating action. So based upon that, there is a group of us that have formed an organization. Besides being Muslims, we have gotten together and formed an organization that has nothing to do with religion at all; it is known as the Organization of Afro-American Unity.

In this organization we involve ourselves in the complete struggle of the Afro-American in this country, and our purpose in becoming involved with a non-religious group is to give us the latitude to use any means necessary for us to bring an end to the injustices that confront us. I believe in any means necessary. I believe that the injustices that we have suffered and will continue to suffer will never be brought to a halt as long as we put ourselves in a strait-jacket when fighting those injustices.

Those of us in the Organization of Afro-American Unity have adopted as our slogan "by any means necessary" and we feel we are justified. Whenever someone is treating you in a criminal, illegal, or immoral way, why, you are well within your rights to use anything at your disposal to bring an end to that unjust, illegal, and immoral condition. If we do it like that, we will find that we will get more respect and will be further down the road toward freedom, toward recognition and respect as human beings. But as long as we dillydally and try to appear that we're more moral by taking a beating without fighting back, people will continue to refer to us as very moral and well-disciplined persons, but at the same time we will be as far back a hundred years from now as we are today. So I believe that fighting those who fight us is the best course of action in any situation.

Again, if the Government doesn't want Negroes fighting anyone who is fighting us, then the Government should do its job; the Government shouldn't put the weight on us. If the Ku Klux Klan in Mississippi is carrying on criminal activities to the point of murdering black people, then I think if black people are men, human beings, the same as anybody else, you and I should have the right to do the same thing in defense of our lives and our property that all other human beings on this earth do in defense of their lives and in defense of their property, and that is to talk the language that the Klan understands.

So I must emphasize, we are dealing with a powerful enemy, and again, I am not anti-American or un-American. I think there are plenty of good people in America, but there are also plenty of bad people in America and the bad ones are the ones who seem to have all the power and be in these positions to block things that you and I need. Because this is the situation, you and I have to preserve the right to do what is necessary to bring an end to that situation, and it doesn't mean that I advocate violence, but at the same time I am not against using violence in self-defense. I don't even call it violence when it's self-defense, I call it intelligence.

So what impact or effect does the African Revolution have upon you and me? Number one, prior to 1959, many of us didn't want to be identified with Africa in any way, not even indirectly or remotely. The best way to curse one of us out was to call us an African; we'd get insulted. But if you've noticed, since 1959 and in more recent years, that's changed. It's changing among us subconsciously faster than we even realize.

The reason for this change is that prior to 1959 the

African image was not created by Africans. The image of Africa was created by European powers. These Europeans joined with America and created a very negative image of Africa and projected this negative image abroad. They projected Africa as a jungle, a place filled with animals, savages, and cannibals. The image of Africa and the Africans was made so hateful that 22 million of us in America of African ancestry actually shunned Africa because its image was a hateful, negative image. We didn't realize that as soon as we were made to hate Africa and Africans, we also hated ourselves. You can't hate the root and not hate the fruit. You can't hate Africa, the land where you and I originated, without ending up hating you and me.

And the man knew that. We began to hate African features. We hated the African nose and the African lips and the African skin and the African hair. We hated the hair so much we even put lye on it to change its looks. We began hating ourselves. And you know, they accuse us of teaching hate.

What is the most inhuman or immoral: a man that teaches you to hate your enemies or a man that skillfully maneuvers you into hating yourself? Well, I think teaching a man to hate himself is much more criminal than teaching him to hate someone else. Look at you—who taught you to hate yourself? If you say we're hate teachers, you tell me who taught you to hate so skillfully, so completely, until we have been maneuvered today so that we don't even want to be what we actually are. We want to be somebody else, we want to be someone else, we want to be something else. Many of us want to be somewhere else.

Then after 1959, as Africans began to get independence, they began to change the image of the African. They got into a position to project their own image abroad. The image began to swing from negative to positive and to the same degree that the African image began to change from negative to positive, the Afro-American's image also began to change from negative to positive. His behavior and objectives began to change from negative to positive to the same degree that the behavior and the objectives of the African changed from negative to positive. They had a direct bearing upon the attitude that we here in America began to develop toward each other and also toward the man, and I don't have to say what man.

There were elements in the State Department that began to worry about this change in image. As Africa became militant and uncompromising, you and I became militant and uncompromising, and even the most bourgeois Uncle Tom Afro-American was happy when he heard about the Mau Maus. [Applause.] Yeah, he was happy when he heard it. He wouldn't say so openly because it wasn't a status symbol to identify with it in some quarters. In other quarters, it was. But all of this uncompromising and militant action on the part of the Africans created a tendency among our people in this country to be the same way, but many of us didn't realize it. It was an unconscious effect, but it had its effect.

That racist element in the State Department became worried about this. And you are out of your mind if you don't think that there's a racist element in the State Department. I'm not saying that everybody in the State Department is a racist, but I'm saying they sure got some in there and they got them in powerful positions. And this is the element that became worried about the changing Negro mood and the changing Negro behavior. Especially if that mood and behavior became one of violence, and by violence they only mean when a black man protects himself against the attack of the white man.

When it comes time for a black man to explode, they call it violence, but white people can be exploding against black people all day long and it's never called violence. I have even had some of you come to me and ask if I'm for violence. I'm the victim of violence and you're the victim of violence. In fact, you've been so victimized by it, you can't recognize it for what it is today.

The fear was that the changing image of the African would have a tendency to change your and my image much too much, and they knew you and I tended to identify with Africa where we didn't formerly do so. Their fear was that sympathy and that identity would eventually develop into sort of an allegiance for African hopes and aspirations above and beyond America's hopes and aspirations. So they had to do something to create a division between the Afro-American and the African so that you and I and they could not get together and coordinate our efforts and make faster progress than we had been making up to that time.

They don't mind you struggling for freedom as long as you struggle according to their rules. As long as you let them tell you how to struggle, they go for your struggle. But as soon as you come to one of them who is supposed to be for your freedom and tell him you're for freedom by any means necessary, he gets away from you. He's for his freedom by any means necessary, but he'll never go along with you to get your freedom by any means necessary.

United States history is that of a country that does whatever it wants to by any means necessary, to look out for its interest by any means necessary, but when it comes to your and my interest, then all of the means become limited. And we can't go along with that. We say what's good for the goose is good for the gander. If we are going to be non-violent, then let America become non-violent. Let her pull her troops out of Saigon and pull her troops out of the Congo and pull back all her troops everywhere and then we will see that she is a non-violent country, that we're living in a non-violent society. But until they get non-violent themselves, you're out of your mind to get non-violent. That's all I say on that.

I'm for peace, but I don't see how any black people can be at peace before the war is over, and you haven't even won a battle yet. If I have to follow a general who is fighting for my freedom and the enemy begins to pin peace medals on him before I've gotten my freedom, I'm afraid I'll have to find another general because it's impossible for a general to be at peace when his people don't get no peace. It is impossible to give out peace medals when the people who are oppressed don't have any peace.

The only man who has peace is the man at the top. And I don't think that black people should be at peace in any way; there should be no peace on earth for anybody until there's peace also for us.

As the African nations began to get very nationalistic, very militant, and very uncompromising in their search for freedom, the European powers found they couldn't stay on the African continent any longer. It's like someone in a football game or a basketball game: When he's trapped or boxed in, he doesn't throw the ball away, but he has to pass it to someone who's in the clear. And this is the same thing the Europeans did.

The Africans didn't want them anymore, so they had to pass the ball to one of their partners who was in the clear and that partner was Uncle Sam. Uncle

Sam caught the ball and he's been carrying it ever since. All you have to do is go to the African continent, travel from one end of it to the other, and you'll find out that the American position and influence has only replaced the position and influence of the former colonial powers and they did it very skillfully.

They knew that no non-African could stay on that continent against the will of the African, so they had to use a better, more subtle method. They had to make friends with the African. They had to make the African think they were there to help them, so they started pretending like they wanted to help you and me over here. They came up with all these pretty slogans about integration which they haven't produced yet.

They came up with slogans about this kind of program and that kind of program, but when you analyze it very closely, you find that they haven't produced it yet. It hasn't produced what it was supposed to produce. It's so hard for them to produce results that when they get that much of it, it makes headlines.

The law was handed down by the Supreme Court. They said you could go to any school you want, but when you get out there and get ready to go to a school like the law says, the law is the one busting you upside your head, or turning the water hose on you, or the cattle prod, so this kind of shook the Afro-American up. He wondered whether the Supreme Court was really in a position to say what the law of the land was supposed to be. They passed a law they could not enforce. And I don't mean they couldn't enforce it in Mississippi, I mean they couldn't enforce it in New York City. They couldn't even desegregate the schools in New York City, so how in the world are they going to enforce it in Louisiana, Mississippi, and some of these other places?

These were token moves, designed to make you and me cool down just a little while longer by making us think that an honest effort was being made to get a solution to the problem. And then as they began to appear as if they were for the black man in this country, abroad they were blown up. Especially the United States Information Service. Its job abroad, especially in the African continent, is to make the Africans think that you and I are living in paradise, that our problems have been solved, that the Supreme Court desegregation decision put all of us in school, that the passage of the Civil Rights Bill last year solved all of our problems, and that now that Martin Luther King, Jr., has gotten the peace prize, we are on our way to the promised land of integration.

I was over there when all of this happened and I know how they used it. They don't use it in an objective, constructive way; they use it to trick and fool the African into thinking that most of their time is spent in loving you and me and trying to solve your and my problem with honest methods, and that they were getting honest results.

So I would like to say in my conclusion why we in the Organization of Afro-American Unity feel that we just can't sit around and rely upon the same objectives and strategies that have been used in the past.

If you study the so-called progress of the Afro-American, go back to 1939, just before the war with Hitler, most of our people were dishwashers, waiters, and shoeshine boys. It didn't make any difference how much education we had. We worked downtown in those hotels as bellhops and on the railroad as waiters and in Grand Central Station as redcaps. Prior to 1939, we knew what our position was going to be even before we graduated from school.

In those days our people couldn't even work in a factory. In Michigan where all of the factories were, they were primarily shining shoes and working at other menial tasks. Then when Hitler went on a rampage, America was faced with a manpower shortage. This is the only time you and I got a break. Some of you are too young to remember it, and some of you are so old you don't want to remember it.

They let us in the defense plants, and we began to get jobs as machinists for the first time. We got a little skill, made a little more money. Then we were in a position to live in a little better neighborhood, we had a little better school to go to and got a little better education. This is how we came out of it; not through someone's benevolence and not through the efforts of organizations in our midst. It was the pressure that Uncle Sam was under. The only time that man has let the black man go one step forward has been when outside pressure has been brought to bear upon him. It has never been for any other reason. World pressure, economic pressure, political pressure, military pressure: When he was under pressure, he let you and me have a break.

So the point that I make is that it has never just been on our own initiative that you and I have made any steps forward. And the day that you and I recognize this, then we see the thing in its proper perspective because we cease looking just to Uncle Sam and Washington, D.C., to have the problems solved and we cease looking just within America for allies in our struggle against the injustices.

When you find people outside America who look like you getting power, my suggestion is that you turn to them and make them your allies. Let them know that we all have the same problem, that racism is not an internal American problem, but an international problem. Racism is a human problem and a crime that is absolutely so ghastly that a person who is fighting racism is well within his rights to fight against it by any means necessary until it is eliminated.

When you and I can start thinking like that and we get involved in some kind of activity with that kind of liberty, I think we'll get some ends to some of our problems almost overnight.

Address to the 1988 Democratic National Convention

by Jesse Jackson

Du Bois was committed to gaining voting rights and full political equality for African Americans. Had he been alive, he probably would have been happy to hear the name of Jesse Jackson entered as a candidate for the 1988 Democratic Presidential nomination. Jackson gave this stirring speech, "Common Ground and Common Sense," at the Democratic convention on July 20, 1988.

Tonight we pause and give praise and honor to God for being good enough to allow us to be at this place at this time. When I look out at this convention, I see the face of America, red, yellow, brown, black and white, we're all precious in God's sight—the real rainbow coalition. All of us, all of us who are here and think that we are seated. But we're really standing on someone's shoulders. Ladies and gentlemen. Mrs. Rosa Parks.

The mother of the civil rights movement.

I want to express my deep love and appreciation for the support my family has given me over these past months.

They have endured pain, anxiety, threat and fear.

But they have been strengthened and made secure by a faith in God, in America and in you.

Your love has protected us and made us strong.

To my wife, Jackie, the foundation of our family; to our five children whom you met tonight; to my mother Mrs. Helen Jackson, who is present tonight; and to my grandmother, Mrs. Maltilda Burns; my brother Chuck and his family; my mother-in-law, Mrs. Gertrude Brown, who just last month at age 61 graduated from Hampton Institute, a marvelous achievement; I offer my appreciation to Mayor Andrew Young who has provided such gracious hospitality to all of us this week.

And a special salute to President Jimmy Carter.

President Carter restored honor to the White House after Watergate. He gave many of us a special opportunity to grow. For his kind words, for his unwavering commitment to peace in the world and the voters that came from his family, every member of his family, led by Billy and Amy, I offer him my special thanks, special thanks to the Carter family.

My right and my privilege to stand here before you has been won—in my lifetime—by the blood and the sweat of the innocent.

Twenty-four years ago, the late Fannie Lou Hamer and Aaron Henry—who sits here tonight from Mississippi—were locked out on the streets of Atlantic City, the head of the Mississippi Freedom Democratic Party.

But tonight, a black and white delegation from Mississippi is headed by Ed Cole, a black man, from Mississippi, 24 years later.

Many were lost in the struggle for the right to vote. Jimmy Lee Jackson, a young student, gave his life. Viola Luizzo, a white mother from Detroit, called nigger lover, and brains blown out at point blank range.

Schwerner, Goodman and Chaney—two Jews and a

black—found in a common grave, bodies riddled with bullets in Mississippi. The four darling little girls in the church in Birmingham, Ala. They died that we might have a right to live.

Dr. Martin Luther King Jr. lies only a few miles from us tonight.

Tonight he must feel good as he looks down upon us. We sit here together, a rainbow, a coalition—the sons and daughters of slave masters and the sons and daughters of slaves sitting together around a common table, to decide the direction of our party and our country. His heart would be full tonight.

As a testament to the struggles of those who have gone before; as a legacy for those who will come after; as a tribute to the endurance, the patience, the courage of our forefathers and mothers; as an assurance that their prayers are being answered, their work has not been in vain, and hope is eternal; tomorrow night my name will go into nomination for the presidency of the United States of America.

We meet tonight at a crossroads, a point of decision.

Shall we expand, be inclusive, find unity and power; or suffer division and impotence.

We come to Atlanta, the cradle of the old south, the crucible of the new South.

Tonight there is a sense of celebration because we are moved, fundamentally moved, from racial battlegrounds by law, to economic common ground, tomorrow we will challenge to move to higher ground.

Common ground!

Think of Jerusalem—the intersection where many trails met. A small village that became the birthplace for three great religions—Judaism, Christianity and Islam.

Why was this village so blessed? Because it provided a crossroads where different people met, different cultures, and different civilizations could meet and find common ground.

When people come together, flowers always flourish and the air is rich with the aroma of a new spring.

Take New York, the dynamic metropolis. What makes New York so special?

It is the invitation of the Statue of Liberty—give me your tired, your poor, your huddled masses who yearn to breathe free.

Not restricted to English only.

Many people, many cultures, many languages—with one thing in common, the yearn to breathe free.

Common ground!

Tonight in Atlanta, for the first time in this century we convene in the South.

A state where governors once stood in school house doors. Where Julian Bond was denied his seat in the state legislature because of his conscientious objection to the Vietnam War.

A city that, through its five black universities, has graduated more black students than any city in the world.

Atlanta, now a modern intersection of the new South.

Common ground!

That is the challenge to our party tonight.

Left wing. Right wing. Progress will not come through boundless liberalism nor static conservatism, but at the critical mass of mutual survival. It takes two wings to fly.

Whether you're a hawk or a dove, you're just a bird living in the same environment, in the same world.

The Bible teaches that when lions and lambs lie

down together, none will be afraid and there will be peace in the valley. It sounds impossible. Lions eat lambs. Lambs sensibly flee from lions. But even lions and lambs find common ground. Why?

Because neither lions nor lambs want the forest to catch on fire. Neither lions nor lambs want acid rain to fall. Neither lions nor lambs can survive nuclear war. If lions and lambs can find common ground, surely, we can as well, as civilized people.

The only time that we win is when we come together. In 1960, John Kennedy, the late John Kennedy, beat Richard Nixon by only 112,000 votes—less than one vote per precinct. He won by the margin of our hope. He brought us together. He reached out. He had the courage to defy his advisors and inquire about Dr. King's jailing in Albany, Georgia. We won by the margin of our hope, inspired by courageous leadership.

In 1964, Lyndon Johnson brought both wings together. The thesis, the antithesis and to create a synthesis and together we won.

In 1976, Jimmy Carter unified us again and we won. When we do not come together, we never win.

In 1968, division and despair in July led to our defeat in November.

In 1980, rancor in the spring and the summer led to Reagan in the fall. When we divide, we cannot win. We must find common ground as a basis for survival and development and change and growth.

Today when we debated, differed, deliberated, agreed to agree, agreed to disagree, when we had the good judgment to argue our case and then not self-destruct, George Bush was just a little further away from the White House and a little closer to private life.

Tonight, I salute Governor Michael Dukakis.

He has run a well-managed and a dignified campaign. No matter how tired or how tried, he always resisted the temptation to stoop to demagoguery.

I've watched a good mind fast at work, with steel nerves, guiding his campaign out of the crowded field without appeal to the worst in us. I've watched his perspective grow as his environment has expanded. I've seen his toughness and tenacity close up. I know his commitment to public service.

Mike Dukakis' parents were a doctor and a teacher; my parents, a maid, a beautician and a janitor.

There's a great gap between Brookline, Massachusetts and Haney Street, the Fieldcrest Village housing projects in Greenville, South Carolina.

He studied law; I studied theology. There are differences of religion, region, and race; differences in experiences and perspectives. But the genius of America is that out of the many, we become one.

Providence has enabled our paths to intersect. His foreparents came to America on immigrant ships; my foreparents came to America on slave ships. But whatever the original ships, we're in the same boat tonight.

Our ships could pass in the night if we have a false sense of independence, or they could collide and crash. We would lose our passengers. But we can seek a higher reality and a greater good apart. We can drift on the broken pieces of Reaganomics, satisfy our baser instincts, and exploit the fears of our people. At our highest, we can call upon noble instincts and navigate this vessel to safety. The greater good is the common good.

As Jesus said, "Not my will, but thine be done." It was his way of saying there's a higher good beyond personal comfort or position.

The good of our nation is at stake—its commitment

to working men and women, to the poor and the vulnerable, to the many in the world. With so many guided missiles, and so much misguided leadership, the stakes are exceedingly high. Our choice, full participation in a Democratic government, or more abandonment and neglect. And so this night, we choose not a false sense of independence, not our capacity to survive and endure.

Tonight we choose interdependency in our capacity to act and unite for the greater good. The common good is finding commitment to new priorities, to expansion and inclusion. A commitment to expanded participation in the Democratic Party at every level. A commitment to a shared national campaign strategy and involvement at every level. A commitment to new priorities that ensure that hope will be kept alive. A common ground commitment for a legislative agenda by empowerment for the John Conyers bill, universal, on-site, same-day registration everywhere—and commitment to D.C. statehood and empowerment—D.C. deserves statehood. A commitment to economic set-asides, a commitment to the Dellums bill for comprehensive sanctions against South Africa, a shared commitment to a common direction.

Common ground. Easier said than done. Where do you find common ground at the point of challenge? This campaign has shown that politics need not be marketed by politicians, packaged by pollsters and pundits. Politics can be a marvel arena where people come together, define common ground.

We find common ground at the plant gate that closes on workers without notice. We find common ground at the farm auction where a good farmer loses his or her land to bad loans or diminishing markets. Common ground at the schoolyard where teachers cannot get adequate pay, and students cannot get a scholarship and can't make a loan. Common ground, at the hospital admitting room where somebody tonight is dying because they cannot afford to go upstairs to a bed that's empty, waiting for someone with insurance to get sick. We are a better nation than that. We must do better.

Common ground. What is leadership if not present help in a time of crisis? And so I met you at the point of challenge in Jay, Maine where paper workers were striking for fair wages; in Greenfield, Iowa, where family farmers struggle for a fair price; in Cleveland, Ohio, where working women seek comparable worth; in McFarland, Calif., where the children of Hispanic farm workers may be dying from poison land, dying in clusters with cancer; in the AIDS hospice in Houston, Texas, where the sick support one another, 12 are rejected by their own parents and friends.

Common ground.

America's not a blanket woven from one thread, one color, one cloth. When I was a child growing up in Greenville, S.C., and grandmother could not afford a blanket, she didn't complain and we did not freeze. Instead, she took pieces of old cloth—patches, wool, silk, gabardine, crockersack on the patches—barely good enough to wipe off your shoes with.

But they didn't stay that way very long. With sturdy hands and a strong cord, she sewed them together into a quilt, a thing of beauty and power and culture.

Now, Democrats, we must build such a quilt. Farmers, you seek fair prices and you are right, but you cannot stand alone. Your patch is not big enough. Workers, you fight for fair wages. You are right. But your patch labor is not big enough. Women, you seek comparable worth and pay equity. You are right. But your patch is not big enough. Women, mothers, who seek Head Start and day care and pre-natal care on the front side of life, rather than jail care and welfare on the back side of life, you're right, but your patch is not big enough.

Students, you seek scholarships. You are right. But your patch is not big enough. Blacks and Hispanics, when we fight for civil rights, we are right, but our patch is not big enough. Gays and lesbians, when you fight against discrimination and for a cure for AIDS, you are right, but your patch is not big enough. Conservatives and progressives, when you fight for what you believe, right-wing, left-wing, hawk, dove— you are right, from your point of view, but your point of view is not enough.

But don't despair. Be as wise as my grandmama. Pool the patches and the pieces together, bound by a common thread. When we form a great quilt of unity and common ground we'll have the power to bring about health care and housing and jobs and education and hope to our nation.

We the people can win. We stand at the end of a long dark night of reaction. We stand tonight united in a commitment to a new direction. For almost eight years, we've been led by those who view social good coming from private interest, who viewed public life as a means to increase private wealth. They have been prepared to sacrifice the common good of the many to satisfy the private interest and the wealth of a few. We believe in a government that's a tool of our democracy in service to the public, not an instrument of the aristocracy in search of private wealth. . . .

That's classic Reaganomics. It believes that the poor had too much money and the rich had too little money.

So, they engaged in reverse Robin Hood—took from the poor, gave to the rich, paid for by the middle class. We cannot stand four more years of

Reaganomics in any version, in any disguise.

How do I document that case? Seven years later, the richest 1 percent of our society pays 20 percent less in taxes; the poorest 10 percent pay 20 percent more. Reaganomics.

Reagan gave the rich and the powerful a multibillion-dollar party. Now, the party is over. He expects the people to pay for the damage. I take this principled position—convention, let us not raise taxes on the poor and the middle class, but those who had the party, the rich and the powerful, must pay for the party!

I just want to take common sense to high places. We're spending $150 billion a year defending Europe and Japan 43 years after the war is over. We have more troops in Europe tonight than we had seven years ago, yet the threat of war is ever more remote. Germany and Japan are now creditor nations—that means they've got a surplus. We are a debtor nation—it means we are in debt.

Let them share more of the burden of their own defense—use some of that money to build decent housing!

Use some of that money to educate our children!

Use some of that money for long-term health care!

Use some of that money to wipe out these slums and put America back to work!

I just want to take common sense to high places. If we can bail out Europe and Japan, if we can bail out Continental Bank and Chrysler—and Mr. Iacocca makes $8,000 an hour, we can bail out the family farmer.

I just want to make common sense. It does not make sense to close down 650,000 family farms in this country while importing food from abroad subsidized by the U.S. government.

Let's make sense. It does not make sense to be escorting oil tankers up and down the Persian Gulf paying $2.50 for every $1.00 worth of oil we bring out while oil wells are capped in Texas, Oklahoma and Louisiana. I just want to make sense.

Leadership must meet the moral challenge of its day. What's the moral challenge of our day? We have public accommodations. We have the right to vote. We have open housing.

What's the fundamental challenge of our day? It is to end economic violence. Plant closing without notice, economic violence. Even the greedy do not profit long from greed. Economic violence. Most poor people are not lazy. They're not black. They're not brown. They're mostly white, and female and young.

But whether white, black or brown, the hungry baby's belly turned inside out is the same color. Call it pain. Call it hurt. Call it agony. Most poor people are not on welfare.

Some of them are illiterate and can't read the want-ad sections. And when they can, they can't find a job that matches their address. They work hard every day, I know. I live amongst them. I'm one of them.

I know they work. I'm a witness. They catch the early bus. They work every day. They raise other people's children. They work every day. They clean the streets. They work every day. They drive vans with cabs. They work every day. They change the beds you slept in these hotels last night and can't get a union contract. They work every day.

No more. They're not lazy. Someone must defend them because it's right, and they cannot speak for themselves. They work in hospitals. I know they do. They wipe the bodies of those who are sick with fever and pain. They empty their bedpans. They clean out their commode. No job is beneath them, and yet when they get sick, they cannot lie in the bed they made up every day. America, that is not right. We are a better nation than that. We are a better nation than that.

We need a real war on drugs. You can't just say no. It's deeper than that. You can't just get a palm reader or an astrologer; it's more profound than that. We're spending $150 billion on drugs a year. We've gone from ignoring it to focusing on the children. Children cannot buy $150 billion worth of drugs a year. A few high profile athletes—athletes are not laundering $150 billion a year—bankers are.

I met the children in Watts who are unfortunate in their despair. Their grapes of hope have become raisins of despair, and they're turning to each other and they're self-destructing—but I stayed with them all night long. I wanted to hear their case. They said, "Jesse Jackson, as you challenge us to say no to drugs, you're right. And to not sell them, you're right. And to not use these guns, you're right."

And, by the way, the promise of CETA—they displaced CETA. They did not replace CETA. We have neither jobs nor houses nor services nor training—no way out. Some of us take drugs as anesthesia for our pain. Some take drugs as a way of pleasure—both short-term pleasure and long-term pain. Some sell drugs to make money. It's wrong, we know. But you need to know that we know. We can go and buy the drugs by the boxes at the port. If we can buy the drugs at the port, don't you believe the federal government can stop it if they want to?

They say, "We don't have Saturday night specials any more." They say, "We buy AK-47s and Uzis, the latest lethal weapons. We buy them across the counter on Long Beach Boulevard." You cannot fight a war on drugs unless and until you are going to challenge the bankers and the gun sellers and those who grow them.

Don't just focus on the children, let's stop drugs at the level of supply and demand. We must end the scourge on the American culture.

Leadership. What difference will we make? Leadership cannot just go along to get along. We must do more than change presidents. We must change direction. Leadership must face the moral challenge of our day. The nuclear war build-up is irrational. Strong leadership cannot desire to look tough, and let that stand in the way of the pursuit of peace. Leadership must reverse the arms race.

At least we should pledge no first use. Why? Because first use begat first retaliation, and that's mutual annihilation. That's not a rational way out. No use at all—let's think it out, and not fight it out, because it's an unwinnable fight. Why hold a card that you can never drop? Let's give peace a chance.

Leadership—we now have this marvelous opportunity to have a breakthrough with the Soviets. Last year, 200,000 Americans visited the Soviet Union. There's a chance for joint ventures into space, not Star Wars and the war arms escalation, but a space defense initiative. Let's build in space together, and demilitarize the heavens. There's a way out.

America, let us expand. When Mr. Reagan and Mr. Gorbachev met, there was a big meeting. They represented together one-eighth of the human race. Seven-eighths of the human race was locked out of that room. Most people in the world tonight—half are Asian, one-half of them are Chinese. There are 22 nations in the Middle East. There's Europe; 40 million Latin Americans next door to us; the Caribbean; Africa—a half-billion people. Most people in the world today are yellow or brown or black, non-Christian, poor, female, young, and don't speak English—in the real world.

This generation must offer leadership to the real world. We're losing ground in Latin America, the Middle East, South Africa, because we're not focusing on the real world, that real world. We must use basic principles, support international law. We stand the most to gain from it. Support human rights; we believe in that. Support self-determination; we'll build on that. Support economic development; you know it's right. Be consistent, and gain our moral authority in the world.

I challenge you tonight, my friends, let's be bigger and better as a nation and as a party. We have basic challenges. Freedom in South Africa—we've already agreed as Democrats to declare South Africa to be a terrorist state. But don't just stop there. Get South Africa out of Angola. Free Namibia. Support the front-line states. We must have a new, humane human rights assistance policy in Africa.

I'm often asked, "Jesse, why do you take on these tough issues? They're not very political. We can't win that way."

If an issue is morally right, it will eventually be political. It may be political and never be right. Fannie Lou Hamer didn't have the most votes in Atlantic City, but her principles have outlasted every delegate who voted to lock her out. Rosa Parks did not have the most votes, but she was morally right. Dr. King didn't have the most votes about the Vietnam war, but he was morally right. If we're principled first, our politics will fall in place.

Jesse, why did you take these big bold initiatives? A poem by an unknown author went something like this: We mastered the air, we've conquered the sea, and annihilated distance and prolonged life, we were not wise enough to live on this earth without war and without hate.

As for Jesse Jackson, I'm tired of sailing by little boat, far inside the harbor bar. I want to go out where the big ships float, out on the deep where the great ones are. And should my frail craft prove too slight, the waves that sweep those billows o'er, I'd rather go down in a stirring fight than drown to death in the sheltered shore.

We've got to go out, my friends, where the big boats are.

And then, for our children, young America, hold your head high now. We can win. We must not lose you to drugs and violence, premature pregnancy, suicide, cynicism, pessimism and despair. We can win.

Wherever you are tonight, I challenge you to hope and to dream. Don't submerge your dreams. Exercise above all else, even on drugs, dream of the day you're drug-free. Even in the gutter, dream of the day that you'll be up on your feet again. You must never stop dreaming. Face reality, yes. But don't stop with the way things are; dream of things as they ought to be. Dream. Face pain, but love, hope, faith, and dreams will help you rise above the pain.

Use hope and imagination as weapons of survival and progress, but you keep on dreaming, young America. Dream of peace. Peace is rational and reasonable. War is irrational in this age and unwinnable.

Dream of teachers who teach for life and not for a living. Dream of doctors who are concerned more about public health than private wealth. Dream of lawyers more concerned about justice than a judgeship. Dream of preachers who are concerned more about prophecy than profiteering. Dream on the high road of sound values.

And in America, as we go forth to September, October and November and then beyond, America must never surrender to a high moral challenge.

Do not surrender to drugs. The best drug policy is a no first use. Don't surrender with needles and cynicism. Let's have no first use on the one hand, or clinics on the other. Never surrender, young America.

Go forward. America must never surrender to malnutrition. We can feed the hungry and clothe the naked. We must never surrender. We must go forward. We must never surrender to illiteracy. Invest in our children. Never surrender; and go forward.

We must never surrender to inequality. Women cannot compromise ERA or comparable worth. Women are making 60 cents on the dollar to what a man makes. Women cannot buy meat cheaper. Women cannot buy bread cheaper. Women cannot buy milk cheaper. Women deserve to get paid for the work that you do. It's right and it's fair.

Don't surrender, my friends. Those who have AIDS tonight, you deserve our compassion. Even with AIDS you must not surrender in your wheelchairs. I see you sitting here tonight in those wheelchairs. I've stayed with you. I've reached out to you across our nation. Don't you give up. I know it's tough sometimes. People look down on you. It took you a little more effort to get here tonight.

And no one should look down on you, but sometimes mean people do. The only justification we have for looking down on someone is that we're going to stop and pick them up. But even in your wheelchairs, don't you give up. We cannot forget 50 years ago when our backs were against the wall, Roosevelt was in a wheelchair. I would rather have Roosevelt in a wheelchair than Reagan and Bush on a horse. Don't you surrender and don't you give up.

Don't surrender and don't give up. Why can I challenge you this way? Jesse Jackson, you don't understand my situation. You be on television. You don't understand. I see you with the big people. You don't understand my situation. I understand. You're seeing me on TV but you don't know the me that makes me, me. They wonder why does Jesse run, because they see me running for the White House. They don't see the house I'm running from.

I have a story. I wasn't always on television. Writers were not always outside my door. When I was born late one afternoon, October 8th, in Greenville, S.C., no writers asked my mother her name. Nobody chose to write down our address. My mama was not supposed to make it. And I was not supposed to make it. You see, I was born to a teen-age mother who was born to a teen-age mother.

I understand. I know abandonment and people being mean to you, and saying you're nothing and nobody, and can never be anything. I understand. Jesse Jackson is my third name. I'm adopted. When I had no name, my grandmother gave me her name. My name was Jesse Burns until I was 12. So I wouldn't have a blank space, she gave me a name to hold me over. I understand when nobody knows your name. I understand when you have no name. I understand.

I wasn't born in the hospital. Mama didn't have insurance. I was born in the bed at home. I really do understand. Born in a three-room house, bathroom in the backyard, slop jar by the bed, no hot and cold running water. I understand. Wallpaper used for decoration? No. For a windbreaker. I understand. I'm a working person's person, that's why I understand you whether you're black or white.

I understand work. I was not born with a silver spoon in my mouth. I had a shovel programmed for my hand. My mother, a working woman. So many days she went to work early with runs in her stockings. She knew better, but she wore runs in her stockings so that my brother and I could have matching socks and not be laughed at at school.

I understand. At 3 o'clock on Thanksgiving Day we couldn't eat turkey because mama was preparing someone else's turkey at 3 o'clock. We had to play football to entertain ourselves and then around 6 o'clock she would get off the Alta Vista bus; then we would bring up the leftovers and eat our turkey—leftovers, the carcass, the cranberries around 8 o'clock at night. I really do understand.

Every one of these funny labels they put on you, those of you who are watching this broadcast tonight in the projects, on the corners, I understand. Call you outcast, low down, you can't make it, you're nothing, you're from nobody, subclass, underclass—when you see Jesse Jackson, when my name goes in nomination, your name goes in nomination.

I was born in the slum, but the slum was not born in me. And it wasn't born in you, and you can make it. Wherever you are tonight you can make it. Hold your head high, stick your chest out. You can make it. It gets dark sometimes, but the morning comes. Don't you surrender. Suffering breeds character. Character breeds faith. In the end faith will not disappoint.

You must not surrender. You may or may not get there, but just know that you're qualified and you hold on and hold out. We must never surrender. America will get better and better. Keep hope alive. Keep hope alive. Keep hope alive. On tomorrow night and beyond, keep hope alive.

I love you very much. I love you very much.

from Sushi and Grits: Ethnic Identity and Conflict in a Newly Multicultural America

by Itabari Njeri

Njeri, an award-winning journalist from Los Angeles, discusses Du Bois's ideas about race and "double-consciousness," finding that they take on new complexity at the dawn of the 21st century. Njeri considers the growing population of multiethnic Americans and explores conflicts between African Americans and other nonwhite minority groups.

Tagged an "emerging" population by social scientists, multiethnic Americans may be the most significant group to spring from a newly pluralistic America. Their demand for recognition is stimulating what I think will be a decades-long debate—one that may force all Americans to confront the myths that surround "race" and ethnicity in the United States.

High on the political agenda of many now-vocal multiethnic Americans is the demand for a new "multiracial" census category that specifically identifies ethnically and "racially" mixed citizens. The size of the "multiracial" population may be about five million—probably more than twice that number, say multiethnic activists. But the exact figures are unknown because the census requires people to either identify with one "race" or ethnic group or to check "other" when filling out data for the Census Bureau.

The ranks of multiethnic activists are being bolstered by their monoethnic kin—parents, grandparents, and spouses—who have helped form support groups in, among other places, Atlanta, Buffalo, Chicago, Houston, Los Angeles, Omaha, San Diego, Seattle, San Francisco, Pittsburgh, and Washington, D.C. Similar support groups are popping up on college campuses, particularly in California, a center of multicultural activism. While these activists failed to get a new multiethnic designation on the 1990 census, they are pushing to see one established for the year 2000.

In general, supporters of the category want recognition and political representation for people of mixed heritage. Opponents say minority groups would shrink if such a designation is allowed, leading to a loss of political representation and congressionally appropriated funds, based on the census count, used to remedy the effects of past and continuing discrimination.

These multiethnic Americans may be Mexican American and Italian American; Japanese American and Cherokee; Korean American, Armenian American, and Chinese. But the most problematic amalgams are those that include the genes of America's most stigmatized group: Negroes, Blacks, Afro-Americans, African Americans, African heritage people—a "spade" by any other name in the consciousness of still too many White Americans. The issue of a special census designation, and social recognition, is especially important to this group because of the way in which "race" has been traditionally defined in America for people of African descent: socially, any known or perceived African ancestry makes one Black—the one-drop-in-the-bucket theory of descent.

"If you consider yourself Black for political reasons, raise your hand," Charles Stewart said to a predominantly African American audience at a symposium I organized for the National Association of Black Journalists in 1990. "The overwhelming majority raised their hands," said Stewart, a Democratic Party activist in Los Angeles. "When I asked how many people here believe that they are of pure African descent, without any mixture, nobody raised their hands." The point, said Stewart, is this: "If you advocate a category that includes people who are *multiracial* to the detriment of their Black indentification, you will replicate what you saw—an empty room. We cannot afford to have an empty room. We cannot afford to have a race empty of Black people—not so long as we are struggling against discrimination based on our identification as Black people."

But a woman I will call Anna Vale eschews the little-dab'll-do-you school of genetics. She is a Californian of Japanese, African American, and Native American descent. A voice from the sushi-and-grits generation, she represents the new kind of diversity challenging old "racial" conceptions. Her eyes scan me skeptically. She does not trust me. Though I have written often and sympathetically about the issues so-called "multiracial" Americans face and the problem of colorism, she fears that I, too, will "rape" her. That's what Black people have been doing to her all her life, she claims, committing political and psychological rape on her person. And

I'll do it, too, she insists, by writing a piece that distorts the reality of Americans like her who assert their "biological truth" and seek an identity separate from Blacks.

"What I don't appreciate about the African American community," she tells me, "is this mentality of annexing anyone with one drop of African blood. . . . I don't know why African American people seem so obsessed with annexing other people." Yet, says Anna, when "multiracial" people want to voice their unique concerns—political support for Amer-Asian refugees, many of whom have African American fathers, funding for works of art that present the complex cultural views of, for instance, a Black-Korean American—they are told to "be quiet," and "just carry out the political and cultural agenda of African Americans."

As she sits in a Santa Monica café, Vale's delicate body belies the dragon within. "African Americans want us to be their political slaves," she says with the intensity of water at a low boil. "They are saying, 'Come join us.' But it's not because of some great brother or sister love—it's political. If their numbers decrease, their chance of getting public funds decrease—as well as political representation. To me, that's a totally unethical way of saying that you want people to be a member of your community. As far as I am concerned all slavery is over—whether it's physical slavery on the plantation or political slavery that gives one group, like African Americans, the audacity to say that they own people because they have one drop of African blood."

Of course, it was White slave owners in the antebellum South who perpetuated the little-dab'll-do-you rule. They wanted to make sure that Blacks of mixed heritage—usually the products of White masters' raping of enslaved Black women—had no special claim to freedom because their fathers were free. They inherited the status of their slave mothers and were categorized with "pure" Blacks to assure the perpetuation of the slave population. In the postslave era, the alleged inferiority of African blood—no matter how little of it one possessed—was used to rationalize the continued social and political subordination of Blacks. Wisely, Blacks made a political virtue out of a necessity, asserting that we would not allow our heterogeneous ancestry to divide and render us politically dysfunctional—as many argue has been the case with Brazil's "Black" population.

I looked at Anna and listened to her ahistorical and apolitical diatribe. Her comments were a more extreme form of the kind of Black bashing I've often heard from multiethnics of African descent—usually ones who have had little contact with, or understanding of, the Black side of their heritage. I fear that the increasingly acrimonious nature of the debate among multiethnic Americans and African Americans is turning into a dialogue of the deaf. Pain and rage are the barriers. And though Anna often sees me as the enemy, I have always viewed her as a wounded sister. I understand the source of her rage.

Born in Japan and brought to the U.S. while in grade school, she knew little about her father's African American and Native American family. He died when she was young. Her mother, a Japanese war bride, raised Anna as only she could: to be a good Japanese daughter.

On the days Anna brought sushi to lunch, African American children teased her. But their mild teasing escalated to schoolyard terrorism: a group of Black girls pushing her down . . . cutting off her long, dark hair 'cause she swung it like a White girl. . . .

. . . a Black cop in L.A. ignoring her pleas for help after a fender bender injured her light-skinned son, then calling her a "half-breed bitch." . . .

From her perspective, the dark-brown, long-haired Polynesian-looking and Japanese-speaking woman has had the foot of an African American on her neck all her life.

"Communities of color are the most severe in doling out this kind of oppression," she says grimly. "The oppressed seem to oppress more."

In 1903, when Du Bois wrote that the "problem of the twentieth century is the problem of the color-line—the relation of the darker to the lighter races of men in Asia and Africa, in America and the islands of the sea," he referred to the domination of Whites over darker peoples. This remains true. But that domination has bred an insidious offspring: internalized oppression, that is, the installing of the oppressor's values within the psyche of oppressed people, so that—in a system of structured inequality such as ours—the psychological dynamics that help to keep the system in place function on automatic pilot. In effect, the mind becomes the last plantation.

One wonders if the assertion of a unique, multiethnic identity—particularly for a person of African heritage in the United States—is the ultimate expression of (or, through a synthesis of competing identities, an escape from) the divided consciousness that Du Bois said defined American Blacks. For where, save the United States—the New World—could an Anna be forged? Not just in the particulars of her ethnicity, but in the clear anguish, for many like her, such an amalgamation in an African-tinged package causes? Where else but in the United States does a slave master's economically motivated definition of identity reign so completely? Multiple souls, multiple thoughts, multiple "unreconciled strivings" warring "in one dark body, whose dogged strength alone," Du Bois wrote, "keeps it from being torn asunder."

Such contradictory feelings were not unknown to Du Bois. In *The Art & Imagination of W. E. B. Du Bois,* Arnold Rampersad notes that the twentieth century's greatest African American scholar was "not immune to the psychological subversions of white racism," often seeming ambivalent about his own "racial" identity. Aiming at this vulnerable psychic spot, the color-conscious Garvey sought to "discredit Du Bois before the bar of black public opinion" in 1921, writes Rampersad. Garvey insisted that the "mulatto" Du Bois was trying to be everything but a Negro. Sometimes, Garvey dug in, Du Bois claims he's a Frenchman, on another day Dutch, and only "when it is convenient is he a Negro."

In a 1929 issue of *The Crisis,* a less hostile commentator, writes Rampersad, noted ironically Du Bois's resemblance to "a sunburnt Jew, a Turk, an Italian, a Cuban or a German," anything but what he was supposed to look like: a Negro.

What is a Negro supposed to look like, then and now? How is one supposed to talk, walk, laugh, love, live—be?

Du Bois confronted these issues personally and politically throughout his life, providing a blueprint, at the jump of this century, for the "race" in *The Souls of Black Folk.*

But as a new century nears, ushering in the next millennium and unprecedented ethnic and "racial" diversity in the U.S., millions like Anna sound a disturbing and potentially potent riff on Du Bois's classic statement of color division. Further, given the tense, competitive relations between Blacks and other people of color vying for the dubious status of America's most significant minority, acute observers of the social landscape have correctly predicted that intraminority group conflicts will be a key factor leading to the fire next time. As Richard Rubenstein, former director of the Center for Conflict Analysis and Resolution at George Mason University, said in a July 12, 1990, *Los Angeles Times* article that anticipated the 1992 Los Angeles "riots" (specifically citing tensions between Blacks and Korean immigrant merchants and police brutality as causes), the nation is on the brink of "civil war."

Hedging so powerful an assertion in customary journalistic fashion, the article continued: "That grim prediction doesn't necessarily mean riots in the streets but a combination of [individual] sociopathic behavior" and "intensified intergroup conflict."

In California, which provides a microcosm of existing and, perhaps, future intraminority group relations, neighborhoods once predominantly Black, such as Watts, are shifting to Latino majorities. Typical of conflicts in these changing neighborhoods is the Latino charge that they are underrepresented on the staffs of hospitals in changing neighborhoods that have large numbers of Latino patients but too few Spanish-speaking nurses. In 1990, for example, the U.S. Equal Employment Opportunity Commission found "significant disparities" in the promotion of Latinos at the Los Angeles County-University of Southern California medical center. There, Latinos accounted for 14 percent of registered nurses but occupied only 4 percent of nursing-supervisor positions. In contrast, Blacks represented 20 percent of the nurses but 29 percent of the supervisors. Whites, however, still outnumbered everybody, accounting for 40 percent of the nurses and 46 percent of the supervisors.

Blacks argue that they should not have to give up jobs they fought for and won in the afterglow of the civil rights struggle and in the wake of the Watts rebellion. As one Black activist complained, "You don't see us going into East L.A. trying to take jobs from Latinos."

And then there is the much-publicized, sometimes deadly, conflict between Korean immigrant merchants and Blacks in many impoverished urban neighborhoods. Many of these merchants view Blacks as violent, ignorant, and unwilling to work, while Blacks see them as among the most arrogant and rude in a succession of exploitative middlemen entrepreneurs.

These variations on intraminority group conflict are related phenomena, in great part a consequence of what that brilliant analyst of the colonized mind, psychiatrist Frantz Fanon, called internalized oppression. . . .

But Re-Evaluation Counseling theory has gone beyond the purely psychological consequences of oppression that Fanon explored. The theory weds the concept of internalized oppression to class analysis, creating what I think of as liberation psychology.

"I define internalized oppression as that process whereby a set of beliefs, attitudes, and misinformation about members of a target or oppressed group are put out by the dominant group to justify their subordination," says [Barbara] Love, both a professor of education at the University of Massachusetts at Amherst and a leader in the Re-Evaluation Counseling community. That misinformation becomes embedded in the psyche—the emotional domain of that target group, she explains.

"There is extensive internalized oppression within the Black community," Loves states unequivocally. "It was a deliberate part of the system of dehumanizing Africans who were brought to the United States and making them fit to be slaves. We were not fit to be slaves when we came here, so we had to be made to be fit—that is to go along with and participate in an oppressive system. And that process continues to this day."

Among the consequences of internalized oppression are "the ways in which we put each other down. The ways in which we play out the dehumanization that got inflicted on *us,* at *each other,*" Love continues. It's the flip side of the oppression itself.

Tall, possessing skin with the soft patina of polished mahogany and disposed to wearing flowing African gowns, Love relates that her own sister had long hair and light skin. "If she tossed her hair in a certain way, she"—like Anna—"was accused of trying to act like a White girl. And the other kids jumped her." Why? "Because we have internalized this set of notions about what it means to be beautiful," says Love. "And what it means to be beautiful in this society is to be like Whites.

"The oppression says that by definition Black people cannot be beautiful. But if someone—because of our genetically mixed heritage—comes along looking like the dominant group, we say, 'If you're Black you are not beautiful—that is, you can't have long hair and here you've got long hair. It's wrong. We'll fix it. We'll cut it off and we'll put you back in your place. Because your place is to be like us: nobody.'"

Looking to the broader community of color, what happens when two historically subjugated people, culturally dissimilar, collide? In one notorious case, a Black teenage girl in Los Angeles was killed by a Korean American merchant after a dispute over a

$1.79 bottle of orange juice.

The merchant, a then fifty-year-old woman named Soon Ja Du, was the daughter of a doctor and a literature major in college before she came to the United States with her husband and three children. She never adjusted to her loss of status as an immigrant who, because of language barriers, was compelled to work in a knitting factory for many years before her family saved enough to buy two combination liquor-and-food markets.

A devout Christian, Du reportedly never felt comfortable selling liquor or having to keep a gun in the stores, one of which was in the midst of gang-plagued South-Central Los Angeles—the Empire Market and Liquor Store. And she later told a probation officer she was afraid of, and didn't understand, the poor Blacks who frequented her store. "They look healthy, young," she said through an interpreter. "Big question why they don't work. Didn't understand why got welfare money and buying alcoholic beverages and consume them . . . instead of feeding children . . . Didn't understand at first," she said. Eventually, she explained, "paid less attention," and decided that it was "their way of living."

Days after Black gang members had terrorized her adult son, Du saw fifteen-year-old Latasha Harlins walk into the Empire Market, take a container of orange juice from a refrigerated case, and placed it in her open backpack. With the juice visible, the girl walked to the counter with two dollars in her hand. Du accused her of stealing the juice. Harlins turned halfway to show her the exposed juice container and said she was paying for it. Du did not believe her, yanked Harlins toward her, pulling the arm of the girl's sweater.

What happened then?

Years before and months after the incident, commentators insist on calling the tensions between Blacks and Koreans an essentially cultural conflict.

At root, I think the conflict stems from economic and political inequality *exacerbated* by cultural differences. And the nation's White elite are not just *tsk-tsk-tsking* spectators. It has much to do with the way capitalism works. As Edna Bonacich, professor at the University of California in Irvine and an expert on the role of middleman minorities around the world, points out, "Korean Americans, to a certain extent, are fronting for the larger White power structure. They are both beneficiaries of the arrangement and the victims of it." The sale of liquor in the Black community is but one example of how Korean immigrant merchants, like Jews before them and Arab immigrants in others parts of the country, fulfill their middleman role.

Corporate-owned liquor companies sell their products through Korean-owned liquor stores in the Black community, Bonacich says. Koreans, who then distribute liquor in a community plagued by substance abuse, "bear the brunt of the anger the African-American community rightfully has against the larger system of oppression. Koreans become sort of foot soldiers of internal colonialism," asserts Bonacich.

Cultural and ethnic difference "are no doubt a small factor in these types of conflict," Bonacich contends, "but unless you deal with the structural problems, you do not solve the conflict."

But I would argue that we have to move on all these fronts—cultural (which includes psychological issues) and structural—simultaneously. Actions rooted in bigotry usually turn these simmering hostilities into social conflagrations. Even when people of apparent goodwill try to cooperate, an aide to Los Angeles

Mayor Tom Bradley admitted, there is this "impenetrable veil" of hostility, based on ethnic stereotyping, that undermines joint economic and cultural ventures.

Traditional mediation and bridge-building efforts are too superficial to penetrate that veil. They don't get at the psychological terror, fed by bigotry, that lead the Soon Ja Dus of the world to shoot the Latasha Harlinses who inhabit the planet's inner cities.

A significant part of the problem lies in a failure to address the exaggerated psychological dimensions of intraminority group tensions. Most interethnic conflicts have a psychological aspect—rigidity of thinking, low self-esteem, compensatory behavior. But I think these are especially significant in disputes between historically subordinate groups.

In the case of Korean immigrants, they carry not only the historical memory of subjugation under the Japanese but the day-to-day reality of anti-Asian prejudice in the United States and the isolation caused by language and cultural differences. African Americans carry not only the historical memory of slavery but their status as American's most stigmatized minority.

In many respects, I believe Korean Americans and African Americans to be very similar. Accustomed to being targets of abuse, members of both groups are quick to defend themselves if anyone seems ready to violate their humanity. I see it especially in the often swaggering, chip-on-the-shoulder posture of African American and Korean immigrant men. I saw it in the quick defense of Latasha Harlins when she slugged Soon Ja Du three times in the face after Du grabbed her. I saw it when the battered Du threw a stool at Harlins . . . then took a gun . . . braced herself on the counter, and as Harlins turned to leave . . . shot the girl in the back of the head. Over and over, I watched the now infamous videotape of the incident in Du's store and saw the consequences of "internalized oppression."

In other words, when a battered wife stabs her husband in the chest after he's complained that the eggs are overdone again, it's a safe bet that the murder was over more than breakfast.

There are few safe places where oppressed groups can express their distress. The nation's power elite are not going to let poor people of any color riot on Rodeo Drive. Instead, much of that rage is turned inward—alcoholism, drug abuse, suicide—or directed toward those equally or more marginalized—Black-on-Black crime, child abuse, spouse abuse, violence against Korean merchants, ethnic-bashing between Blacks and Latinos.

The model I've seen that best addresses this phenomenon of internalized oppression is RC [Re-Evaluation Counseling].

RC communities exist worldwide, with head-quarters in Seattle. What Love and other RC counselors do, first one on one at the level of peer counseling, then in larger support groups, is help the "client" "discharge" the distress, born of the hurt, that keeps them numb or enraged and often irrational. Each person takes turns being a client and being a counselor. The goal is self-healing and clear thinking. When used by organizations, that clear thinking can be wedded to a pragmatic program of social change.

Says Love: When people are able to identify, talk about, and discharge their pain with the help of an aware, supportive human being, they "can take the information, minus the painful emotions" and reevaluate behavior. It's when the information is covered over with all that painful emotion that we get stuck and end up hurting one another rather than responding to one another from a rational place of thinking."

The healing work that RC communities and RC-influenced prejudice-reduction programs utilize (and there are many of the latter around the country, often presented by independent diversity consultants contracted by governmental agencies, schools, and corporations) is essential work; but it is not enough. I've yet to come across a conflict-resolution model that clearly connects the dots.

I believe we need a holistic conflict analysis and resolution model, one that comprehends the psychological issues that RC identifies but that more clearly articulates the need for institutional change and gives people the skills to do it.

Further, the model should show that it is only through building coalitions within communities and across all types of communities that structural change can occur—and this can only happen if the profound hurts all of us have suffered and the dehumanizing myths we have internalized about each other are "discharged."

Perhaps programs utilizing what people find valuable in RC should be established in every neighborhood, as accessible as twelve-step programs are. But unlike RC, which is not a political organization, the clear thinking that peer counseling facilitates should be applied to an agenda that participants develop themselves for social change—whether it be transforming the policing of neighborhoods, the nation's system of public education, or the United States government.

Certainly, people already engage in the work of social change everywhere—personal epiphanies happen and sometimes the people who have them join forces—but it's always too few doing too much. People get burned out, exhausted from the physical effort, drained by the negativity of others who attack those who do choose to lead.

People are not going to heal overnight, or, perhaps, even in a lifetime. But it's a process, once initiated and carried out systematically, as RC members do, that can give people enough "slack"—emotional and intellectual space—to act in their own best interest, which, politically, is to find common ground with other groups. In the post-L.A. rebellion era—in that city and elsewhere—few people have the slack to think in their best interest. They have circled the wagons, staked out tribal positions, and their hurt and rage are frozen. What that leads to is the societal equivalent of the criminal beating of White truck driver Reginald Denny by several Black men the first few hours of the L.A. "riot"—political revenge.

Even free, as is RC, relatively few people will make the effort to seek counseling of any sort. So what can we do? I write, and I hope that, just as I was influenced and inspired by Alice Walker to investigate the significance of colorism, what I say rouses people, beyond the halls of academe, to discuss in beauty parlors and barbershops, on radio and TV shows and in church, color conflict among our own people and relations with other ethnic groups of color—remember, we are likely to be the majority one day. We should, as well, reconnect with allies in the White community. The latter are often marginalized by their own community when they take progressive and honorable stands against racism. And as many young African Americans work through the morass of our own oppression, we push them away with the orthodoxy of a vulgar, compensatory nationalism—

this era's version called Afrocentrism—that often denies their humanity.

These tensions have no easy remedies. But we have to work toward an atmosphere of cooperation rather than antagonism. If we don't, the bottom line for African Americans is this: our numbers are shrinking relative to the growth of other minorities. Like the poor, troublesome Black people are always with us, lament many Whites. But as one elderly Black xenophobe acknowledged, White people have some "new niggers" now ("I'm just a high-tech coolie," said one politically conscious Chinese American engineer)—ones that look more like them, act more like them, and don't haunt their days and nights with cries of "No justice, no peace." Know something else, in some parts of the country they vote more like conservative Whites. And when they marry into White families, some grandpas and grandmas (happy that at least their new child-in-law is not Black) are more than willing to lobby for a new mixed-race census category that might take some of the taint off their grandchild's color and may, eventually, make them honorary White people. (That's already the case with large numbers of Latinos, East Indians, and Arabs.)

Not long ago, I heard about a bumper sticker spotted on a car cruising down a Los Angeles freeway: *If I had known then what I know now, I would have picked my own cotton.*

Tired of reaping what they've sown, many White Americans will happily embrace the proliferating Asian American and Latino population in an effort to exploit intraminority conflicts and permanently marginalize Blacks, if we can't reach honorable political, social, and cultural compromises with other groups, particularly people of color.

As we approach this mine-laden social-psychological terrain, among the questions we should be asking is, What does it mean to be an African American at the end of the twentieth century? In the same breath we should ask, What does it mean to be an American? These questions are at the heart of the unresolved tension in discussions about cultural pluralism: balancing what is perceived to be universal with ethnic particularism.

Examine the lived American culture—as opposed to what usually gets funded by public television. It has been shaped by many groups and at its base is European, African, and Native American. It is not the exclusively Eurocentric artifact that Patrick Buchanan, for example, extolled during campaign speeches for the Republican presidential nomination in 1992.

Buchanan even sounded un-American to many other conservative Whites who cherish the notion of the melting pot. But most Americans don't really know what the "pot" represents: a process of assimilation that results in a homogenized end product. You know, the same Big Mac you get here you get in Oshkosh. If this were an accurate representation of America, as newspaper headlines commonly suggest—MIAMI MELTING POT BOILS OVER—the country would not be the contentious place that it is.

Jazz, the only uniquely American music, represents the cultural synergy that is the best part of the melting-pot process but the one least celebrated. What we embrace as "high" culture is European. The all-American social identity that we celebrate is the ethnic smelter's alleged "everyman": Jimmy Stewart in 1940, Kevin Costner today.

The New World synergy that produced jazz, tap, as well as the essentially creolized African American population and the mestizo-California culture seldom seems understood by the creators of tourist propaganda in prerebellion Los Angeles. They presented the "multi-cultural" city as either a paradise of separate but harmonious ethnic groups or, in an updated version of Anglo-dominated assimilation, a zesty tossed salad served on the American flag.

But, as a nation, we are more bound to each other than the metaphor of a mosaic, for instance, suggests. We seem more a tapestry with a series of patterns, some more dominant than others.

African American music, literature, dance, and our struggle to extend democracy have been central to that tapestry.

While the official culture pretends otherwise, we all know what Elvis was about, Fred Astaire, too. And in White suburbia, people still watch *Moonlighting* in reruns and smile approvingly at a favored American male image: Bruce Willis's hip White/Black man.

On this score, I am reminded as well of the recent evidence strengthening the claim that the voice of Mark Twain's Huckleberry Finn—the book from which "all modern American literature comes," claimed Hemingway—was inspired by a ten-year-old African American boy named Jimmy.

"This shows a real black root in a white consciousness," one literary scholar claimed. The actor Hal Holbrook, who for thirty-eight years has played Twain, told one interviewer he had sensed a Black strain in Huck's voice but never knew for sure.

"It's almost like the truth about something is so clear," he said, "that you look right through it."

It would seem, at this point in our history, African Americans can calm the warring identities in our consciousness. Assimilation is not a one-way street. It's a boulevard with multiple lanes of traffic, flowing two ways, intercut by persistent jaywalkers. But our trucks are so big we've been jamming the boulevard for decades. If we understand that, especially our young people, then we have the consciousness to engage, with confidence, in the political struggle (which multiculturalism represents) to assert the authority of our claim: We are central to the notion of an American identity.

If, then, America is largely us, who are we?

Clearly, African Americans are not just the descendants of enslaved Africans in the United States. My cousin Jeffrey looked like one of Ozzie and Harriet's kids. But what's unusual about that? African Americans are the product of a New World culture. It's been estimated that 80 percent of us have polygenetic backgrounds. And while U.S. custom and law have denied that multiethnic reality to perpetuate its own system of apartheid, calling America on it wouldn't be the first time Black people got hip to a trick bag—and out of it.

While many Blacks argue that they know they have mixed ancestry, they (1) don't acknowledge it because it would appear that they are trying to distance themselves from a socially stigmatized Black identity, of which they are not ashamed; (2) their non-Black ancestry is so distant they could not identify it precisely; (3) if they did know their non-Black ancestors, their descendants wouldn't accept them as kin; (4) most of their non-Black ancestors were White men who raped enslaved Black women and they want nothing to do with a kinship forged by brutality.

For these reasons, as well as the dictates of U.S. social customs and sometimes law, we have not *embraced* the fact that we are generically a creolized population. And the rise of Afrocentrism has encouraged the science fiction that we are an unadulterated ethnic group. No ethnic group is pure, as Du Bois pointed out long ago. For centuries, Africans mixed with myriad ethnic groups before any were enslaved and shipped to the New World.

While rape of Black women by White men was pervasive once we got here, not every sexual encounter between individuals of the two groups was coerced—to think so displays a fundamental misunderstanding of human nature.

But when rape did occur, we must remember that it is the perpetrator of the crime, not the victim, who bears the shame. And to constantly cast this criminal aspect of New World history as the cruel burden the descendants of slaves must bear is like stigmatizing a contemporary victim of sexual assault.

As far as I am concerned, every Black person with White ancestry should, no matter how they came by it, own it. That is not a rejection of African American identity, but an affirmation of the complex ancestry that defines us as an ethnic group. It will normalize what is erroneously treated as an exotic and, consequently, divisive characteristic among African Americans. Further, the acknowledgment of our ties by blood and culture puts the lie to the official silence on America's historically miscegenated identity.

But again, carnal knowledge of each other "across the color line" not only goes beyond rape but includes other non-Whites. Zora Neale Hurston once wrote: "I am colored but offer nothing in the way of extenuating circumstances except the fact that I am the only Negro in the United States whose grandfather on the mother's side was not an Indian chief." So where we once tried to find every drop of non-Black blood as a buffer against our caste status, we now tend to proclaim that all of us are exclusively the descendants of African princes, princesses, kings and queens. (You notice how no one ever claims descent from the village thief.) In reality, many social scientists estimate that most of our non-African ancestry is Native American.

As demographers point to the growth of the non-White population and the consequent "browning" of America, the already heterogeneous African American gene pool will become more so: Black, Korean American, Hispanic; Japanese, African American, and East Indian; Ethiopian, African American, Chinese, and Euro-American. In Los Angeles, I meet people with these and similar backgrounds frequently.

Is the African American community capable of embracing such diversity? Is it too much of a stretch for the traditionally defined African American population, which is essentially monocultural, to include people of African descent whose consciousness has been shaped by a multicultural family?

What should we expect if the Annas of the world meet African Americans who continually vent their own pain through the physical and psychological abuse of multiethnic people who have African ancestry but do not identify solely with the African American community? Is there any alternative but for people like Anna to reject us and work for a separate census designation and the social and political recognition that will result?

Certainly getting the personal pain that arises from these conflicts healed is essential. When that process is begun perhaps people can think more clearly about the question of a "multiracial" census category, and the notion of "race," period.

Says Love: "The question of whether there should be a new racial category has to be considered aside from personal pain and personal history."

Love believes, as I do, that "personal wishes have to be viewed in the context of what it means to live in an oppressive society where inequality is based on social identity groups. And where race is the fundamental criterion on which those groupings, and thus divisions, are made.

"If you go at it from a sociological rather than a personal standpoint, it is disastrous to create a new category, because the oppression itself is based on exactly that kind of division," Love argues. "We should be putting our energies into using the historic juncture of the year 2000 as a time when we will abolish all racial categories."

I know many multiethnic activists would argue that this is a progressive-sounding argument to deny them recognition and representation. But if their interest is the elimination of oppression—and not social vengeance against Blacks—then the elimination of classifications based on "race" is the only solution that makes sense. We should be challenging the nomenclature of oppression and attacking the philosophical underpinnings of racism—all a necessary part of dismantling institutionalized discrimination.

Finally, the exorcising of the psychological consequences of oppression that divide communities of color is a painful matter that many of us would rather deny or argue should be done out of sight and earshot of the enemy. But Black folks are among the most studied people on the planet. Who *doesn't* know our business?

As long as colorism and conflicts with other minority groups distract us from the larger issues of social and economic justice, the nation's system of structured inequality prevails. Which is why so many among the country's White power elite smile indulgently at the notion of a "browner," "newly multicultural" America. They know what the last plantation is, too.

Acknowledgments

Continued from page ii

CMG Worldwide Inc.: "Communication and Reality" by Malcolm X. Copyright © 1998 Family of Malcolm X c/o CMG Worldwide Inc., Indianapolis, IN, 46256, www.cmgww.com. Reprinted by permission of CMG Worldwide Inc.

Itabari Njeri: Excerpt from "Sushi and Grits: Ethnic Identity and Conflict in a Newly Multicultural America" by Itabari Njeri. First published in *Lure and Loathing: Essays on Race, Identity and the Ambivalence of Assimilation,* edited by Gerald Early (Penguin Books, 1993). Copyright © 1993 by Itabari Njeri. Reprinted by permission of the author.